P9-CAT-309

A House for My Name

A House for My Name

A Survey of the Old Testament

Peter J. Leithart

Canon Press
MOSCOW, IDAHO

Peter J. Leithart, *A House for My Name: A Survey of the Old Testament*

Published by Canon Press, P.O. Box 8729, Moscow, ID 83843
800-488-2034 / www.canonpress.org

05 04 03 02 01 00 9 8 7 6 5 4 3 2 1

Cover design by Paige Atwood Design, Moscow, ID

Printed in the United States of America.

ISBN: 1-885767-69-2

To Lindsey

ישׂמךְ אלהים
כרות וכאסתר
אם בישׂראל

Contents

Acknowledgments

Readers familiar with the work of James B. Jordan, especially his *Through New Eyes*, will recognize his fingerprints on every page of this book. I even toyed with the notion of entitling this book *Through New Eyes For Dummies*, but feared that would infringe some kind of copyright or patent. Over nearly two decades, Jim has been a continual source of stimulation and insight, as well as being a generous and helpful critic. If this book does nothing more than encourage readers to buy and read Jim's books and papers, it will have served a useful purpose.

Thanks also to Professor Tremper Longman, III of Westmont College, who read the manuscript and made encouraging comments. Rev. Jeffrey Meyers of Providence Presbyterian Church in St. Louis read portions of the book and offered correctives at a number of points.

I am grateful to Doug Jones of Canon Press, who commissioned the book and whose generosity and enthusiasm for the project kept me going through those moments when I was sure the whole thing was a very bad mistake.

My oldest son, Woelke, helped at the early stages by turning old teaching outlines into prose. I owe thanks to all my children. I have been teaching them the Bible since they were very young and have learned more from them than they or I can possibly know.

Preface

I learned the characters and events of the Old Testament in Lutheran Sunday School, and though profoundly grateful for this training, I realize now that there were some significant weaknesses. The least important of these was that the teaching was very selective. Selectivity in itself is not a problem. Unless a writer simply wants to reproduce the entire Old Testament, he must highlight some events rather than others. The problem had more to do with the principle of selection. We learned about Samson's strength and power, but we were never taught about Ehud's sword disappearing into fat Eglon or about Jael pounding a tent peg through Sisera's head. Doubtless, the curriculum writers were protecting us from something. What would Mom think if I brought home a picture of splattered brains from Sunday School? But leaving out these stories impoverishes one's understanding of and interest in the Old Testament.

A more serious problem was that the story was never quite finished. The curriculum almost always stopped at Solomon or shortly thereafter, so that I received only the vaguest idea of the history of the divided kingdom and the exile. A few scattered stories from the latter part of Israel's history made it into the Sunday School pamphlets, but I had little sense of the setting of Elijah and Elisha or of Jonah and Haggai. If I was taught about the Babylonian exile, I forgot somewhere along the line and had to relearn it. Daniel just popped up in the court of Nebuchadnezzar and that was that.

Perhaps I was taught all these things, but my failure to retain any memory of them points to the most serious problem with many Sunday School curricula: They do not connect the dots. Children learn a story here, a story there, but they do not get the sense that the Bible is telling one story and that each of the little stories is an episode of something bigger. And this weakness is rooted in an even more fundamental hermeneutical flaw. Christians teaching the Old Testament are constantly tempted to treat it as a collection of moral fables. Abram "lies" to Pharaoh in Genesis 12, and we draw the conclusion that Abram's faith was not sufficiently strong, and that lying is a bad thing. But the story ends with Abram being treated well by Pharaoh and receiving all manner of livestock (Genesis 12:16). How such an ending discourages lying is not exactly clear: Abram does not just get away scot free—he is richly rewarded for his "lack of faith." To make this work, the moralizer has to say that the riches Abram receives are "deceptive riches," rather than the true riches received by faith. Moral piles on moral, all of them obscuring the passage they are supposed to illuminate. If we cut through the layers of moralizing, we realize that the story is not well-designed as a warning against lying. Why does Abram have to go to Egypt to lie? Why *this* lie? Why is he rewarded? One must simply say that something else is going on in Genesis 12, something that a moralistic reading of the Bible does not even hint at (see chapter 2 following).

This book is also selective, and necessarily so. I do not try to tell every story in the Old Testament, and, in fact, I give short shrift to many of the most popular stories or ignore them completely, while I give detailed attention to some of the lesser known books and figures, Jeremiah for instance. For the most part, I have also ignored the historical background to the Old Testament, concentrating instead on the internal workings of the text itself.

I hope to provide a framework for the whole Bible and particular books that will help readers make sense of individual stories and passages. Given this focus, this book will be most useful to readers who already have some basic knowledge of the facts of the Old Testament.

And so, this book lacks balance. In two senses, however, I have attempted to be comprehensive: This book covers the entirety of Old Testament history. Solomon makes his appearance in chapter four, but then the three chapters that follow trace the history of the divided kingdom, the latter days of Judah, and the exilic and postexilic periods. Second, and more importantly, I have attempted to show how the episodes of the Bible fit together into the single story of God's works within the creation and especially with Israel. In this way, I have avoided moralizing. There is, of course, moral instruction to be had in the Bible. But the point is that the events recorded in Scripture happened in real history and are episodes in the outworking of God's plan for humanity and for His world. Moral inferences should be drawn *after* we have grasped the shape of a particular passage and how it fits into the larger sweep of biblical history.

The setting I have in mind for my readers is not the library or even the pastor's study, though I hope this book will be useful to pastors and other teachers. Instead, this book is designed to be read aloud at the dinner table during family devotions, and I have tried to write it in such a way that even very young children will begin to grasp the sweep and beauty of the Bible. Because I want to get across the main point and do it in an understandable way, I have placed technical details in the endnotes that conclude each chapter. This has sometimes produced overstuffed endnotes, but that is preferable in this case to an overstuffed book.

I encourage parents not to underestimate what children can learn about the Bible. Unlike many books of theology, the content of the Bible is fairly easy to grasp. Even (especially?) a two-year-old understands what happens when someone's head is bashed with a tent peg. If trained to read properly, children can begin to see how parts of the Bible are connected to each other and to one big story. I have been teaching the Bible to my children for many years, and years ago they began to teach me by noticing wonders in the Scriptures that I had never noticed.

Though this book is designed for families, it is not, I trust, a simplistic book. For those who want to know, the introduction is an eggheady discussion of the importance of the Old Testament for Christian faith and practice and a description of the rules for reading that guide my work. If you are the type who does not care to know about the gears making things go, you should turn immediately to the first chapter. But if, like me, you are a theological engineer who gets a thrill out of the music of the gears, the introduction may be of interest.

Introduction: The New Concealed

In his lovely study of medieval monasticism, Jean Leclercq notes that the medieval monks studied and commented on the Old Testament even more than the New. They did this not because they confused the Old and New but because of their understanding of what God was doing in the Old Testament. For the medieval monks, the Old Testament was not merely a prefiguration of salvation in Christ, but the beginning of that salvation, albeit in a veiled form. Their study of the Old Testament was closely tied to their understanding of the New, for "the Old and the New Testament taken as a whole tell the same story of the same people of God." If the New Testament was necessary to a proper understanding of the Old, the principle worked in reverse as well: "truth [in the New Testament] unveils the figure [in the Old] and shows forth its meaning; once revealed, the figure in turn illuminates the Truth." Knowing Christ meant knowing Him not only from the pages of gospels and epistles, but knowing Him as He is presented in type and shadow in the Old Testament. Studying the Old Testament was thus never merely an historical interest—never a study of "Hebrew religion"—but a central means for growing in "compunction," the desire for God in Christ that was the goal of the monastic life.[1]

Though the Reformation departed in a number of ways from medieval methods of biblical interpretation, the Reformers treated the Old Testament in much the same way.

Calvin insisted, along with the medieval theologians, that the Old Covenant saints communed with Christ and were saved in and by Him. The Old Testament, as Calvin understood it, was an exhibition of the gospel under the veil of figures and shadows. As with the medieval monks, Calvin's goal in studying the Old Testament was to know Christ and to serve Him, promptly and sincerely.

Modern Christianity, by contrast, has not quite known what to do with the Old Testament; or, better, it has known precisely what to do with the Old Testament—toss it in the rubbish bin. This dismissive attitude toward the Old Testament is seen especially in classic liberalism, a product mainly of the nineteenth century. Two of the key ingredients in the making of theological liberalism were what Stephen Sykes has called the "inwardness tradition" and a sharp separation of Christianity from the religion of the Old Testament. Liberal separation of Old and New was similar to the view of Marcion, the early church heretic who taught that the God of the Old Testament is a different God from that of the New.[2]

Sometimes, the connection of liberalism and Marcionism was very explicit, as in the church historian Adolf von Harnack. Harnack's views also illustrate how the Marcionite division of the Old and New leads to a certain view of the content of Christian faith. In his third lecture on the *Essence of Christianity*, which was delivered at the turn of the century, Harnack offered this description of the kingdom of God:

> Anyone who wants to know what the kingdom of God and the coming of this kingdom mean in Jesus' preaching must read and meditate on the parables. There he will learn what the kingdom is all about. The kingdom of God comes by coming to *individuals*, making entrance into their *souls*, and being grasped by them. . . . Everything externally dramatic, all public historical meaning vanishes here; all external hope for the future fades also. . . . It is not a matter of angels and devils, nor of principalities and powers, but of God and the soul, of the soul and its God.[3]

As Harnack continued, the Marcionite basis for this description of the kingdom became clear. Jesus "severed the connection existing in his day between ethics and external forms of religious worship and technical observance" and traced moral issues to their "root, that is, to the disposition and intention."[4] Religion for Harnack had to do with inner feeling and intentions, not with public worship or questions of political or social concern. Continuing this work, Paul "delivered the Christian religion from Judaism," by virtue of his insight that "religion in its new phase pertains to the individual" and by introducing the dichotomies of spirit/flesh, inner/outer, life/death.[5] Harnack recognized that the gospel has a bearing on the problems of law, society, culture, and work, and he justified the formation of churches by noting that religion cannot remain "bodiless." But these "externals" are not part of Christianity *per se*, and the genius of Christianity is its liberation from externals. Harnack claimed that the church fell when the externals of religion began to take on too much importance. In the West, the church came to be seen as a necessary institution, and in Eastern Christianity, worship turned from "a worship of God in spirit and in truth into a worship of God in signs, formulas, and idols."[6] In his work on Marcion, Harnack was explicit in his endorsement of a modernized Marcionite program.[7] Thus, the "inward" form of Christianity is defined by opposition to the "external" form of religion found in Judaism and the Old Testament. Marcion is brought forward in defense of pure inward piety.

Already at the beginning of the nineteenth century, Friedrich Schleiermacher had set modern Protestant theology off on a similar course. Despite his opposition to the Enlightenment's rationalistic view of religion, he shared its view of the Old Testament. In what has been called the "decisive sentence of his dogmatics," Schleiermacher argued that the connection of Christianity with "Mosaic institutions" was purely historical, while "as far as concerns its historical existence and its aim, [Christianity's] relations to

Judaism and Heathenism are the same." The Old Testament itself, Schleiermacher claimed, "ascribed to the New Covenant a different character from the Old," even an "antithesis" between them. This view of the transition from the Old to the New meant, theologically, that the Old Testament might be safely ignored by the theologian, indeed that it was to be "utterly discard[ed]," since it was merely the "husk or wrapping" and since "whatever is most definitely Jewish has least value." The "most definitely Jewish" elements are "a legalistic style of thought or a slavish worship of the letter," which improperly entered the church when the Old Testament was used for the expression of Christian piety.[8] The medieval monks, in other words, were Judaizers when they used Old Testament terminology to express the faith of the church.

Most important for Schleiermacher, the form of Christianity's piety and of its religious consciousness was wholly different from that of Judaism.[9] The members of what Schleiermacher called the "true church," as opposed to the institutional clingers-on, had no need of text or letter, as was necessary under the old system. This was consistent with Schleiermacher's effort to define an irreducible "essence" of religion and religions. Such a program falters when applied to the religion of Israel, in which the covenant with Yahweh, embodied in its texts, rites, feasts, sanctuary, and religious hierarchy, embraced the whole of the nation's life. The externals in Israel's religion were not a dispensable husk protecting an internal seed but much more like the layers of an onion: Keep peeling away the layers and eventually you're left with nothing. Schleiermacher's definition of religion as a "modification of feeling" or a "taste for the Infinite," however brilliantly qualified to accommodate the social aspects of religion and to explicate the connection of feeling with acting and knowing, simply could not embrace the religion of the Old Testament. Schleiermacher did not follow Immanuel Kant in denying that Judaism was a religion,[10] but he treated the forms of Old Testament religion as rubble that must be removed to find the religious treasure buried beneath. In short, some variation of Marcionism was essential to Schleiermacher's definition of religion and therefore at the heart of his entire system, as Harnack realized.[11]

Evangelicals are rightly horrified by the evils of liberalism, including its hostility toward the religion of Israel. But it is not clear exactly how modern evangelicalism differs from liberalism on these fundamental points. Reading Schleiermacher leaves the evangelical of the late twentieth century with a feeling of eerie familiarity. Attacks on the "external" supports of religion, emphasis on emotional religious experiences, the idea that the kingdom of God is a nebulous and mainly inner reality—all these are themes that can be found in countless books from modern evangelicals. And Schleiermacher's attitude toward the Old Testament, while never stated in so bold a form, is the working assumption of much evangelical theology. When examined on these related issues—treatment of the Old Testament and the emphasis on the "inwardness" of Christianity—liberalism and evangelicalism begin to appear as two aspects of a single theological enterprise. Their wars are civil wars.

In recent years, mainstream theology has begun to recognize the disaster that followed from the Marcionism of classical liberalism. R. Kendall Soulen is a leading figure in efforts to restore the importance of the Old Testament to Christian theology. In his book, *The God of Israel and Christian Theology*, Soulen recognizes that the "standard model" of dismissing the Old Testament fosters a "double impoverishment for Christian theology":

> On the one hand, the standard model has led to a loss of biblical orientation for Christian theology, especially with regard to the Scriptures of Israel. On the other, it has led to a loss of creative theological engagement with the hard edges of human history. As a result, the standard model has fostered and supported a damaging dislocation of the gospel about Jesus Christ. Estranged from its proper context in the Scriptures of Israel and in public history, the gospel has been resettled in

> very different contexts. Alienated from the Hebrew Scriptures, the gospel has been interpreted in the context of accounts of human religiosity more or less foreign to the theological idiom of the Bible. Disconnected from the sweep of public history, the gospel has been contextualized one-sidedly in the realm of the personal and private.[12]

Unfortunately, the target of Soulen's attack includes most of what has counted as orthodox Christianity throughout its history. In Soulen's telling, it is not only modern theology that has wrongly rejected the Old Testament; Christian theology as such is marred by the same "flaw in the heart of the crystal." According to Soulen, Christian theology has always taught a doctrine of "supercessionism," that is, the belief that

> God chose the Jewish people after the fall of Adam in order to prepare the world for the coming of Jesus Christ, the Savior. After Christ came, however, the special role of the Jewish people came to an end and its place was taken by the church, the new Israel. The church, unlike the Jewish people, is a spiritual community in which the carnal distinction between Jew and Gentile is overcome. . . . the Jews failed to recognize Jesus as the promised Messiah and refused to enter the new spiritual Israel. God therefore rejected the Jews and scattered them over the earth, where God will preserve them until the end of time.[13]

By contrast, Soulen endorses the view summarized in a statement of the Presbyterian Church (USA): "The church has not 'replaced' the Jewish people. . . . Hence, when speaking with Jews about matters of faith, we must always acknowledge that Jews are already in a covenantal relationship with God."[14]

There are many problems with Soulen's analysis, but I will limit myself to three criticisms. First, he is simply wrong in his understanding of the covenant with Abraham. Citing the Jewish theologian Michael Wyschogrod, he claims that the "mystery" of the election of Israel is that it "concerns a natural human family." Rather than choosing His people according to faith or moral excellence, "God chose the seed of Abraham, Isaac, and Jacob, a human family neither better nor worse than others." Thus, the election of Israel is a "corporeal election," and even observance of Torah is subordinate to the "fundamental reality of Judaism," which is "the corporeal election of Abraham's children."[15]

Soulen's point contains a profound truth, namely, that when God acts in the world to save mankind, He works "with the grain" of human life as He created it. His grace flows through the created channels of family and descent, through speech and food. But Soulen is arguing that blood descent from Abraham was the backbone of the covenantal arrangements with Israel, and that point is simply false. Right from the beginning, the covenant embraced many who were not in any way related to Abraham by blood. All the male members of Abraham's household were circumcised (Genesis 17:12–14), and in a household that included 318 men of fighting age (Genesis 14:14), this must have been a sizable number of men—far more than the blood descendants of Abraham, who at that time included only Ishmael! When Israel came from Egypt, they came out as a "mixed multitude" (Exodus 12:38) that included thousands of converted Egyptians who did not want to hang around Egypt after it had been nearly destroyed by plagues. It was never the case that "the family identity of the Jewish people as the descendants of Abraham, Isaac, and Jacob" was the foundation of the faith of Israel. That is perhaps the modern Jewish view, but it is not the view of the Bible. This fundamental error leads Soulen off in the wrong direction from the start. He maintains that the Jews continue to have a covenantal identity because they are descended from Abraham, when in fact descent from Abraham was never the criterion of covenantal identity. Within the covenant, those who are not blood descendants of Abraham have *always* outnumbered those who are.

Second, though Soulen thinks he is attacking those who separate Christian theology from the Old Testament, he perpetuates that same error. He is still working within the liberal framework that regards the religion of Israel as a different kind of religion from the religion of the church. Take, for example, his understanding of "redemption." Supercessionism, which Soulen rejects, teaches that the covenant with Israel is part of a larger story that begins with Adam's fall in the garden of Eden; the covenant with Israel is a means for achieving redemption from the effects of Adam's sin. However, Soulen wants to give Israel's covenant with God an independent standing, as a permanent structure in God's dealings with the world. He writes:

> [Within the supercessionist framework] the vast panorama of the Hebrew Scriptures is made to unfold within the basic antithesis of Adam's sin and redemption in Christ. This soteriological framework foreshortens the Hebrew Scriptures both thematically and temporally. Thematically, because the Scriptures are thought to relate a story whose fundamental presupposition is the catastrophe of sin and whose goal is therefore deliverance from the negative conditions of existence. This perspective obscures the possibility that the Hebrew Scriptures are not solely or even primarily concerned with the antithesis of sin and redemption but much rather with the God of Israel's passionate engagement with the mundane affairs of Israel and the nations. . . . the standard model also foreshortens the Hebrew Scriptures in a temporal sense. As perceived through the lens of the standard model, the Hebrew Scriptures do not relate a story that extends indefinitely into the future.[16]

In this context, Soulen quotes Bonhoeffer to the effect that the Hebrew Bible is not a book about redemption from death, but rather about how Israel's God delivers His people "so that it may live before God as God's people on earth."

Again, we give Soulen his due. It is true that the Old Testament is concerned with "God's passionate engagement" with the real world of nations, and it is also true that ignorance of the Old Testament has led Christian theology to miss that crucial point. As noted above, modern theology has treated Christianity as a religion of the inner man rather than an account of God's works in history. But to play God's engagement with the nations off against "redemption," as if the two were opposites, assumes an unbiblical definition of "redemption." For the Bible, delivering Israel from Egypt to live before God on earth is precisely an act of "redemption" (see Exodus 6:6). Soulen has narrowed the scope of terms like "sin" and "redemption" so that they do not encompass God's actions among the nations and in history. Narrowing these biblical terms, however, is precisely the kind of thing that Soulen dislikes in supercessionism, because it detaches scriptural teaching from the "hard edges" of history. The fact that Soulen accepts such truncated meanings for key terms suggests that he is defining them without much reference to the Old Testament. This is a perfect example of the kind of "gnosticism" that Soulen rightly deplores. Will the real "historical gnostic" please stand up?[17]

Finally, Soulen's treatment of New Testament texts announcing the removal of the dividing wall between Jew and Gentile is, to put it mildly, deeply unsatisfying. The church, he claims, is not a place where the identities of Jew and Gentile are erased but the place in which they are reconciled: "Reconciliation does not mean the imposition of sameness, but the unity of reciprocal blessing," and this means that the church is "a particularized form in which the basic relation between Jew and Gentile is actualized."[18] Soulen is clearly right that peoples incorporated into the church are not required, or at least not always required, to give up their distinct cultural identities. Insofar as modern Jews form a subculture, they may join the church and maintain their own traditions, so long as these are consistent with the faith of the church. It is also true, as Soulen says, that "what God has done in Jesus engages Jews as Jews and Gentiles as Gentiles."

Soulen is wrong, however, to suggest that the union of Jews and Gentiles in the church does not produce a "third column of biblical ontology next to that of the Jews and that of the Greeks," for clearly Paul envisions a new sort of human being emerging in the body of Christ (Ephesians 2:15).

More disturbingly, Soulen somehow moves (leaps?) from this recognition of the church as a place of reconciliation of Jew and Gentile to the notion that Christians in the church are in union with Jews who are not: "the church can only desire the faithful preservation of the distinctiveness and integrity of Jewish existence wherever this takes place, whether within or without the church."[19] We are treading on delicate ground here. Jews have suffered enormously in the twentieth century, but sensitivity to Jewish suffering and abhorrence of horrific crimes against the Jews should not lead us to abandon the clear teaching of Jesus and Paul. Absolutely nothing in Soulen's argument supports the idea that Christians should strive to maintain Judaism outside the church. Jew and Gentile are reconciled *in Christ*, in Christ's body, but to suggest that Christians and Jews are reconciled whether or not Jews turn to Christ makes utter nonsense of the New Testament. Perhaps Soulen would respond by saying that "Christ" is bigger than the church, saving some who have never heard the gospel and joined the church, but this leaves him again dangling over the precipice of gnosticism.

Soulen's book offers two challenges to evangelicals, one that we desperately need to heed, another that we need to reject in the strongest possible terms. The positive lesson is that the Old Testament must be our book if we are to be fully Christian. The modern tendency to demean the Old Testament has wrought untold falsehood, misery, incoherence, and oppression. When the Old Testament is ignored, Christianity is conceived as a private "spiritual" religion with little to say to the world, and the world goes on its merry, bloody way. But Soulen wants us to read the Old Testament as a book having an integrity of its own, without reference to the New Testament, and this we must, with the church in every age, reject utterly. We must recover the medieval and reformational way of reading the Old Testament as the crucial early chapters of the single book that is the Bible. We must recover the Old Testament as a book about Jesus.

Interpreting the Old Testament

But reading the Bible as a single book requires some training in the art of reading. Since the Reformation, "grammatical-historical" biblical interpretation has been the main hermeneutical method among Protestants. A development of the medieval idea of "literal" meaning, the grammatical-historical approach attempts to understand Scripture in the light of the grammar of the original languages and the historical and cultural setting in which the text was written. Something like the grammatical-historical method has been foundational to all biblical interpretation throughout the history of the church. Biblical interpretation would be a free play of signifiers without grounding in the vocabulary, grammar, and historical setting of the Bible. But the grammatical-historical method, essential as it is as a foundation, cannot provide the overarching "grammar" for the interpretation of Scripture. If it becomes the sole method of interpretation, the study of the Old Testament will be reduced to a study of "what they did then" rather than a study of the glories of the Christ who was yet to come. Liberal interpretation of the Old Testament can, in fact, be understood as the product of an exclusive reliance on the grammatical-historical method, and evangelical biblical study often has the same narrow focus. Interpretation of the Old Testament must be grounded in grammar and history, but if it does not move to typology, it is not Christian interpretation.

"Typology" is a loaded word. In this book, the word has more baggage than usual, for I use the term not only to highlight the principle that the Old Testament points ahead to Christ, but also to describe the structure of the Old Testament itself. The Old Testament is composed according to a rhythm of "repetition with difference" that is a microcosm of New Testament typology. David is a "type" of Jesus, but he is also an "antitype" of Adam. When I speak of a "typological" understanding of the Old Testament I am further calling attention to the literary devices that the Bible uses to communicate its message. These are "typological" in the sense that they are the means by which the Bible presents the rhythms of history, as well as the means by which the Old Testament in particular points to Christ. The point is difficult to grasp at this level of abstraction, so let me explain more specifically what I mean.

Let me begin with a brief discussion of different approaches to meaning in language. Linguistic theories of meaning can be classified as either "concept" or "system" theories. A concept theory of meaning says that each word has its meaning attached to it by usage and history. Thus, through the usage of English speakers over time, a certain meaning has attached itself to the word "dog." Any competent user of English forms a concept whenever he hears or reads the word "dog." This concept is not necessarily a mental image of a dog, but it is a mental response of some sort, one awakened in the mind by the linguistic unit "dog." The word has sense, though it can have any number of different referents. "Dog" can refer to Maggie, Fluffie, or Phaedeau. In this view, a word can be used metaphorically, but when it is used metaphorically, it is referring to a thing in the world other than its normal referent or with a meaning other than its normal meaning, as when a teenage boy calls a teenage girl a "dog."

Most linguists in this century have operated with a "field" or "system" orientation. Each word has a place in the system of words within a language, and the word takes its meaning by its place in the system. Meaning is not "attached" to the word, rather it is established by the difference that one word has with another. The word "few" does not have a packet of meaning attached to it but is understood by contrast to related words like "many," "some," "all," and "several." Similarly, the word "dog" has meaning not because it has inherent sense but because it fills a place within the system of language and within a variety of subsystems. "Dog" means what it does by contrast to "wolf," "fox," "canine," "Great Dane," and so on. Here, meaning is not located in the word but in the differences between this word and that.

Like many dilemmas in philosophy and theology, this is a false one. Both the "concept" and the "system" viewpoint capture some truths about the mystery of communication. Though I believe that the meanings of words are constituted by some combination of system and concept, here I want to focus on the "system" orientation. The point I wish to make about biblical interpretation is this: We come to understand the words, sentences, paragraphs, and books of the Bible by examining them within a set of overlapping "systems" or contexts. Many studies of hermeneutics focus on what I will call the "lexical" context. Determining the meaning of a word in its "lexical context" not only means looking it up in the dictionary, though it does mean that. It also has to do with determining which of the possible dictionary meanings of a word is being used in a particular sentence or paragraph.

Several sorts of problems arise when dealing with a word's place in a lexical system. When a word has several lexical meanings, we are faced with a problem of "ambiguity," a possible confusion of meaning. If someone says, "He's blue," that could mean he is sad, or it could mean he is painted up for a Duke University basketball game, or it could mean that he has held his breath for just a moment longer than he should have. Several solutions to ambiguity are possible. Normally, the word is being used in one or the other of its senses, and we determine which one is being invoked by looking at the context in a text or the situation in which a statement is made.

There are cases when ambiguity is deliberate, however. The apostle John, for example, is very fond of deliberate ambiguities. In John 1:5, the word translated as "comprehended" can mean either "comprehend" or "seize." Did the darkness fail to "comprehend" the light come into the world, or did the darkness fail to "seize" the light? As we go through John's gospel, it becomes clear that both meanings are in play. Jesus is constantly slipping away from His enemies, so that they fail to "seize" Him until His hour comes. (He is, after all, the one born of the Spirit who, like the wind, blows where He will, though no one knows where it is coming from or where it is going.) Yet, it is also clear in the gospel that Jesus' opponents do not comprehend or understand Him. Another famous example occurs in John 3, where Jesus tells Nicodemus that he must be born *anothen*, a word that can mean either "from above" or "again." Given John's track record, we are safe in concluding that he is being deliberately ambiguous. Being born again is being born from above, by the Spirit, through the One who was sent from above.

Another sort of problem for the lexical meaning of words is "synonymity," which is when two or more words are very close in meaning ("house" and "home," for example). Here the problem is to determine why the author has chosen one word rather than another, and how significant a choice it is. Again, a number of resolutions are possible. Grammar or usage sometimes determines why one word is used and another is not. In the dictionary, "strong" and "powerful" are synonymous, but there are certain contexts where one is the right word and the other sounds strange to a native English speaker. "My car has a strong engine" sounds odd, as does "This coffee is too powerful." If I say, "My employer is a strong man," you think my employer works out during his lunch hour. But if I say, "My employer is a powerful man," I am making a statement about his influence, prominence, or clout. Moises Silva, whose book on semantics provided these examples, discovered from a study of Paul's use of different words for "know" that the particular word used is almost always determined by the constraints of Greek grammar. When "know" occurs with a direct object, Paul uses one verb, but when he writes "know that," he uses another. When Paul uses the words according to this rule, his choice is not an important one. But it may be significant to notice when he departs from this normal usage. Variations like this do not arise from any subtly different shade of meaning, but from grammatical considerations, and this means that you should not put a lot of weight on a particular use of the word "know" in Paul.[20]

In general, the greater the difference between the uses and meanings of the words, the more significance you may attach to the choice of one over another. "Writer" and "author" are close synonyms, but if I call someone a "poet," I have made a more specific designation. Secondary shades of meaning and nuance also help to determine a word choice; connotations of similar words can be quite different. In English, "house" and "home" overlap a great deal, but they have a different feel. A "home" is where your heart is, where people welcome you, but a "house" is just the bricks and wood that provide the physical setting for a "home." "Horse" and "steed" are no different in denotation or dictionary meaning, but they differ markedly in nuance. If I say, "He mounted his steed," you will picture a knight in armor. But if I say "He mounted his horse," you think of a jockey.

I am giving rather cursory treatment to issues of lexical context because others have treated this issue much more thoroughly than I am capable of doing.[21] But if, in our study of Scripture, we remain fixed on seeking to understand words in their "lexical context," we will be missing much of the richness and beauty of Scripture. In addition to the "lexical context," this book will be based on the study of words in their "literary context." This can be subdivided into several levels. Most hermeneutics texts will include extensive discussions of "non-literal" uses of words. Puns, metaphors, similes, and other "tropes" fall into this category, and the Bible is full of them. The Bible's tropes, however, are never merely artistic adornments; they carry significant theological content. For example, in 2 Samuel 7, David, having defeated the Philistines and Jebusites, wants to build a "house" for the Lord. Instead, the Lord says He will build a "house" for David. The word "house" (*bayit*) is used in both a literal sense (house = temple) and in a figurative sense (house = dynasty), and the two are playing off each other. A substantial part of the meaning of the passage comes out in the interplay of these different senses of "house." This is "play" with words, but it is play of the most serious kind.

The Bible's tropes, furthermore, fit into a system of imagery and metaphor. When Isaiah compares the growth of righteousness to the earth's bringing forth fruit like a garden (61:11), the garden reference is not just a homely metaphor but is linked with the pervasive garden theme of the Bible. It refers ultimately to the garden of Eden, picks up on the imagery of the Pentateuch and Psalms that compares Israel to a garden or a vineyard, and is linked to Isaiah's notion that Israel has become a wilderness because of her sin. Isaiah's prophecy is thus a promise of restored Edenic righteousness and fruitfulness. In Psalm 1, to take another example, the simile comparing the righteous man to the tree by streams of water is again rooted in the garden setting of Genesis 2. A righteous man is like a tree not only in His stability and firmness and fruitfulness, but also because his life, in some measure, recaptures human life in its integrity.

Tropes can be recognized by examining the immediate context of a sentence, but in addition to this level of context, an interpreter has to examine how words are used throughout entire books of the Bible. Like great novelists, the biblical writers repeat a theme, word, or image throughout a book, and it accumulates significance as it goes. Looking at the use of a word or image in chapter twenty-five without first tracing how the author has packed meaning into the word in chapters 1–24 is like seeing the end of a movie first. We might get some of it, but mainly we will be left confused. On occasion, looking at an author's use of a word or phrase is essential to an accurate grasp of its meaning in a particular passage. A good example of this is Jesus' use of the phrase "this generation" in Matthew 24:34. Studied solely in its lexical context (i.e., looking it up in the dictionary) and in the immediate context of Matthew 24, it is possible (though just barely) to understand the phrase as "this race." What Jesus is saying, on this interpretation, is that the things He predicts will occur before the Jewish race disappears from the world. Once we see how Matthew uses the phrase, however, this interpretation becomes quite impossible. Throughout the gospel, Matthew has used "this generation" to refer specifically to the generation that witnessed the ministries of John and Jesus (11:16; 12:39ff; 16:4; 17:17; 23:36). By the time we get to chapter twenty-four, we should not be confused about it anymore.

Seeing the repeated use of a word or image is sometimes important not for grasping precisely what is being said, but for grasping the fullness of what is being said. For example, in 1 Samuel, we frequently see Saul holding a spear (18:10–11; 19:9–10; 22:6; 2 Samuel 1:6). This seems an entirely unnecessary detail, added perhaps to make Saul a more vivid character. If we begin to examine the "spear" motif through 1 Samuel, we realize that most Israelites are without spears (1 Samuel 13:22). The first character who has a spear is Goliath, a Philistine, who wants to kill David with it (17:7). Through the rest of the book, Saul is the one with the spear, and he too wants to kill David with it. David, by contrast, never uses a spear (see 17:45–47). The writer has noted several specific incidents that involved spears in order to associate the spear with oppressive power. As Samuel warned, Saul-of-the-long-ash-spear is a king like the kings of the nations; he acts like a Philistine giant. We will grasp this important theme only if we read "with the grain" of the text, paying attention to the accumulating associations of words and phrases as we go. If we read stories in isolation from one another, we will miss this.

The third level of literary context is the whole Scripture. Here we are dealing with what Michael Fishbane, a Jewish scholar, has called "innerbiblical interpretation." This refers to the way biblical writers interpret their own times through the lenses of earlier events in Israel's history. Sometimes, this takes the form of direct allusion. In Exodus 2, the baby Moses is placed in an "ark," and the Hebrew word is the same as the word for Noah's ark in Genesis 6–8. Like Noah's ark, the "ark" of Moses is covered with pitch too. This allusion to the flood story is not window dressing but is intended to tell us something about the nature of the ministry of Moses. Like Noah, he will pass through the waters unharmed, both in infancy and later in adulthood; more importantly, like Noah (whose name means "rest"), Moses will be the one who brings Yahweh's people from slavery to Sabbath. Like Noah, Moses will be the instrument for destroying the old world of Egypt and bringing Israel into a "new creation."

Sometimes, the allusions are found not in verbal quotations but in analogous situations, events, and settings. Here at last we get to something that looks like typology in the traditional sense, but here "typology" is not merely describing the relation between the Old and New Testaments; rather it but is operating already within the Old Testament. It is remarkable, for example, to note the incidence of "death by head wound" in the Old Testament. Sisera, Abimelech, Goliath, Absalom—many of the enemies of God have their heads crushed. When a scene or event is repeated in this way, it is deliberate and theologically grounded. All these are types of the serpent, whose head the Seed of the woman will crush (Genesis 3:15).

Thus far, we have been examining interpretation at the word level. But the Spirit is responsible not only for the words of Scripture, but also for the way the words are ordered. If we want to grasp the full meaning of the Scriptures, we must pay attention not only to the way words are being used, but also to how the Scripture is structured at larger levels. Here I wish to discuss two main categories: One is "literary structure" and the other is "plot structure." By the former, I mean a formal and abstract pattern in the text, a pattern that can be applied to a number of different types of writing. A "chiasm," for instance, can be used to organize a story, a Psalm, an exhortation in an epistle, or even a single sentence. By "plot structure," I mean recurring stories. The "death and resurrection" story is an example of a plot structure, though the death and resurrection can take very different forms from one specific story to another.

Let me begin with an example of a chiasm from Deuteronomy 12. Examined as a whole, the chapter follows this outline:

A. Observe carefully in land, v. 1
  B. Destroy Canaanite worship, vv. 2–4
    C. Worship at central sanctuary, vv. 5–14
      D. Meat and blood, vv. 15–18
        E. Don't neglect Levites, v. 19
      D´. Meat and blood, vv. 20–25 ("well with you"; "do what is right," v. 25)
    C´. Worship at central sanctuary, vv. 26–28 ("well with you"; "do what is right," v. 28)
  B´. Beware Canaanite worship, vv. 29–31
A´. Be careful to do commands, v. 32

John Breck has argued in his fascinating study, *The Shape of Biblical Language*,[22] that chiasms proper always have a central section that contains the main point of the passage. Here, strikingly, the reference to the Levite stands at the center. The centralization of worship is prominent, but supporting the Levite at the central sanctuary is the main point.

Alternatively, the first fourteen verses of Deuteronomy 12 can be outlined into two smaller chiasms, as follows:

I. Eliminate Canaanite worship, vv. 1–4
  A. Observe statutes and judgments, v. 1
    B. Destroy places of false worship, v. 2
    B´. Destroy objects of false worship, v. 3
  A´. Don't act like Canaanites, v. 4

II. Establish true worship, vv. 5–14
  A. Seek Lord in place He chooses, v. 5
    B. Bring offerings and contributions, v. 6
      C. Rejoice with house, v. 7
        D. Rest given, vv. 8–9
    B´. Brings offerings and contributions, vv. 10–11
      C´. Rejoice with house, v. 12
  A´. Offer offerings in place Lord chooses, vv. 13–14

In verses 5–14, the main point is to emphasize the rest that the Lord promises to provide Israel when they have entered the land. It is not unusual for biblical texts to be organized by several overlapping structural principles, which enables the text to teach a number of things simultaneously.

Another sort of "literary structure" is called a "panel" construction. Here, instead of the chiastic pattern of "ABCBA," we have an ABC-ABC pattern as the text follows through the same sequence two or more times. As with the chiasm, the panel structure is often a clue to theological significance and sometimes uncovers the theological point of a passage that may seem to be arranged arbitrarily. In 2 Samuel 5–7, for instance, the text cycles through the same topics three times, with some important variations. In chapter five, David is first anointed as king over all Israel, then he fights the Jebusites and conquers Jerusalem, then we are told that Hiram helps him build a palace, and finally there is a list of the sons born to him in Jerusalem. In verse seventeen, we have a reference to his anointing, which suggests that the story is starting over where it began. Again, we follow through the same cycle: After the reference to David's anointing, he fights the Philistines, takes the ark into Jerusalem, and then decides to build a house for Yahweh. The Lord responds by saying that He will build a house for David (chapter 7). Thus, we have two sections following this same sequence: Anointing, battle and victory, house-building. The pattern continues in a somewhat different form into chapter eight, which records David's victories over the Philistines and Hadadezer and then lists the members of his administration, his royal "house." When we see that the text is structured as a set of variations on similar themes, it takes on a considerable weight of significance. David fights and then builds a house from the spoils, just as Jesus will later build His church from the spoils of His victory on Golgotha.

A final "literary structure" is the Bible's use of sequences of seven, all of which are rooted in the creation account of Genesis 1. A sevenfold pattern can be used to structure a narrative, a letter, or a set of speeches. In Exodus, for example, the description of the tabernacle is divided into seven speeches, which are marked by the phrase "Yahweh spoke to Moses, saying" (25:1; 30:11; 30:17; 30:22; 30:34; 31:1; 31:12). Some of these sections correspond in striking ways to the creation week, but the mere fact of seven "words" of God suggests that the tabernacle is to be understood as a new creation or as an aspect of a new creation. Similarly, in Leviticus 8, the description of the ordination of Aaron and his sons as priests is divided into seven speeches that are marked off by the phrase "as the Lord commanded Moses" (8:5, 9, 13, 17, 21, 29, 36). As Aaron is brought through these seven "words," he is made a new man. This pattern continues into the New Testament, especially in Revelation, which is structured by a complicated set of sevens. Some of the sequences of seven in Revelation are ironically related to the creation account, although they depict a "decreation" rather than a "recreation."

In addition to these and other literary patterns, the Bible also makes use of repeated plot or story lines. The Bible tells the same story over and over, though never in exactly the same way twice. One of the main story-lines of the Bible is the "Creation-Recreation" story. The clearest example of this is found in the early chapters of Genesis. God creates the world (Genesis 1–2); then Adam sins and an initial judgment is passed when Adam is thrown out of the Garden (Genesis 3). There follows a period in which sin ripens and grows, a period of decline (Genesis 4–5); finally, God passes a "final" judgment, destroying the world corrupted by sin, in this case by the flood (Genesis 6–8). On the other side of the judgment, however, the Lord brings in a new creation with a new Adam, Noah, who is sent out to rule, multiply, and fill it (Genesis 9). We see this pattern repeated in the rest of the Bible, both in large sections of text and in smaller stories. As James Jordan has suggested, the whole Bible can be organized by this pattern:

Creation	*Fall*	*Initial Judgment*	*Decline*	*Final Judgment*	*Recreation*
Creation	Fall	Gen. 3	Gen. 4–5	Flood	Noah
Exodus	Kadesh	no entry	40 years	death of first generation	conquest
Conquest	failure to conquer, Judg. 1	nations remain	Judges	capture of ark	return of ark
David/Sol	Solomon	division	divided K	exile	return
Return	Jews reject Jesus	turn to Gentiles	Jews reject apostles	Jerusalem, A.D. 70	Church

Recognizing this kind of repeated story-line helps us to see the analogies between different parts of the Bible. From the chart, we see the "typological" relation between Adam and Solomon, for example. Sometimes the Bible makes explicit allusions that indicate these connections. Deuteronomy 32:11 speaks of the Lord "hovering" over Israel at the time of the Exodus, and this is the same (rare) word used in Genesis 1:2 to describe the Spirit's hovering over the deep of the original creation.[23] This allusion, in short, indicates that the Exodus is a new creation and that Israel is being formed by the Spirit as the people of the new creation. Another example is found in Jeremiah 4:23, where Jeremiah describes the judgment on Jerusalem and Judah with another allusion to Genesis 1:2: The land is "formless and void," and there is no light. This suggests that the judgment on Judah returns the world to a pre-creation state, to a "prime matter" that will be formed into a new cosmos.

Another common story-line follows this pattern: God speaks a word of command or promise, people respond to the Lord's command, and then God evaluates the response, passing a judgment of innocence or guilt. Again, this story is, in a sense, the story of the entire Bible. God commanded Adam not to eat from the tree of knowledge; Adam disobeyed, so God pronounced curses and cast him from the garden. The gospel is that another Adam obeyed perfectly and therefore was judged righteous and readmitted to the Garden. Sometimes, the command or promise is implicit, and therefore it is necessary to compare Scripture with Scripture to determine what command is being broken. 2 Samuel 6 describes David's first attempt to bring the ark into Jerusalem, which leads to disaster as Uzzah reaches out to touch the ark to keep it from toppling over and is struck dead. This seems to be a harsh judgment until we read the text against the background of Numbers 4:15 and 7:9, where we learn that the Levites were not supposed to be carrying the ark on a cart in the first place and that no Levite was allowed to even see, much less touch, the ark.

When we get to the book of Exodus in chapter two, we will look in more detail at the "exodus story-line," which is very frequent in Scripture. In a sense, this is a variation on the "victory-housebuilding" story. Yahweh fought against and defeated Pharaoh and the gods of Egypt and then commanded Israel to build His house with the spoils of victory. Other exodus stories in the Old Testament—preeminently, the exodus from Babylon—also follow this pattern of Yahweh's victory followed by the building of a house. And this points, typologically, to the victory of Jesus over Satan and His project of building His house, the Church.

Conclusion

Recovering the Old Testament as a text in which Christians live and move and have their being is one of the most urgent tasks before the church. Reading the Reformers is good and right. Christian political activism has its place. Even at their best, however, these can only bruise the heel of a world that has abandoned God. But the Bible—the Bible is a sword to divide joints from marrow, a weapon to crush the head.

[1] *The Love of Learning and the Desire for God: A Study of Monastic Culture* (Fordham University Press, 1974), pp. 87–109.

[2] I have developed this point at greater length in my article, "Marcionism, Postliberalism, and Social Christianity," *Pro Ecclesia* 8:1 (Winter 1999) 85–97.

[3] *What is Christianity?* (5th ed.; trans. Thomas Bailey Saunders; London: Ernest Benn, 1958), pp. 49–50.

[4] *Ibid.*, p. 60.

[5] *Ibid.*, p. 130.

[6] *Ibid.*, pp. 153–154, 169.

[7] *Marcion: The Gospel of the Alien God* (trans. John E. Steely and Lyle D. Bierma; Durham, NC: Labyrinth, [1924] 1990), pp. 133–142.

[8] *The Christian Faith* (2d ed.; trans. H. R. MacIntosh and J. S. Stewart; Edinburgh: T&T Clark, 1928), pp. 60–62, 608–611.

[9] In *On Religion*, Schleiermacher claimed that the leading idea of Judaism was its belief in "universal immediate retribution," that God disciplines individual sins. By contrast, Christianity's leading idea is that God overcomes all obstacles and the resistance of finite being to unity with the Whole

(*On Religion: Speeches to its Cultured Despisers* [trans. John Oman; New York: Harper Torchbooks, 1958], pp. 239–241). It should be noted that Schleiermacher was not personally anti-Semitic; he took the unpopular stance of defending the extension of full civil rights to Prussian Jews.

[10] According to Kant, "The *Jewish faith* was, in its original form, a collection of mere statutory laws upon which was established a political organization; for whatever moral additions were then or later *appended* to it in no way whatever belong to Judaism as such. Judaism is not really a religion at all but merely a union of a number of people who, since they belonged to a particular stock, formed themselves into a commonwealth under purely political laws, and not into a church; nay, it was *intended* to be merely an earthly state so that, were it possibly to be dismembered through adverse circumstances, there would still remain to it (as part of its very essence) the political faith in its eventual reestablishment (with the advent of a Messiah)."

Christianity "completely" forsook Judaism and was "grounded upon a wholly new principle" that required "a thoroughgoing revolution in doctrines of faith," though this was a revolution for which Judaism somehow prepared. Typological and allegorical efforts to connect Judaism and Christianity are not theologically substantive but only provide evidence of the sensitivity of Christians to the prejudices of the first-century; early Christianity sought to introduce a "purely moral religion in place of the old worship, to which the people were all too well habituated, without directly offending the people's prejudices" (*Religion Within the Limits of Reason Alone* 2d ed.; trans. Theodore M. Greene and Hoyt H. Hudson; LaSalle, IL: Open Court, 1960), pp. 116–118).

[11] According to Harnack, critical philosophy, as developed by Schleiermacher and others, implies that the Old Testament cannot have any authority in Christianity. He commended Schleiermacher for recognizing this and giving Marcion his due (*Marcion*, p. 137).

[12] *The God of Israel and Christian Theology* (Minneapolis: Fortress, 1996).

[13] *Ibid.*, pp. 1–2.

[14] Quoted in *ibid.*, p. 3.

[15] *Ibid.*, pp. 5–6.

[16] *Ibid.*, p. 53.

[17] With regard to "temporal foreshortening," it is difficult to see how supercessionism has this effect, even if it is wrong. The church has always taught that the story of the Hebrew Bible continues indefinitely into the future.

[18] Soulen, *God of Israel*, p. 170.

[19] *Ibid.*, pp. 169–171.

[20] For further examples and discussion, see Moises Silva, *Biblical Words and their Meaning: An Introduction to Lexical Semantics* (rev. ed.; Grand Rapids: Zondervan, 1994).

[21] See, in addition to *ibid.*, James Barr, *The Semantics of Biblical Language* (Oxford: OUP, 1961); Dan McCartney and Charles Clayton, *Let the*

Reader Understand: A Guide to Interpreting and Applying the Bible (Wheaton, IL: Victor Books, 1994).

[22] Subtitled *Chiasmus in Scripture and Beyond* (Crestwood, NY: St. Vladimir's Seminary Press, 1994).

[23] Meredith Kline, *Images of the Spirit* (Published by the author, 1986), pp. 14–15.

1
Book of Beginnings

The Bible tells one story. It is a long and complicated story about events that took place over several thousand years, but even so it is one story. Like most good stories, the most exciting and important parts come toward the end. In this case, the most important part comes when Jesus is born, lives, dies on the cross, rises again, and ascends to heaven. But to know why Jesus comes and what He is doing when he dies and rises again, we need to know the story that goes before. A man kisses a sleeping woman in a wood and she awakes. That's a nice ending to a story, but if we don't know the woman is Sleeping Beauty and the man is Prince Philip, then we don't know the story very well. A beginning is nothing without an ending, but an ending without a beginning isn't worth much either. To tell the story of Jesus, we need to start with Genesis, the first book in the Bible, a book whose name means "Beginnings."

Three-Story House, Genesis 1:1–2:4[1]

The Bible's story begins by telling us about the world where the story takes place. In the Bible, the world is the real world that we live in, the world that God created. But the Bible describes the world in a particular way. In some places, the Bible describes it as a house. Talking to Job from the whirlwind, Yahweh asks:

> Where were you when I laid the foundation of the earth!
> Tell me, if you know understanding,
> Who set its measurements, since you know?
> Or who stretched the line on it?
> On what were its bases sunk?
> Or who laid its cornerstone,
> When the morning stars sang together,
> And all the sons of God shouted for joy? (Job 38:4–7)

Earth, and especially mountains, are set on "foundations" (Deuteronomy 32:22; 2 Samuel 22:8, 16; Psalm 104:5) just like the foundations that hold up a house. Blue sky is stretched out above like a "tent curtain" (Isaiah 40:22). Pillars support the earth (Job 9:6) and heaven (Job 26:11). When God first appears in the Bible, He is building a house.

God makes His house through His Word and Spirit. All three Persons of God are working to build His house. The Father speaks and things are made. He says, "Let there be light," and there is light. Other places in the Bible, we learn that the "Word" that makes the world is the "Word" that is God (John 1:1–5). And this Word becomes man in Jesus. The Spirit is mentioned too in Genesis 1:2: "the Spirit of God was moving over the face of the waters." What does the Spirit look like when He "hovers" over the waters? In other places in Scripture, we learn that the Spirit makes His appearance looking like a cloud that sometimes glows with light.[2] The cloud that leads Israel out of the wilderness is the Spirit. He "hovers" over Israel, as He hovered over the waters, to make a new creation (cf. Deuteronomy 32:11). Later, this same "glory-cloud" appears in the Most Holy Place of the tabernacle and temple of Israel. And much later, the Spirit "hovers" in the form of a dove at Jesus' baptism (Matthew 3:16), because in Jesus, God is again making the world new.

It takes God six days to build His house, six days that are just like our days with the sun coming up in the morning and going down in the evening. After that, God rests on the seventh day, a day known as the Sabbath day.[3] During the first three days, God makes a three-story house by dividing one thing from another. On the first day, He divides light and darkness; on the second, He divides waters in heaven from waters on the earth and puts the sky or firmament in between, and on the third day, he divides the waters on the earth to make the dry land and the sea. The next three days, He fills up the three stories of His house. On the fourth day, He puts the sun, moon, and stars in the sky to fill up daytime and nighttime. On the fifth day, He creates birds to fly across the sky and fish to swim in the waters. On the sixth day, He makes Adam and animals that live on land. What's interesting is that the first three days match the second three days:

Dividing	**Filling**
Day 1: Light/dark	Day 4: Sun, moon, stars
Day 2: Waters above/below	Day 5: Birds and fish
Day 3: Waters/land	Day 6: Land animals and man

7. Sabbath

And so, at the end of the six days of creation, God has finished a "three-story" house. Above is the "tent curtain" of blue sky, then the dry land, and finally the waters "below" the earth.

The Bible mentions this three-story house many times. In the second commandment, God forbids us to bow down to an image of anything in "heaven above, or on the earth beneath, or in the waters under the earth" (Exodus 20:4). That means we must not bow down to images of *anything*. "Heaven, earth, and sea" means "the whole universe." Sometimes when the Bible mentions the three-story house, it's not as obvious as it is in the second commandment. In Psalm 77:16–18, for example, we read:

> The waters saw Thee, O God;
> The waters saw Thee, they were in anguish;
> The deeps also trembled.
> The clouds poured out water;
> The skies gave forth a sound;
> Thy arrows went here and there.
> The sound of Thy thunder was in the whirlwind;

> The lightnings lit up the world;
> The earth trembled and shook.

Each story of the house is mentioned. When the Lord appears, the waters tremble and shake with anguish. The Hebrew word for "anguish" can refer to the pain of a woman who is having a baby. When the Lord comes, the waters thrash about like a woman in labor. Then the Psalm describes the sky: God comes riding on clouds that are like a chariot, rumbling with thunder, and flashing with arrows of lightning. God is coming on the scene like a great warrior entering a battle.

Finally, the earth "trembled and shook" at the coming of the Lord. Waters, sky, and earth: God comes and the whole house begins to shake.[4]

When we read this Psalm, it sounds like the world is breaking apart. But that's not what the Psalm is talking about. Instead, it's talking about an event that happened in the Old Testament. At the end of the Psalm, we read this:

> Thy way was in the sea,
> And Thy paths in the mighty waters,
> And Thy footprints may not be known.
> Thou didst lead Thy people like a flock,
> By the hand of Moses and Aaron (vv. 19–20).

The Psalm is talking about Israel's Exodus through the Red Sea, but it describes it as something that makes the whole universe tremble. Asaph, who wrote the Psalm, is telling us that the Exodus is a world-shaking event. We think that World War II is a big event, but the Psalm says that the Exodus is even bigger. When Israel is brought out of Egypt, the whole world trembles. And when God shakes the world, it means that God is making a new world (Hebrews 12:26–27). In the Exodus, the cloud and "whirlwind" hover over the waters as the Spirit hovers over the waters at creation (Genesis 1:2). Out of the "anguish" of the waters, a new Israel, and a new world, is born.

Sometimes the Bible talks about a nation or empire as if

it were the three-story house. Each nation is a "world." Like the creation, a nation is built on "pillars." In Hannah's prayer at the birth of Samuel, she looks forward to what the Lord is going to do in Israel:

> He raises the poor from the dust,
> He lifts the needy from the ash heap
> To make them sit with nobles,
> And inherit a seat of honor;
> For the pillars of the earth are the Lord's,
> And He set the world on them. (1 Samuel 2:8)

Here the "pillars of the earth" are pillars that hold up the "house" of Israel (see Psalm 75:3). Nobles and other important people are the "pillars" of Israel, but in Hannah's day, the pillars are wicked men. Hannah looks forward to a time when the evil pillars will be torn down and the righteous will be set up as columns. Two decades later, Samson tears down the pillars of the temple of Dagon and, in the process, destroys most of the "columns" of the nation of Philistia (Judges 16:23–31). When Samson brings down the "house" of Dagon, he also brings down the "house" of Philistia. Hannah, it seems, has good reason to hope that the pillars will be shaken.

So, the world is a house, and each nation is also a house. And this is why the Bible sometimes seems to be talking about the fall of the universe when it's talking about the fall of a nation. The plagues are attacks on the "three-story house" of Egypt. There are ten plagues, with the killing of the firstborn as the climax. The first nine are arranged in three sets of three plagues (all references are to Exodus):

	First Cycle	*Second Cycle*	*Third Cycle*
Water	1. Nile to blood	4. Flies (by water, 8:20)	7. Hail (ice)
Land	2. Frogs (8:5–7)	5. Pestilence (land animals)	8. Locusts (10:5)
Sky	3. Gnats (flying)	6. Boils (9:8)	9. Darkness (sky)[5]

Egypt's water, land, and sky are being shaken until Egypt falls to the ground.

Sometimes the Bible focuses attention on only one of the floors of the three-story house. Sun, moon, and stars—which are set in the "upper room" of the universe—often picture rulers and kings. Already in Genesis 1:16, the heavenly bodies are described as "governing" the day and night. Isaiah the prophet talks about the sun, moon, and stars falling from the sky:

> Behold, the day of the Lord is coming,
> Cruel, with fury and burning anger,
> To make the land a desolation;
> And He will exterminate its sinners from it.
> For the stars of heaven and their constellations
> Will not flash forth their light;
> The sun will be dark when it rises,
> And the moon will not shed its light. (Isaiah 13:9–10)

Like Psalm 77, it sounds as if Isaiah is talking about the end of the world. And he is, in a sense. But the world that's coming to an end is Babylon (Isaiah 13:1), not the whole universe. What Isaiah describes as the fall of the heavens is a prophecy of the collapse of Babylon as a "heavenly" power.

Very often the land pictures Israel and the sea pictures the nations (see Psalm 46:1–3, 6; 65:7–8). Isaiah talks about Assyria as an overflowing river that threatens Judah. The people of Judah have to decide between two rivers:

> Inasmuch as these people have rejected the gently flowing
> waters of Shiloah,
> And rejoice in Rezin [king of Aram] and the son of Remaliah
> [Pekah of Israel];
> Now therefore, behold, the Lord is about to bring on them
> The strong and mighty waters of the [Euphrates] River,
> Even the king of Assyria and all his glory;
> And it will rise up over all its channels and go over all its
> banks.
> Then it will sweep on into Judah, it will overflow and pass
> through,

> It will reach even to the neck;
> And the spread of its wings will be the fulness of the breadth
> of your land, O Immanuel. (Isaiah 8:6–8)

Yahweh is the "river whose streams make glad the city of God" (Psalm 46:4), but Judah has rejected these waters, trusting in Aram and Israel for protection from Assyria. Because they have rejected the Lord's living water, the Lord will let the Euphrates overflow and engulf Judah. God is turning back creation as He did in Noah's flood: Instead of separating land and water, the water is now going to overflow the land.[6]

Jeremiah also compares the sea to the Gentile nations when he warns Judah that Babylon is coming to destroy her. Nebuchadnezzar, the Babylonian emperor, is a sea monster who swallows up the Lord's people (Jeremiah 51:34–35). But the Lord will not allow Babylon to overflow His people forever: "Behold, I am going to plead your case and exact full vengeance for you; and I shall dry up her sea, and make her fountain dry" (v. 36). Though once a sea herself, Babylon will be overcome by the sea: "The sea has come up over Babylon; she has been engulfed with its tumultuous waves" (v. 42). This flood, strangely, turns Babylon into "a parched land and a desert, a land in which no man lives." Though the Gentile sea monster has swallowed Judah, the Lord promises to "punish Bel [a Babylonian god] in Babylon, and I shall make what he has swallowed come out of his mouth; and the nations will no longer stream to him" (v. 44). The Lord is going to make Babylon vomit Israel back onto the land.

When God finishes building His house, it is "good" (Genesis 1:4, 10, 18, 21, etc.). But He doesn't want the house to stay exactly as it is. He makes a good house, but He wants it to get better and better. In the next section, we'll see how, instead of getting better and better, His first house is spoiled.

Review Questions.

1. How is the world like a house?
2. How do the first three days of creation match the second three days?
3. What are the stories of God's three-story house?
4. What is Psalm 77 talking about? Why does it describe this event as if it were the end of the world?
5. How does Hannah's song compare Israel to a house?
6. What do the sun, moon, and stars represent? What is Isaiah talking about when he describes heavenly bodies falling from the sky?
7. What does the land often represent? What is the sea?
8. How does Isaiah describe the Assyrian invasion of Judah?
9. How does Jeremiah describe Nebuchadnezzar and Babylon?

Thought Questions.

1. What does Psalm 82:5 mean by "the foundations of the earth"?
2. Compare Genesis 1:2 and Genesis 8:1. Note that the word for "Spirit" is the same as the word for "wind." In light of this, explain what's happening in Genesis 8:1.
3. Notice the references to the three-story house in Revelation 8:1–13. Notice also that there are seven trumpets being sounded. Explain how this connects to Genesis 1.
4. Why is it significant that Noah's ark has three levels (Genesis 6:16)?
5. If the land pictures Israel, what do land animals represent? Look at Psalm 77:20 and 80:1.

***Junior Architects,* Genesis 1:26–28; 2:1–25; 6–9**

Once God has made His three-story house, He puts Adam and Eve in it and gives them a job to do. In Genesis 1:26–28, God makes Adam and Eve in His "image and likeness." An image is a copy, and Adam and Eve are created to be like

God. As God is king of the whole creation, so Adam is to be king of the animals and birds, with Eve the queen at his side. Being like God also means that Adam is supposed to work as God works. As we have already learned, God builds the creation as His house, and Adam, as the image of God, is also to be a builder. This is what God intends when He says that Adam should be fruitful and multiply; fill the earth and subdue it; and rule over the fish of the sea, the birds of the sky, and every living thing that moves on the earth (Genesis 1:28).

Adam's job is to "subdue" and "rule." The word "subdue" is especially interesting. In the Old Testament, the same word is used to describe victory in a war, as when David "subdues" his enemies. And the word also means "subduing" someone to slavery (see Jeremiah 34:11, 16; 2 Chronicles 28:10). When God creates the world, it is all good, so Adam does not have to "subdue" wicked enemies. Still, Adam has to work hard to subdue the world. Even before Adam sins, it is not easy to rule creation. Animals need training, trees are tough to cut, the earth is hard to dig, and rocks are hard to break. By working hard, Adam is to make creation a "slave." He is supposed to find new ways to use what God has made, so that the whole creation serves man more and more. In Genesis 4:22, we learn that Tubal-cain is "the forger of all implements of bronze and iron." He is the first to "enslave" the metals that God has created and make them useful. Today, thousands of years later, we are still learning new ways to "subdue" creation.

Of course, Adam's job is not only to make the world more useful for him, but also to make the world pleasing to God. God does not want Adam simply to have children; He wants Adam to have faithful, godly children who worship and serve Him. God does not want Adam to use iron to hurt other people; He wants Adam to use iron to make useful tools and musical instruments. Adam is the king of the world, but he is always a servant to a higher King. If Adam subdues the world as God commands, he will be building a house for

God within the house that God has built for him.

When Adam is first created, he is put in the garden of Eden. The Garden is one of several different areas that God makes in the world. Remember that God initially makes a "three-story" world. In Genesis 2, we learn that the middle floor, earth, is divided into three "rooms." The Garden is only one of them. Genesis 2:8 tells us that the Lord God plants a garden "toward the east, *in* Eden," which means that the Garden is on the east side of the land of Eden. Eden is larger than the Garden, and outside Eden there were other lands, which are named in Genesis 2:11–13. If Adam had taken time on the first day to make a map, he would have drawn a map with several areas: the Garden, the land of Eden, and the larger world.

It is interesting to notice how these three "rooms" of earth match up with the three "stories" of the universe. To see fully how this works, another portion of the creation has to be considered, namely, the "firmament." Made on the second day of creation (Genesis 1:6), the firmament is not just the flat surface of the sky but the whole region that we call "outer space." We know this because the sun, moon, and stars are "in" the firmament (Genesis 1:14–19). It is also called "heaven" (Genesis 1:8). This means that God created a world with two "heavens": The heavens where God dwells and the visible heavens of outer space. When we add this to our picture of the three-story house, we see that the "attic" is divided into two sections.

With this in mind, we can compare the order of the universe to the map of the earth as follows:

World	Earth
Heaven	Land of Eden
Firmament	Garden
Earth	Land to east
Sea	Outlying lands

We have already looked at some places in the Bible that compare the "earth" to the "land," that is, the land of Palestine where Israel lives. We have also seen that the sea pictures the Gentile world outside of Israel. How Eden and the Garden match with the two heavens isn't obvious yet, but we'll get to that in the next chapter.[7] This picture implies that Adam's highest achievement will be to move from the garden into the land of Eden. He was not created to serve in the Garden only but to rule in the land.

We have learned already that the three-story house is mentioned in many passages of Scripture, and the same is true of the garden of Eden. After the fall, cherubim are placed at the gate of the Garden, which is on the east side (Genesis 3:24). This means the entrance to the Garden is toward the east. If you want to return to the Garden, you have to travel west, and moving east is moving away from the Garden. All through the Bible, east and west have this meaning. Cain is cast out of the land and wanders in Nob, which is east of Eden (Genesis 4:16). Lot moves east and settles near Sodom (Genesis 13:11). When Israel enters the land from Egypt, they circle around to Moab and cross the Jordan from the east. This shows that entering the land flowing with milk and honey is like returning to the Garden. Later, when Israel goes into exile, they are taken to the east, away from the land, and to return they travel west. In the New Testament, the wise men come from east to west, seeking the Garden and Jesus, the real Tree of Life (Matthew 2:1).

The Garden is on a mountain. The river that runs into the Garden comes from the land of Eden and then flows through the Garden (Genesis 2:10). Eden is on higher ground than the Garden, but since the water runs from the Garden to outlying lands, the Garden too is a high place. Ezekiel states this plainly. He prophesies against Tyre, describing the "prince of Tyre" as an Adam who is in the garden of God (v. 13) on the holy mountain of God (v. 14). Throughout the Bible, mountains and hills are places where God meets with man. During the time between the collapse of the tabernacle and the building of the temple, Samuel conducts worship in "Ramah," which means "high place" (cf. 1 Samuel 7; 9). David brings the ark to Jerusalem and sets it in a tent on Mount Zion, and later, the Lord instructs Solomon to build His temple on a mountain in Jerusalem. Every time God meets with man on a mountain, it is a return to the Garden.

Adam has a job in the world—to subdue and rule it. In Genesis 2, he is given a job in the Garden. According to Genesis 2:15, he is to "guard" and "work" the Garden. Through much of the Old Testament, these words describe the work of priests. Priests are called to "guard" the Lord's house (see Numbers 1:53; 3:8), and the "service" of worship is often described using the same Hebrew word found in Genesis 2:15 (see Exodus 20:5; Numbers 8:15; Deuteronomy 7:4, 16). Adam's job is not only to build for God in the world, but also to serve God as priest in the Garden. When God divides the earth into a "garden" and the "world" outside, He is pointing to the two jobs of Adam: king and priest. In the Garden, Adam meets with God and worships Him; in the world, Adam is to rule and subdue.

Water and trees, a man and woman on a mountaintop—these features of the Garden come up again and again later in the Bible. Throughout Genesis, the patriarchs, the forefathers of Israel, meet their wives by wells in oases. A servant from Abraham goes to the city of Nahor and finds a wife for Isaac while waiting by a well to water his camels (24:10). Jacob flees from the wrath of Esau and meets Rachel coming to get water from a well at Haran (29:1–12). Moses fights off the shepherds who attack Jethro's daughters at a well in Midian and ends up marrying one of those daughters (Exodus 2:16–22). These are all garden scenes, with a man and a woman and animals at a well. This shows us that the patriarchs are new Adams, with their wives new Eves; they will be fruitful and multiply, rule and subdue. This scene reappears in the New Testament when Jesus meets with the Samaritan woman at the well and discusses marriage with her (John 4). Jesus is the new Jacob and the new Moses, but also the Last

Adam, inviting Samaritans and Gentiles into the Garden and offering them the water of life.

For this same reason, we find the patriarchs preoccupied with digging wells. Isaac has to reopen wells of water that the Philistines stop up (Genesis 26:18–22). When he digs new wells, the herdsmen of Gerar contend about the water, so he moves to Sitnah, where there is another quarrel. Finally, they dig a third well, and here there is no dispute, which leads Isaac to say, "Now we can be fruitful in the land." "Fruitful" reminds us of the command to Adam and Eve in Genesis 1:26–28. Isaac has to dig wells because he and his animals and his family need water. But digging wells is also a sign that Isaac is like a new Adam who seeks for a well-watered place in the land, a place where he can be fruitful and multiply.

Though Adam is created good and given every privilege and blessing, he sins by taking the fruit of the tree of the knowledge of good and evil. Adam is allowed to eat from the tree of life, but he prefers to reach out for the tree that the Lord has forbidden. Adam's sin occurs in the Garden, and it is a failure having to do with his priestly task. Called to guard the Garden, Adam lets in a serpent who tempts Eve while he stands by, watching (Genesis 3:6). Called to "serve" God in the Garden, he listens to the voice of Satan. Because of this, Adam and Eve are driven from the Garden and cherubim are set up to prevent their return (Genesis 3:24). All through the Old Testament, no man was ever able to return to the Garden. Adam messes up the world not just for himself but for everyone who follows him.

But God doesn't leave mankind in that condition. Right away, God promises to send the "seed of the woman," who will crush the serpent's head and lead God's people back into the garden (Genesis 3:15). This is the first promise of a Savior in the Bible, and it shows us that the Savior will be a great warrior who will be victorious over Satan. But God does not keep that promise right away. The rest of the Old Testament is all about what God does to prepare for the coming of the Seed of the Woman.

Adam's sin is not the only sin that we find in the early chapters of Genesis. Cain kills his brother in the field, and because of his sin, he is cast out of the land and forced to wander in Nob to the east of Eden (Genesis 4:16). Genesis 4–5 trace the generations of Cain and Seth, a history that ends with the whole world full of wickedness (Genesis 6:5). Evil fills the world because the "sons of God" intermarry with the "daughters of men" (Genesis 6:2). The "sons of God" are the descendants of Seth, the faithful believers who fall into sin by marrying the women who have descended from Cain. The Lord responds by reversing the creation, flooding it with water to return it to its original condition (cf. Genesis 1:2). Thus, Genesis 3–6 record a series of "falls," moving from the Garden, to the land, to the world. Sin and death spread until the three areas of the original creation are spoiled and therefore have to be wiped away:[8]

Place	*Sinner*	*Sin*	*Judgment*
Garden	Adam	Eats fruit	Cast out of Garden
Land	Cain	Kills brother	Cast out of land
World	Sons of God	Marry unbelievers	Cast out of world (Flood)

Of course, the Lord preserves Noah and his sons during the flood and then sends them out into a new creation. Noah is a new Adam. Like Adam, he is told to "be fruitful and multiply and fill the earth" (Genesis 9:1). Yahweh promises that Noah will have successful dominion over the animals (Genesis 9:2) and forbids him to eat blood (Genesis 9:3–4). Yet, Noah also receives authority beyond Adam's. The Lord gives Noah permission to execute murderers (9:5–6), and instead of being given a garden that the Lord has planted, Noah plants his own vineyard-garden (9:20). In the last episode of Noah's story, we see him drinking wine and taking rest in his tent (9:20–21). Noah, whose name means "bringer of rest," has brought the world from violence to Sabbath peace.

After the three falls and the ruin of the whole earth, God has given man a new start. But the stories of Adam, Cain, and the sons of God make us wonder, "How long will it last?"

Review Questions.

1. What does it mean for Adam to be the "image" of God?

2. What does "subdue" mean? What is Adam supposed to "subdue"? What is the result supposed to be?

3. Describe the map of the original creation in Genesis 2.

4. In what part of the land of Eden is the Garden? Why is this significant?

5. How do we know that the Garden was on a mountain? Give some examples of how this appears later in the Bible.

6. What is Adam's job in the Garden?

7. In what ways is Adam's sin a failure to be a priest?

8. What is the difference between Cain's sin and Adam's? Between Cain's sin and the sin of the "sons of God"?

9. Explain how the flood is a "reversal" of creation.

10. How is Noah a new Adam? In what ways does Noah advance beyond Adam?

Thought Questions.

1. Read Ephesians 1:21–23, noticing how Paul refers to Genesis 1:26–28. What is Paul telling us about Jesus?

2. Read Revelation 21–22. How is the city similar to the garden of Eden? How does it differ? What does this tell us about the direction of history?

3. How is the Song of Solomon related to the creation of Adam and Eve in Genesis 2? See Song of Solomon 4:12–16; 5:1; 6:2.

4. Hebrews 5:14 speaks of the "mature" who have their senses trained "to know good and evil." How does this verse help us understand the "tree of the knowledge of good and evil" in Genesis 2?

5. Consider how the story of Israel in Judges, Kings, and Ezra-Nehemiah moves through the three areas described in Genesis 2 (garden and worship, land and brother, world and unbelievers).

***Between Babel and Bethel,* Genesis 11–12; 17; 35**

As the apostle Peter teaches, the flood is the watershed between one world and another. It brings an end to the world that was formed out of water and by water and starts a new "heavens and earth" (2 Peter 3:5–7). In the baptism of the flood, the world dies and rises again (1 Peter 3:18–22). But the story of the "world that then was" sets the pattern for the history that follows. Just as sin ruined the world before the flood, so sin ruins the new world. Yet, where sin is great, God's love and mercy is greater. When the new world is ruined, God immediately takes steps to set things back on track.

Genesis 10 lists the seventy nations of the new world that come into being after the flood. In chapter eleven, however, there is another "fall" of man at the tower of Babel.[9] The story in Genesis 11:1–9 follows what is called a "chiastic" outline, where the second half of the story matches the first half, in reverse order:[10]

A. The *whole earth* has one *language* (v. 1)
  B. Settled *there* (v. 2)
    C. Said to *one another* (v. 3)
      D. *Come, let us* make bricks (v. 3)
        E. Let us *build* (v. 4)
          F. *City* and *tower* (v. 4)
            G. Lord came down (v. 5)
          F´. *City* and *tower* (v. 5)
        E´. That man had *built* (v. 5)
      D´. *Come, let us* confuse (v. 7)
    C'. *One another's* speech (v. 7)
  B´. Scattered from *there* (v. 8)
A´. Confused *language* of the *whole earth* (v. 9)

When God makes His appearance in the central section ("G"), everything changes.

The story of Babel focuses on the fall of one clan of Shem's descendants. Genesis was not originally divided into chapters, so in the Hebrew Bible the story goes straight from

10:26–31 to 11:1–9. Genesis 10:30 describes the journeys of the descendants of Joktan and says that they settle in the "hill country of the east." A few verses later, we learn that "they were journeying east" (11:2), and since it's a continuation of the same story, "they" means the descendants of Joktan who have just been mentioned. Though Joktan's descendants fall at Babel, this has consequences for the whole world, confusing the "lip" and scattering the nations who cooperate with the project. Just as the sons of Seth fall into sin with the daughters of Cain (Genesis 6:1–4), so here a faithful line of descendants, the line of Shem, joins with Nimrod (Genesis 10:10) to rebel and bring ruin to the world. In Genesis 12, however, the Lord calls another Shemite, this time a member of the clan of Eber, whose seed will bring together the nations divided at Babel.

The Shemites who assemble at Babel want to build a tower that will not only become famous throughout the world but will also connect heaven and earth. Babel's tower, in other words, is a temple, and Babylonian books describe the building of a great tower, Esagil (which means "tower with its top in the sky"), as a "dwelling" for Babylonian gods.[11] Though in the east, in the land of exile from God's presence, the children of Joktan are trying to reestablish the Garden.[12]

But this house for the gods is built in rebellion. The men of Babel want to reach to heaven and make a name for themselves, not exalt the name of Yahweh. Besides, they disobey God's command to "fill the earth." They want to stay put, "lest we be scattered abroad over the face of the whole earth." God's response to this rebellion is funny. Verse five says, "Yahweh came down to see the city and the tower." The "tower that reaches to the sky" is so far from heaven that the Lord has to "come down" to see it. "Seeing" in Scripture often means making a judgment (Genesis 1:4, 12, 18, etc.; Psalm 11:4). When the Lord draws near to "see," He is inspecting the tower and deciding whether or not it will stand.[13] Their reason for building the tower is to avoid being "scattered," but the end result is that they are scattered more widely than they were to begin with. They want to make a name for themselves, but the name they receive is Babel, which means "confusion." The name "Babylon" means "gate of God," but the Old Testament name for these efforts to establish a gate to heaven is "confusion" and "folly."

The ruins of the tower and city of Babel loom in the background throughout the stories of Abraham, Isaac, and Jacob. God calls Abram immediately after the fall at Babel, and there are a number of connections between Babel and Abram. The story of Babel is part of the genealogy of the Shemites, which begins in Genesis 10:21 and resumes in 11:10. Abraham comes at the end of this genealogy (11:27–32). The line of Shem takes a detour through Babel, but it ends with Abram.[14] God's promises to Abram also reflect back on the story of Babel. The Babelites intend to achieve a great name, but Yahweh tells Abram that He will make his name great (12:2). At Babel, the Shemites hope to unite the whole world, but it is Abram who will be the father of a great nation. The true "United Nations" is found among the descendants of Abram.[15]

God makes two great promises to Abram, and both are connected with the promise that Abram's seed will build the true "Babylon." First, God promises Abram a "seed." This is the promise of a son, and it is a promise that seems impossible to fulfill because of Sarai's barrenness and her advancing age. Most of the stories about Abram have to do with his hope for a child. Lot is initially Abram's heir, and so their relationship has to do with the promise of a seed (Genesis 13–14, 18–19). Abram's decision to have a son by Hagar is also a response to the Lord's delay in fulfilling the promise of a son (Genesis 16). When Isaac is finally born, the Lord commands Abraham to offer Him as a sacrifice on Mount Moriah (Genesis 22), and Abraham obeys, believing that God will raise Isaac from the dead (Hebrews 11:19).

This promise of the seed is part of God's response to the fall of the nations at Babel. Though Abram is not given the task of building God's house, having a son is the first stage in building God's house. In 2 Samuel 7, as we'll see in chapter four, the Lord answers David's plan to build a house by saying that He intends to build a house for David. What He means is that He will build David's family into the royal family of Israel. The house that God builds for David is a house made of people. Then the people that God makes into a house turn around and build a house for God. This is the story we find in the history of Israel: The Lord builds a great nation in Egypt and then sets them to work building His house. And this is the same pattern we find in the stories of Abram: God promises to build a house for Abram, a large household that includes many nations. In light of the events at Babel, this promise implies that Abram's household will one day build the Lord's house. More specificially, the Lord promises that the son will build the house.

Another way to say this is to notice that God promises to multiply Abram's house. Remember that Adam and later Noah are commanded to "be fruitful and multiply and fill the earth." The same words are repeated when the Lord appears to Abram and other patriarchs, but instead of being a command ("be fruitful"), it is a promise ("I will make you fruitful"). Adam is told to build himself a large household, but the Lord promises Abram, the head of a new human race, that He will build a house for him (Genesis 17:2, 6).

The other great promise to Abram is the promise of land. Abram begins his life in Ur but is called to come to Canaan. When he arrives, the Lord appears to him to say, "To your seed I will give this land" (Genesis 12:7). Later, God tells Abram that this promise will be delayed:

> Know for certain that your seed will be strangers in a land that is not theirs, where they will be enslaved and oppressed four hundred years. But I will also judge the nation whom they will serve; and afterward they will come out with many possessions. . . . Then in the fourth generation they shall return here. . . . To your seed I have given this land. (Genesis 15:13–14, 16, 18)

Israel's land is going to be a new Eden, a land flowing with milk and honey. And within the land, Israel is going to build a new garden, the temple, the house of God. It's no accident that Abram came to the land from Ur, a pagan city to the east. Traveling west from Ur, Abram is making his way back toward the Garden.

Circumcision, the "sign of the covenant" that God gives to Abram (Genesis 17), brings these two promises together.[16] Yahweh has promised land, but here it is called the land of Canaan for the first time (17:8). The Lord has promised an abundant seed, but here Abram is father not only of a "great nation" (12:2) but also of "a multitude of nations" (17:5). He will father a new set of "seventy nations" (cf. Genesis 10) to replace the nations that have fallen at Babel. Abram has been told that descendants will come from him, but here it is emphasized that "kings shall come from you" (17:6). Yahweh has already entered into a covenant with Abram, but here the covenant is extended to Abram's "descendants after you throughout your generations" (17:9). From this point on, Abram is a new man with a new name. Abram has been replaced by Abraham, and Sarai by Sarah.

Fittingly, the passage centers on circumcision as the sign of the covenant.[17] Circumcision is a cut in the flesh, and it speaks of the cutting off of the old in order to receive the new. Circumcision cuts off Abram and replaces him with Abraham. Having been cut off from the flesh, Abraham is ready to father the "child of the promise" (see Galatians 4). But it is not just Abraham who begins a new stage of life here; his entire household is involved. Circumcision marks out the house of Abraham as the house in covenant with Yahweh (17:12–13). Circumcision shows that the flesh is powerless and points to the need for God to be the Giver of the seed. Only God can open Sarah's womb and fulfill His promise to multiply Abraham's seed. Circumcision shows that Yahweh alone can build the house of Abraham.

Promises of seed and land are also given to Isaac and Jacob, but in the case of Jacob, the connection of the land to the "house of God" is clearer. As Jacob is leaving the land to get away from Esau, he stops at a "certain place" to spend the night and sees a vision of a "ladder" reaching to heaven (Genesis 28). Like the tower of Babel that is to reach its "head" into heaven (Genesis 11:4), the "head" of the "ladder" that Jacob sees reaches to heaven (28:12). Jacob's ladder is the true "tower" that connects heaven and earth, but it is built by Yahweh, not by Jacob. Furthermore, there is an emphasis on the word "place" in Genesis 28 (vv. 11, 16–17, 19). Initially, the location is an undisclosed "place," but the Lord's appearance there turns it into a holy "place." This reminds us of the emphasis of Genesis 11 on the Shemites' settlement "there," at the place on the plains of Shinar. When Jacob awakes from his dream, he calls the place the "gate of heaven" (28:17), which is reminiscent of the Babylonian "gate of God." By the end of the story, Jacob has changed the name of the "place" from Luz to Bethel, which means "house of God." At Bethel, the Lord reveals His answer to Babel: He will build a way to connect earth and heaven; He will build it in the land; and He will build it through Jacob's seed (28:13–14).

From the "house of God," Jacob moves on to Haran, where he works for his uncle Laban for over a decade. Between Genesis 28 and 32, the story of Jacob follows a roughly chiastic story-line:

A. Jacob fleeing land; God appears at Bethel (28:10–22)
  B. Jacob arrives at Haran, marries (29:1–30)
    C. Jacob's children (29:31–30:24)
    C´. Jacob's flocks (30:25–43)
  B´. Jacob leaves Haran (31:1–55)
A´. Jacob reentering land; God appears at Peniel (32:1–32)

Here, the multiplication and prosperity of Jacob's house is central to the story. Though oppressed and mistreated by Laban, Jacob nonetheless receives the Lord's blessing and returns from his exile in two large companies. The Lord is keeping the promise of Bethel. He is building Jacob a house.

Jacob sets out from Bethel, and in returning to the land,

he returns to Bethel. When the Lord appears at Bethel the first time, Jacob vows to return a tenth to the Lord if the Lord will be with him. In the closing chapter of the Jacob story, Genesis 35, he makes his way back to Bethel to fulfill the vow (vv. 1–4). At Bethel, Jacob again sets up a pillar and anoints it, and the Lord promises again to bless him. Most of Jacob's life takes place between these two visits to Bethel.

As we have seen, the early chapters of Genesis tell us of three sins: one in the Garden, one in the land, and one in the world. Adam's sin is against God, Cain's is a sin against His brother, and the sons of God sin in their relations to unbelievers in the world. The stories of the patriarchs focus on these same three areas. But the patriarchs, instead of sinning, act rightly in each area. Abraham shows that he is a righteous man by being willing to sacrifice his son to the Lord. He is faithful as a priest in the garden. Jacob's life is taken up with conflicts with his relatives: his brother Esau and his uncle Laban. Joseph, whose story comes at the end of Genesis, is faithful even when he goes as a slave into a foreign land and among unbelievers in Egypt. For this reason, the story of Joseph is a good ending to the book of beginnings. Joseph is the true "son of God" who resists the daughters of men (Genesis 39:7–12).

It's a good ending for another reason too. The book of Genesis begins with God telling Adam to "subdue and rule" the earth, and it ends with Joseph, a man who rules the vast empire of Egypt. Joseph is a picture of what Adam is supposed to become. Everywhere he goes he serves faithfully and ends up running the show. Even as a young man, his father gives him authority over his brothers and puts a robe on him as a sign of his position (Genesis 37:2–3). His brothers strip off his robe, but once he is in Potiphar's house, he again begins to rule (Genesis 39:1–6). Again his robe is stripped off, this time by Potiphar's wife. After two years in prison, Joseph is called upon to interpret Pharaoh's dream:

> Then Pharaoh took off his signet ring from his hand, and put it on Joseph's hand, and clothed him in garments of fine linen,

> and put the gold necklace around his neck. And he had him ride in his second chariot; and they proclaimed before him, "Bow the knee!" And he set him over all the land of Egypt. (Genesis 41:42–43)

Joseph is not naked as Adam was when he was created. Joseph is like the Last Adam, clothed like a king and ruling over the Gentiles.

Like all great kings in the Bible, Joseph rules in order to serve. When he becomes the second ruler of Egypt, he does not use his power to do selfish things. Instead, he uses his power to give bread to the world. He does not take revenge against the brothers who mistreated him. Instead, he feeds them too and invites them to come live with him in Egypt. Here too, Joseph is like the Last Adam, who is raised up above all kings and rulers to give Himself as the bread of life to hungry sinners.

At the very end of Genesis, Joseph is no longer a ruler in Egypt. The very last verse tells us: "Joseph died at the age of one hundred and ten years; and he was embalmed and placed in a coffin in Egypt" (Genesis 50:26). Great as Joseph is, his life is not the end of the story of Israel. It is only the beginning. Time moves on. Joseph is not just the end of the book of beginnings; he is the beginning of a new story. That's the story of the Exodus, which we'll look at in the next chapter.

Review Questions.

1. Who is involved in building the tower of Babel? What are they trying to build?
2. Explain how the story of the tower of Babel is put together. What happens in the middle of the story?
3. How is God's call to Abram connected to the story of Babel?
4. What are the main promises given to Abram? How are these connected with the story of Babel? How are they connected with Adam?
5. What is circumcision? What does it mean?

6. Explain the connections between Jacob's dream and the tower of Babel.

7. What does Jacob call the place where he sees the dream? Why is this important?

8. What happens while Jacob is in Haran working for Laban?

9. Explain how the three patriarchs are related to the three sins early in the book of Genesis.

10. Why is it fitting for Joseph's story to be at the end of Genesis?

Thought Questions.

1. Yahweh tells Abram that his seed will be like the stars (Genesis 15:5). In light of the three-story house, what is the Lord telling Abram?

2. Where does Abraham go to sacrifice Isaac? (Genesis 22:2). Compare to 2 Chronicles 3:1. What is the significance of this connection?

3. Read Genesis 25:23. In light of what the Lord says here, evaluate Isaac's preference for Esau. See also 25:34; 26:34–35.

4. Judah becomes one of the most prominent sons of Jacob. Yet, he is not the firstborn but the fourth son of Leah. Why? Look at Genesis 34 and 35:22.

5. Genesis 38 is a story about Judah, yet it comes in the middle of the section of Genesis that is dealing with Joseph. Why? Look at Genesis 39:7–18 and 44:14–34.

[1] Much of this chapter is a summary of James B. Jordan, *Through New Eyes: Developing a Biblical View of the World* (Eugene, OR: Wipf and Stock, [1989] 1999).

[2] For a full defense of this conclusion, see Meredith Kline, *Images of the Spirit* (Published by the author, 1986).

[3] Some people today don't believe this. They think that God took thousands or even billions of years to make His house. But the Bible says that it took Him six days, and that's the way it happened. For an examination of the alternative viewpoints, see James B. Jordan, *Creation in Six Days: A Defense of the Traditional Reading of Genesis One* (Moscow, ID:

Canon Press, 1999). Incidentally, Jordan finds a chiastic organization in Genesis 1 and contests the "two-panel" arrangement I am using here. Both structures, it seems, are valid.

[4] The reference to "deeps" (Hebrew, *tehom*) reminds us of the deep of the original creation (Genesis 1:2).

[5] For discussion of the three plague cycles, see Nahum M. Sarna, *Exploring Exodus: The Origins of Biblical Israel* (New York: Schocken, 1996), pp. 76–77. In his taped lectures on Exodus, James B. Jordan suggests that the cycles are related to the three-story universe.

[6] The king of Assyria, like some bird of prey, will spread his "wings" over Judah, an instrument of anti-creation (cf. Genesis 1:2)and anti-exodus (Deuteronomy 32:11).

[7] To anticipate briefly, we shall see that the Garden is transformed in the Mosaic covenant into the tabernacle, so that the tabernacle is, at least in one aspect, an architectural garden. Further, the tabernacle is modeled on the "pattern" that Moses was shown while on Sinai, and thus the tabernacle is an architectural embodiment of a heavenly archetype. Putting these two associations together, we conclude that the Garden too is patterned after heaven.

[8] See James B. Jordan, *Crisis, Opportunity, and the Christian Future* (Niceville, FL: Transfiguration Press, 1998).

[9] My discussion is based on the careful work done by J. P. Fokkelman, *Narrative Art in Genesis: Specimens of Stylistic and Structural Analysis* (2d edition; Sheffield: JSOT Press, 1991), pp. 11–45; U. Cassuto, *A Commentary on the Book of Genesis: Part Two: From Noah to Abraham* (Jerusalem: The Magnes Press, [1964] 1992), pp. 225–249; and Gordon J. Wenham, *Genesis 1–15* (Word Biblical Commentary #1; Waco, TX: Word, 1987), pp. 232–246.

[10] Wenham, *Genesis 1–15*, p. 235. Overlapping this structure is a two-panel construction:

v. 1	one language	v. 6	one people
	one kind of speech		one language
v. 2	there	v. 7	there
v. 3	each other		each other
v. 4	build a city	v. 8	building a city
v. 5	name	v. 9	its name
	scattered	v. 10	scattered

[11] See the quotation from the *Enuma Elish* in Wenham, *Genesis 1–15*, p. 237. See also Cassuto, *Genesis*, pp. 226–230.

[12] The repetition of "there" in verses two and nine, therefore, has a specific significance. This "there" was to become a new sanctuary.

[13] In response to the Babelites' call, "Come, let us build," the Lord says, "Come, let us confuse" (vv. 4, 7). In the Hebrew, the contrast is sharper, because the verbs for "build" and "confuse" alliterate ("build" is *nibneh* and

"confuse" is *nabelah*), and the latter also punningly refers to the Hebrew word for "folly" (*nebalah*).

[14] Abraham is the tenth from Shem, just as Noah is the tenth from Adam. Both Abraham and Noah are "new Adams" who will be God's instruments for bringing in a new world.

[15] This is the way the apostle Paul interprets the promises to Abraham. According to Galatians 3, Abraham hears the gospel when the Lord promises that "all the nations shall be blessed in you" (see Genesis 12:3). Galatians 3:14 implies that Abraham is promised the Spirit: Jesus endured the curse of the tree "in order that in Christ Jesus the blessing of Abraham might come to the Gentiles, so that we might receive the promise of the Spirit through faith." How is the promise to Abraham connected to the promise of the Spirit? And how are these connected with the tower of Babel story? If we look at the story of Pentecost in Acts 2, we can answer these questions. Acts 2, which is the story of the outpouring of the Spirit on the apostles, is like Genesis 10–11. Like Genesis 10, Acts 2 contains a "table of nations" (vv. 9–11), and like Genesis 11, Acts 2 tells about a miracle of language. But the language miracle is exactly the opposite of the judgment at Babel. At Babel, people were unable to understand each other because of their different languages; at Pentecost, they are able to understand each other, in spite of their different languages. At Pentecost, God fulfilled His promise to Abraham: the promise that the curse of Babel will be reversed, that many nations would name Abraham as their father, and that the nations would be reunited in Abraham's Seed.

[16] David A. Dorsey has suggested that Genesis 17 is the center of a chiastic pattern that structures much of the Abraham narratives. With some modifications, the following represents his outline of Genesis 12–21:

A. Promise of seed, 12:1–9
  B. Abram in Egypt, 12:10–20
    C. Lot settles in Sodom, 13:1–18
      D. Abram intervenes on behalf of Lot, 14:1–24
        E. Promise of a son, 15:1–21
          F. Ishmael's birth, 16:1–16
            G. Covenant of circumcision, 17:1–17
          F´. Ishmael and Abraham circumcised, 17:22–27
        E´. Promise of a son, 18:1–15
      D´. Abraham intercedes on behalf of Sodom and Lot, 18:16–33
    C´. Lot flees from Sodom, 19:1–38
  B´. Abraham in Gerar, 20:1–18
A´. Birth of Isaac, 21:1–7

The Literary Structure of the Old Testament: A Commentary on Genesis–Malachi (Grand Rapids, MI: Baker, 1999), p. 56.

[17] Gordon Wenham (*Genesis 16–50* [Word Biblical Commentary #2; Waco, TX: Word, 1994], pp. 17–18) has analyzed the structure of Genesis 17

itself in much the same way that he analyzes the structure of Genesis 11:1–9, as a combination of chiastic and panel construction. With some modifications, I am adopting Wenham's outline:

A. Abraham is 99 (v. 1a)
B. Yahweh appears (v. 1b)
C. Yahweh's first speech (vv. 1b–2)
D. Abraham falls on his face (v. 3a)
E. Second speech: name change, nations, kings (vv 4–8)
F. Third Speech (vv. 9–14)
E′. Fourth Speech: name change, nations, kings (vv. 15–16)
D′. Abraham falls on his face (v. 17)
C′. Fifth speech (vv. 19–21)
B′. Yahweh departs (v. 22)
A′. Abraham is 99, Ishmael is 13 (vv. 24–25)

The panel construction also centers on the third speech, verses 9–14:

vv. 1–2 Yahweh promises to multiply	v. 16 Yahweh promises to bless Sarai
v. 3 Abram falls on his face	vv. 17–18 Abraham falls on his face
vv. 4–6 Abraham father of nations	v. 19 Sarah mother of Isaac
v. 7 Yahweh will carry out oath	vv. 19–21 Yahweh will carry out oath
v. 9–14 Sign of the covenant	vv. 23–27 Sign of the covenant

2
Out of Egypt Have I Called My Son

Jacob has lived in Laban's household for many years, and Laban has treated him badly. Finally the Lord tells Jacob to flee, and he leaves secretly at night. In the morning, Laban realizes what has happened, chases Jacob, and angrily confronts him. "Give me back my household gods," he demands. Jacob knows nothing of the household gods and invites Laban to look through his tent. He says, "The one with whom you find your gods shall not live." Without Jacob knowing it, Rachel, Jacob's wife, has taken Laban's idols and hidden them in her tent. Laban searches tent by tent until he comes to Rachel's:

> Then he went out of Leah's tent and entered Rachel's tent. Now Rachel had taken the household idols and put them in the camel's saddle, and she sat on them. And Laban felt through all the tent, but did not find them. And she said to her father, "Let not my lord be angry that I cannot rise before you, for the manner of women is upon me." So he searched, but he did not find the household idols (Genesis 31:33–35).

What is this story doing in the Bible? What is this supposed to teach us?

One thing it teaches is that the gods of Laban are no gods. Rachel is sitting on them and they can't get up. As Psalm 115 says, idols have eyes but cannot see, mouths but cannot speak, ears but cannot hear, arms but no strength. But this story is not only telling us that these gods are nothing. The story is showing us that the gods of Laban are becoming unclean. Normally, a daughter in the ancient world stands up when her father comes into her tent, but Rachel says she can't get up because the "manner of women" is on her. Rachel is talking about the monthly flow of blood that comes from a woman's body. In the law of Moses, a woman who is having her monthly flow of blood is unclean. Anything a woman sits on during this time becomes unclean, and her seat also makes other things unclean (Leviticus 15:19–24). Laban's gods are unclean because Rachel is sitting on them. But the people who worship them also become unclean.

This is not the only story in the Bible that shows us that idols have no power. In the book of Exodus, God attacks some of the main gods of Egypt with the plagues. Egyptians worship the Nile, but the Lord turns the Nile to blood. Egyptians worship frogs, so God gives them lots and lots of frogs. Egyptians worship Pharaoh, so the Lord kills Pharaoh and his firstborn son. When He judges Pharaoh, Yahweh also executes judgments against the gods of Egypt (Exodus 12:12; Numbers 33:4), and His mighty acts lead Israel to sing, "Who is like thee among the gods?" (Exodus 15:11). Moses' father-in-law, Jethro, also confesses that God has shown He is greater than all gods (Exodus 18:11).

A King Who Knows Not Joseph, Exodus 1–2

God displays His power and shows that idols are powerless by saving His people from their enemies. The stories that tell about God rescuing His people are called "exodus stories." The story of Jacob is an exodus story: He goes out of the land, spends time with Laban, who treats him badly, and then returns to the land more wealthy than before. And Jacob is not the first patriarch to leave the land and return. Abram leaves twice, and the first exodus in Genesis 12 reminds us of what happens to Israel later on:

> Now there was a famine in the land; so Abram went down to Egypt to sojourn there, for the famine was severe in the land. . . . And it came about when Abram went into Egypt, the Egyptians saw that the woman [Sarai] was very beautiful. And Pharaoh's officials saw her and praised her to Pharaoh; and the woman was taken into Pharaoh's house. Therefore he treated Abram well for her sake; and gave him sheep and oxen and donkeys and male and female servants and female donkeys and camels. But the Lord struck Pharaoh and his house with great plagues because of Sarai, Abram's wife. . . . And Pharaoh commanded his men concerning him; and they escorted him away, with his wife and all that belonged to him. (Genesis 12:10–20)

Why do Jacob and his sons go down to Egypt? Because there is no food in Canaan, and Abram goes to Egypt for the same reason. Pharaoh enslaves them, as Pharaoh takes Sarai into his house. So, the Lord strikes Pharaoh with plagues until he is willing to let Yahweh's people go. Like Abram, Israel leaves Egypt with great wealth. Shortly after Abram returns, he fights against the kings of the land to rescue Lot (Genesis 14), just as later Israel leaves Egypt and then conquers the kings of Canaan (see Joshua 10:5, 16, 22; and Genesis 14:9). Like a preview at the movie theater, the exodus of Abram is a preview of the Exodus of Israel. Long before Israel goes to Egypt, God is the God of exodus, the God who delivers His people from slavery.

Israel is in Egypt for over two centuries, and the exodus stories of Abram and Jacob give hope to the Israelites while they wait for the Lord to redeem them. And they need hope because, since the days of Joseph, things have gotten very bad for the people of God. When the book of Exodus begins, Israel is prospering and multiplying in Egypt. The first verses of the book tell us that seventy from the "loins of Jacob" went to Egypt, along with the members of their households (Exodus 1:1, 5). The number seventy is the number of the nations in Genesis 10. When we learn there are seventy in the household of Jacob, we are learning that Israel replaces the "seventy nations" that fell at the tower of Babel

(Genesis 11:1–9). Even after Joseph and all his brothers die, Israel is still being blessed and prospering in the land of Goshen. They are "fruitful, increased greatly, multiplied exceedingly, became numerous, and filled the land" (Exodus 1:7). In the Hebrew, these are seven words that tell us over and over that Israel is doing well in Goshen. Words are multiplied to tell us about Israel multiplying. Israel is a new Adamic race, multiplying and filling the land.

But suddenly everything changes (v. 8). A new king arises who doesn't know Joseph and doesn't care about the people. This Pharaoh is also afraid of Israel because they are multiplying so fast. He fears that if a nation invades Egypt, the Hebrews will switch sides and fight against him (vv. 9–10). And he fears that they are "spreading out," taking over land that belongs to the Egyptians (v. 12). So, Pharaoh makes life very hard for the Israelites, forcing them to make bricks without straw, then making them slaves, and then trying to kill their male children. Notice Exodus 1:13–14: "And the Egyptians compelled the sons of Israel to labor rigorously; and they made their lives bitter with hard labor in mortar and bricks and at all kinds of labor in the field, all their labors which they rigorously imposed on them." Words are piled up again, just like in verse seven. But here the words describe the burdens piling up on Israel, not the Israelites spreading out and multiplying. Elsewhere in the Bible, we learn that the Israelites worship idols in Egypt (Joshua 24:14; Ezekiel 20:5–8). The Lord puts them under a wicked ruler because they have turned from Him. We'll see that this is something He often does during the history of Israel.

Pharaoh's plan doesn't work. Even though Pharaoh makes the Israelites work harder and harder and tries to kill all their sons, the midwives save many of the boy babies so that "the people multiplied and became very mighty" (1:20). More importantly, the Lord is working to raise up a deliverer to bring Israel out of slavery and into rest. That deliverer is Moses.

Like many boys of his time, Moses has to be saved from

Pharaoh, and he is saved by his mother, Jochebed. The woman preserves the "seed of the woman" who will grow up to crush Pharaoh's head. Jochebed sees that Moses is "good" or "beautiful" and wants to save him. This doesn't mean that she would have killed him if he had been ugly. But for some reason the Bible tells us that Moses is a beautiful child. Why? Part of the reason is to remind us of Joseph, who is also handsome (Genesis 39:7). Joseph is a deliverer of his people, bringing food to his brothers and to the world, and Moses is another Joseph. Like Joseph, he will be a prince in Egypt and bring salvation to the sons of Jacob. Of course, he is a Joseph in reverse. Instead of bringing Israel into Egypt, he will bring them safely out. Moses' beauty also says that he is a special child. Stephen the martyr says in his sermon that Moses was "lovely to God" (Acts 7:20). His beauty as an infant is a sign that God has chosen him to be a savior.

Jochebed puts her "beautiful son" in a basket lined with pitch. This reminds us of Noah's ark. In Hebrew, the word for "basket" is the same as the word for "ark," and this word is used only in these two places in the Old Testament. Noah's ark, like Moses', is lined with pitch (see Genesis 6:14). Moses is a new Noah. All around him the children of Israel are drowning, but Moses' ark passes through the waters of death and gets to safety. The same water that kills other Israelite children saves Moses. After the flood, Noah and his family come out from the ark and enter a new creation. Moses, the one who has passed through the waters in an "ark," is going to bring Israel out of Egypt and into a new world.

Moses begins right away trying to deliver Israel. When he grows up, he kills an Egyptian who is beating a Hebrew slave (Exodus 2:11–15). Many Christians think that Moses commits a horrible sin here. But that's not what the Bible says. It says that Moses "went out to" or "visited" his brethren (2:11; Acts 7:23). This doesn't mean that he has never visited them before. Moses grows up knowing all along that he is a Hebrew. When God "visits" His people, He saves them and punishes their enemies (see Psalm 106:4). That's what Moses is doing. He is "visiting" the Egyptians with punishment and visiting Israel to bring salvation (Acts 7:25). Moses sees an Egyptian "striking" a Hebrew, and so he "strikes" the Egyptian (Exodus 2:11–12). The same word is used in both verses. This means that the Egyptian is trying to kill the Hebrew, and Moses delivers his Israelite brother from death. Moses uses deadly force to stop the Egyptian from using deadly force. Like Yahweh, Moses acts on the principle of "eye for eye, tooth for tooth, stroke for stroke." Stephen the martyr calls this an act of "vengeance on behalf of the oppressed" (Acts 7:24), and that's a good thing to do. Moses is permitted to do this because he is a prince and ruler in Egypt. He is hoping that killing the Egyptian will be the beginning of Israel's deliverance from Egypt (Acts 7:25). Nothing in the Bible says that Moses is guilty of murder.

The next day, though, Moses gets his first taste of how the Israelites will treat their savior. He tries to stop a fight between two Israelites, as he stopped the fight between the Egyptian and the Israelite the day before, but the Israelites don't want him to be ruler and judge over them (Exodus 2:14). Moses sees that Israel isn't ready to leave Egypt, and so he flees to Midian for forty years. Moses goes into Midian not because he has to pay for *his* sin. He goes into Midian because the Lord is punishing Israel for *her* sins. Israel's salvation from Egypt is delayed for a generation because they do not accept Moses. Stephen sees that Israel treats Jesus the same way they treated Moses: The Jews in Stephen's day are "doing just as your fathers did. Which one of the prophets did your fathers not persecute?" (Acts 7:51–52).

When he comes to the well at Midian, Moses finds shepherds mistreating the daughters of Jethro. So Moses "stood up and helped them" (2:17), just as he had hoped to help the Israelites. He proves himself a true shepherd, fighting off the wicked shepherds. And he shows that he is a true Adam, protecting the "garden" and the women from the serpents who attack. Moses has been saved by a "woman" and now has grown up to be a savior of women. Notice how Jethro treats Moses: While the Israelites reject their savior, the Midianites invite him to stay with them. This is a repeated pattern in the Bible. When Joseph's brothers reject him, he goes to Egypt. When the Jews reject the preaching of Paul and the apostles, he turns to the Gentiles (Acts 28:28). In the end, God turns this to good. Paul says that "all Israel will be saved" after they become jealous of the Gentiles (Romans 11:26). In Egypt, Joseph provides food for his brothers. And Moses, too, returns from Midian to redeem Israel.

Everything that happens to Moses early in the book of Exodus will happen to Israel. Moses is saved through the water, and the whole nation will be saved through the sea. Jochebed places Moses in the "reeds" along the river (Exodus 2:3), and he will bring Israel through the "Sea of Reeds" (Exodus 13:18). He flees to Midian, where he spends forty years (compare Acts 7:23 with Exodus 7:7), just as Israel will have to spend forty years in the wilderness because of her rebellion. While Moses is among the Midianites, Yahweh appears to him in a burning bush on Mount Horeb (Exodus 3:1–2), just as the Lord will appear at Horeb to the whole nation after the Exodus. Moses is the head of Israel, and whatever happens to the head will happen to the body.

Already with the "head," Moses, the fortunes of Israel are changing. The Nile has been a burial ground for Israelite boys, but now it is the water of salvation for Moses. When Moses comes back to Egypt and begins to confront Pharaoh, this reversal continues. The Nile has been filled with the blood of Israelite boys, and now it is turned to blood. Pharaoh has been getting rid of the male Israelite boys, but in the end, all the firstborn sons of *Egypt* are killed. Israelite boys have been drowning in the Nile, but now Pharaoh and his hosts will sink in the sea like stones. The justice of the plagues is plain: Eye for eye, tooth for tooth. Yahweh delivers Israel with a powerful arm, but the Lord's arm is as just as it is strong.

The Marriage Supper of Yahweh, Exodus 20–24

But there's more to the story in the book of Exodus than Moses delivering Israel from slavery. The book doesn't end like the movie *Prince of Egypt*, with Israel crossing through the Sea. Israel passes through the sea in Exodus 14, and there are forty chapters in the book. The end of the story happens at Sinai. If we compare the beginning and end of Exodus, we see how the whole story fits together. At the beginning of Exodus, the sons of Israel are slaves to a wicked king, but at the very end of the book, the Lord takes His throne in the tabernacle as the King of Israel (Exodus 40:34–38). When the book begins, Pharaoh says that Israel belongs to Him. Yahweh says that Israel belongs to Him (4:23; 8:1), and at the end of the book, Israel is serving a new Master.

When Israel gets to Mount Sinai, God "cuts" a covenant with His people. To understand a covenant, think of a wedding. Through a wedding, a man and woman are bound together as husband and wife. Each of them takes a vow promising to do certain things: The man promises to love and care for his wife, and the woman vows to obey and support her husband. If they don't obey, the marriage may come to an end in divorce. What the man and woman are doing is making a covenant. In the Bible, God makes covenants with His people. Israel is the Lord's bride, and at Mount Sinai, Yahweh marries her (see Ezekiel 16:1–14; Hosea 1–3). He promises to provide all good things for His bride, and His people take an oath to obey and honor Him. If His people don't keep the covenant promise that they make, God threatens to bring all kinds of bad things upon them—diseases, famine, drought, death (Leviticus 26; Deuteronomy 28). To say that God is in covenant with Israel is to say that God has a close relationship with Israel, a relationship that includes promises, laws, and threats of curses. Israel's new Master is her Husband, bound to her by the covenant.

The wedding service goes from Exodus 19–24. Moses is the minister officiating at the wedding. He goes up on the mountain to hear the Lord's word and then brings it back down to the people. The Husband's part of the wedding service begins with the Lord reminding His bride of what He has done for her (Exodus 20:1–2). Then Yahweh tells Israel how they are to live as His holy people (Exodus 20–23). When Moses brings these words to the people, they say, basically, "I do": "All the words which the Lord has spoken we will do!" (Exodus 24:3). The wedding ceremony ends with a wedding reception, a feast in the Lord's presence (Exodus 24:9–11). Now that Yahweh and Israel are married, Yahweh decides to move in with His bride. Most of the rest of Exodus is about the kind of house He wants Israel to build for Him (Exodus 25–40).

Getting married means living by new rules. In Exodus 20–23, the Lord tells Israel how they are to live as His servants. Many of these laws are based on the Exodus. God says something like this: Because I have saved you from Egypt, you should live like people who have been saved from Egypt. In the New Testament, Paul teaches the same way. He says that Christians are "dead to sin." Because they are "dead to sin," they should live like people who are dead to sin by putting sin to death (Romans 6:1–11). What God has done for us is the basis of what He commands us to do. The basic command is: Be the kind of people that the Lord has made you; live up to who you are.

Because Israel has been redeemed from slavery, they are to release others from slavery. God does not forbid slavery (Exodus 21:1–11), but He spends a lot of time telling Israel how to set slaves free. In Deuteronomy, God tells Israel that every seventh year they should let Hebrew slaves go free (Deuteronomy 15:12). When the Lord brings Israel out of slavery, they are not empty-handed; God gives them the treasures of Egypt (Exodus 12:35–36). Israelites are supposed to treat their slaves the same way: "when you set him free, you shall not send him away empty-handed" (Deuteronomy 15:13).

The Sabbath commandments are based on the Exodus too. The Sabbath day is the seventh day of the week, and it is a time when all Israelites stop working and rest. They do this to follow God's example in creation, since He rested on the seventh day (Exodus 20:8–11). Resting on the Sabbath is also a reminder of the Exodus (Deuteronomy 5:12–15). When Israel is in Egypt, they are slaves and are not allowed to rest. By rescuing them from Pharaoh, Yahweh gives His people rest, and so every week they are reminded that "you were a slave in the land of Egypt, and the Lord your God brought you out of there by a mighty hand and by an outstretched arm" (Deuteronomy 5:15). But the sons of Israel are not only to take rest for themselves, they are supposed to *give* rest: "you shall not do any work, you or your son or your daughter or your male servant or your female servant or your ox or your donkey or any of your cattle or your sojourner who is in your gates" (Deuteronomy 5:14). Just as God gives Israel rest, so Israel is to give others rest. This shows that Jesus is not breaking the law when He heals people on the Sabbath. Healing people is a way of giving rest. Jesus is showing what real Sabbath-keeping is all about.

Another law based on the Exodus is the law about the "kinsman-redeemer." The kinsman-redeemer is a close relative who has special duties. When one Israelite becomes so poor that he has to sell his land, his "kinsman-redeemer" may buy his land back for him (Leviticus 25:25). If an Israelite becomes a slave, his "kinsman-redeemer" may buy him back from slavery. These laws were to remind Israel of what Yahweh had done for them in the Exodus. He is Israel's "kinsman" (Exodus 4:23) who buys Israel from slavery and gives her a land.

At the beginning of Exodus, Israel is serving Pharaoh by building storage cities (1:11). When we come to the end of the book, Israel is still busy building, but they are building the tabernacle for their new King, Yahweh. We saw in the last chapter how God called Abram to be the answer to the tower of Babel. Finally, at the end of the book of Exodus, Abraham's seed is fulfilling that promise. God has built Israel into a great people. They have multiplied so that they are like the sand on the seashore. Now Israel is ready to build God a house, the true "gate of God."

Review Questions.

1. What is Laban looking for in Genesis 31?
2. What does the story of Laban's gods teach us?
3. Explain how the story in Genesis 31 is like the story in Exodus.
4. How is Abram's exodus like the exodus of Israel?
5. Explain the connections between the beginning and end of Exodus.
6. Explain the "wedding ceremony" of Yahweh and Israel at Sinai.
7. How are the laws of Exodus based on God's rescue of His people?
8. How is the tabernacle related to the tower of Babel?

Thought Questions.

1. The Hebrew midwives deceive Pharaoh in order to protect the Hebrew children (Exodus 1:15–22). Is this right? Does God punish them for doing this? Compare Genesis 12:11–13.
2. When Yahweh strikes Egypt with gnats, the magicians of Egypt recognize that the "finger of God" is at work (Exodus 8:19). Compare Luke 11:20. What does this connection say about Jesus? What does it say about the Jews who oppose Jesus?
3. When Israel crosses the sea, the waters are divided and dry land appears (Exodus 14:22). How is this connected to Genesis 1:9–13?
4. What is the punishment for theft (Exodus 22:4)? How does this illustrate the principle of "eye for eye, tooth for tooth" (Exodus 21:23–25)?
5. Many Christians believe that the Old Testament law was harsh compared to Jesus' emphasis on loving your enemies. Look at Exodus 23:4–9. Was Jesus teaching anything new?

The House of the Lord, Exodus 25–40

The house that Israel builds at Mount Sinai is a tent called the tabernacle. The tabernacle is not merely canvas but has walls made of wooden boards that are set in sockets on the ground (Exodus 26:15ff). Three layers of curtains cover the wooden frame, and the inner layer is a beautiful curtain with figures of cherubim woven into it. Around the tent is a courtyard set off by white curtains hung on posts. The doorway of the tabernacle is to the east, so that anyone who wants to enter the tabernacle has to move from east to west (Numbers 1:53; 3:23, 29, 35, 39).

Within the tent are two rooms. The first is the Holy Place, and the second is the Most Holy Place or "Holy of Holies." The courtyard makes a third area. The tabernacle has three zones, and each of these zones is governed by a different set of rules. Any Israelite layman may enter the courtyard, but only priests may enter the Holy Place. Only the High Priest may enter the Most Holy Place, and he may do it only once a year on the Day of Atonement (Leviticus 16:1).

Each "room" of the Lord's house has furniture in it. In the courtyard is a bronze altar. All the animal offerings are burned on this altar, and blood of most animals is poured out here. Also in the courtyard is the bronze laver filled with water, set between the altar and the tent (Exodus 30:17–21). Priests wash their hands and feet in the water from the laver every time they enter the Holy Place. In the Holy Place are three pieces of furniture. On the North side is a table made of wood and overlaid with gold (Exodus 25:23–30). Twelve loaves of Shewbread or "bread of the presence" are on the table and are replaced each Sabbath day (Leviticus 24:5–9). To the South is a lampstand of pure gold that looks like an almond tree, with branches and bulbs (Exodus 25:31–40). On the West side, in front of the veil that separates the Holy Place and the Most Holy Place, is the golden altar of incense (Exodus 30:1–10). The Most Holy Place contains only one piece of furniture, the ark of the covenant, a box of wood covered inside and out with gold. The cover of the ark is pure gold and has golden cherubim stretching over the top of it (Exodus 25:10–22).

One way to think about the tabernacle is that it is a "house." Its furniture is similar to the furniture that is in the tents of the Israelites. In the court, there is an altar-stove for cooking food, and the altar is also called the Lord's "table" (Ezekiel 44:16). In the Holy Place, there is a lamp to give light, an altar for burning sweet-smelling incense, and a table with bread. But this tent is no ordinary tent. It is full of gold furniture and has beautiful curtains and veils. The Most Holy Place is the throne room. The ark, which contains the two tablets of the Ten Commandments, is God's footstool, and the cherubim above the ark form the Lord's throne. God sits on His throne "above" the cherubim (1 Samuel 4:4; Psalm 80:1; 99:1). It is not just a house, but the house of Israel's King.

The tabernacle is often called a "sanctuary," and this word means "holy place." In the Bible, places become holy when the Lord visits them in His glory. In Exodus 3, the glory of the Lord in the burning bush makes the ground holy. Exodus 29:43–44 tell us that the Lord makes His tabernacle holy by His glory, the glory-cloud that filled the Most Holy Place. Once a place is holy, it is God's special possession and must be used for Him and used only as He wants it to be used. A "sanctuary" is Yahweh's place, and holy things are Yahweh's things. This is why there are a lot of rules about what Israel may and may not do in the tabernacle: You shouldn't mess with Yahweh's things. In the New Testament, the church is the temple of God, made holy by the Spirit. If anyone messes with us, he is attacking God's holy things and messing around with the furniture of God's house. As the history of Israel shows, the Lord gets angry when people mess with His stuff.

The glory of God that fills the Most Holy Place and makes the tabernacle holy comes from the top of Sinai (Exodus 19:16; 24:17; 40:34–38). The tabernacle is like Sinai, a building made like a holy mountain. When Israel leaves the mountain, they take the mountain with them.[1] Like the tabernacle, Sinai is divided into three zones. The people are encamped at the foot of Sinai, but they may not even touch it (Exodus 19:20–25). Elders and priests ascend partway to feast in God's presence (Exodus 24:1–8), but only Moses enters the cloud on the top of the mountain. Similarly, in the tabernacle, the people may only enter the courtyard and are not allowed to touch the altar. Priests work in the Holy Place but are not allowed to enter the Most Holy Place, where only the High Priest, a permanent "Moses," may enter. If the tabernacle is like Sinai, then every time a priest enters the tabernacle, it is like climbing up God's mountain.

The tabernacle is not only a picture of Sinai but also a picture of the people of God. The New Testament tells us that the church is the temple of God, and in the Old Testament, the tabernacle is a picture of the people of God. As the holy things of the tabernacle are "gathered at the throne of God," so also the holy people are arranged around God's throne. Like Sinai and the tabernacle, Israel is divided in three groups. Most of the people of Israel are not priests; the descendants of Aaron are all priests, and one of the priests is the High Priest. So the house of Israel is like the house of the Lord, and the house of the Lord is a picture of the house of Israel. This is why the blood of the animal offerings is always sprinkled or thrown on some piece of furniture in the tabernacle and never on the people. This seems odd at first. How can blood make a sinner clean if the blood is never put on him? The answer is that the tabernacle is a picture of Israel, and so putting blood on the tabernacle is counted as putting blood on the sinner. When the priest puts blood on the altar, God accepts the sinner as clean.

This chart summarizes what we have learned about the tabernacle so far:

Tabernacle	*House*	*Sinai*	*Israel*
Courtyard	"Kitchen"	Base (people)	People
Holy Place	"Living Room"	Middle (elders)	Priests
Most Holy Place	"Throne Room"	Top (Moses)	High Priest

But there's still more. The tabernacle is a picture not only of Israel but of the whole world.[2] Remember that the world is a "three-story house," that the heavens are divided between the "highest heavens" and the "firmament," and that earth is also divided into several areas. With these things in mind, we can understand the arrangement of the tabernacle:

Universe	*Earth*	*Tabernacle Area*
Heaven	Land of Eden	Most Holy Place (throne of God)
Firmament	Garden	Holy Place (lampstand)
Land	Eastern land	Courtyard (altar)
Sea	Other lands	Outside the courtyard

The tabernacle as a whole is like heaven. When Moses goes up on Sinai, the Lord shows Him a "pattern" or model, and Moses builds the tabernacle to match the pattern in heaven (Exodus 25:9, 40). Hebrews 9 emphasizes that the earthly tabernacle is an image of the heavenly tabernacle, and in Psalm 150:1, the Holy Place is linked to the firmament. In building the tabernacle, Israel is doing God's will on earth as it is done in heaven.

A number of things in the tabernacle remind us of the garden of Eden. Like the Garden, it has a doorway on the east side (Genesis 3:24). The cherubim embroidered into the tabernacle curtains and built above the ark remind us of the Garden (Exodus 26:31–37). When a priest enters the Holy Place, he looks at the veil that has cherubim on it and is reminded over and over of the cherubim with the flaming sword in Genesis 3. Like the garden and land of Eden, the tabernacle is mostly off-limits. From the time of Adam to the time of Jesus, no one is allowed to go back into the Garden, past the cherubim, to enjoy God's presence. As Paul put it, the Old Covenant is a ministry of death (2 Corinthians 3:7; see Hebrews 9:8–10). The tabernacle is a way of keeping the people of God at a distance.

Since Jesus has come, there is no longer a tabernacle or temple on earth. This means that God is no longer keeping us away from Him. Because Jesus has offered Himself as the perfect sacrifice for our sins, we may boldly enter the Most Holy Place (Hebrews 10:19–25). We may go back into the garden and eat from Jesus, the Tree of Life. All this is true now because Jesus has died and torn the veil that separated Israel from God. And when we have passed through the "firmament" of the Holy Place, God brings us to the highest heavens to sit on thrones in Christ and rule with Him (Ephesians 2:6).

Review Questions.

1. What is the tabernacle?
2. What are the three zones of the tabernacle?
3. What is in each of the three "rooms" of the tabernacle?
4. How is the tabernacle like a house? Whose house is it?
5. What is a "sanctuary"? What makes the tabernacle a "sanctuary"?
6. How is the tabernacle like Sinai?
7. How is the tabernacle like the "house" of Israel? How does this help explain the sacrifices?
8. How is the tabernacle similar to the original creation?
9. In what ways is the tabernacle like the garden of Eden?

Thought Questions.

1. Notice how the materials of the tabernacle furniture change as you move from the courtyard to the Most Holy Place. What metals are used? Why?
2. Compare the materials of the tabernacle curtains and veils (Exodus 26:31–37) with the materials of the garments of the High Priest (Exodus 28:5–6). What does this tell you about the High Priest? See John 1:14.
3. The Spirit of God is mentioned only a few times in the Pentateuch. Two of the times are Genesis 1:2 and Exodus 31:3. Are these passages connected? How?
4. Israel's sin with the golden calf is recorded in Exodus 32, in the middle of the description of the tabernacle. What does this suggest about the golden calf?

5. Why does Moses break the tables of the law when he sees Israel worshiping the golden calf (Exodus 32:15–20)?

Bread of God, Leviticus 1–7

Once Israel builds the Lord's house and the Lord takes His seat above the cherubim, Israel begins serving Him in His house. "Worship" means "service in the Lord's house." At the tabernacle, Israel worships God mainly through bringing animals, killing them, and burning them on the altar. This kind of worship is often called "sacrifice," but this word is not exactly right. In the Bible, a "sacrifice" is an offering that is followed by a meal. When there is no meal, the offering should not be called a "sacrifice."

To understand Israel's worship, we need to understand two words that are used for all the animal offerings. The first word is the Hebrew word *qorban* (see Leviticus 1:2; 2:1; 3:1–2; 4:23; 5:11; 7:38). This word means a "gift" or "something brought near." For Israel, a gift is a very important thing. It is not just a "present," like we might give on a birthday. When two people exchange gifts, they are forming a friendship or continuing a friendship. Exchanging gifts is one way of making a "covenant" with someone, like a man and woman who exchange rings at a wedding. At Sinai, God makes a covenant with Israel, so that Israel becomes His "bride." Yahweh as the Husband of Israel promises many gifts, and to continue in the "marriage" covenant, Israel is supposed to bring gifts.

The offerings are *qorban* in another way. A *qorban* is something brought near to God. What the worshiper really wants is to draw near to God himself, to be His friend and companion. In the Old Testament, because of the sin of Adam, Israel is kept away from God and may not fully enter into His presence. By offering an animal, however, the Israelite worshiper is offering himself to God. And this is the "gift" that God really wants. Gifts are important, but it is possible to give a gift without caring very much for the person you're giving it to. God wants the Israelites to offer themselves by obeying and serving Him. The Lord is more pleased with obedience than with "burnt offerings" (1 Samuel 15:22–23). When a faithful Israelite brings an animal near, he is saying that he will serve and obey the Lord. He is drawing near through the animal in order to offer himself to the Lord.[3]

The second term used for the offerings is "bread of God" (Leviticus 3:11, 16; 21:6; Numbers 28:2).[4] Offering an animal is bringing a meal to Yahweh. This doesn't mean that God needs offerings to stay alive. In Psalm 50:7–9, the Lord says that He can get along without "young bulls out of your house" and "male goats out of your folds," since "every beast of the forest is Mine, the cattle on a thousand hills." But we don't eat just to stay alive. We eat to enjoy time with family and friends and to celebrate important events like weddings and birthdays and holidays like Thanksgiving and Christmas. This is why God "eats" Israel's sacrifices. He doesn't need them to stay alive, but He eats Israel's food as a sign that He is their friend. He "eats" to make a covenant with Israel, to continue the "wedding" feast that started at Sinai. Of course, what God truly desires is not the flesh of animals but instead people who love and obey Him. God wants us to be thankful, humble, and sorry for our sins. That's the sacrifice that pleases Him (Psalm 51:14–17). God wants to eat *you*.

In the Old Testament, God ate cattle, goats, sheep, and some birds: animals of land and sky. Those animals represent Israel, and so when God "eats" them on His table, He is having fellowship with Israel. When we come to the New Testament, Jesus is always eating fish. In the Old Testament, there are never any fish on God's table. Why is there a change? Remember the three-story universe. Israel is pictured by the land, and the Gentiles by the sea. When Jesus comes eating fish, it is a sign that He is going to bring the Gentiles into His covenant. Jesus comes to change God's menu by adding seafood.

There are several different kinds of animal offerings and a lot of rules about how Israel is supposed to offer them. Basically, though, it is pretty simple. There are five basic steps to each animal offering, and there are four basic kinds of animal offerings. There are less than ten things to remember. So you can learn the basics of Israel's worship if you have two hands with a full set of fingers.

Remember that the worshiper brings the offering, the *qorban*, because he wants to be near to God. The question is, How may sinners draw near to a holy God in His Holy Place? How may sinners, who are unclean and rotten, become tasty meals for Yahweh? We know that sinners are not allowed to come barging into God's house. They must not throw themselves on the Lord's table and offer themselves as bread. If they try that, they're going to end up dead. When Aaron's sons, Nadab and Abihu, try to draw near their own way, God kills them (Leviticus 10:1–2). Drawing near to God is dangerous, but God tells Israel in Leviticus that there is a safe way to come into His house.

First, the safe way is through a substitute. A substitute is someone who takes the place of someone else. If my son is going to be killed and I step in and get killed in his place, I am his substitute. In Israel, the animal is the substitute for the worshiper. The worshiper shows this by leaning his hand on the animal's head.[5] Laying hands on a person's head is a way of giving them a particular job or office (Numbers 27:18ff; Deuteronomy 34:9; Acts 6:6). Here, the animal is set apart to do the job of approaching the Lord on behalf of the worshiper, since the worshiper can't do this for himself. Setting apart the animal for an office is also a way of showing that the animal is a substitute. These two parts of hand-laying—setting apart for office and setting apart a substitute—are both found in Numbers 8:10. There, the Levites, who take the place of the firstborn sons of Israel as servants to the priests, are put in office by the laying on of hands. Notice the wording of Leviticus 1:3–4: The worshiper brings an animal to the doorway of the tent for *his* acceptance before the Lord. In verse four, after he lays his hand on the animal's head, the animal is "accepted" for him. When the animal is accepted into the fire, the worshiper himself will be accepted before the Lord.

Immediately after the worshiper has made the animal his substitute, he kills the animal. By doing this, he's killing himself. The animal's job is to die for the sinner. The only safe way for a sinner to draw near to God and become God's food is through a substitute who dies. In this way, Israel's worship at the tabernacle is a picture of the death of Jesus on behalf of His people. But this is not all that the animal offerings teach us. The substitute animal has died, but the problem is not solved: The worshiper has not yet been able to "draw near," and he has not been turned into the "bread of God."

From this point, the priest takes over. The animal is killed in such a way that the blood can be collected. A priest takes the blood and sprinkles or pours it in various places in the tabernacle. Leviticus 17:11 gives us an important clue to the meaning of the blood: "I have given the blood to you on the altar to make atonement for your souls." Blood atones for sin. Hebrews 9:22 reminds us that without the shedding of blood, there is no forgiveness of sins.

But it's not enough simply to shed blood. The blood has to be put on the tabernacle or some piece of tabernacle furniture. Sprinkling blood is a way of showing that a death has taken place. The worshiper is a sinner who deserves to die. Before he may draw near to God, he has to show that someone or something has died in his place. The blood proves that. We see the same principle at Passover. If an Israelite kills and eats the Passover lamb without putting blood on the door post, his firstborn will be killed. It is not enough just to kill the Passover lamb. Its blood has to be displayed for God to see. Similarly, if the sinner is going to be saved from the wrath of God, blood must be presented before God to stop the angel of death. Even for Jesus, it is not enough for the substitute to die; His blood also has to be presented in the tabernacle in heaven (Hebrews 9:11–12).

The other purpose of blood is for cleansing. In Leviticus 16:19, blood from the offerings on the Day of Atonement cleans the sons of Israel and turns God away from His anger. There is a connection with the laws about the death penalty. Some crimes make the land unclean (Deuteronomy 21:1–9), and the defiled land cries out for the death of the criminal, as Abel's blood cries out against Cain (Genesis 4:10). So also, the defiled altar, which is made of earth, cries out for the death of the sinner and has to be sprinkled with blood.[6]

After the blood has been sprinkled or poured out, the flesh of the animal or part of the flesh is burned on the bronze altar in the courtyard of the tabernacle. Burning the animal does not represent hell or eternal destruction. The word for "burning" an animal on the altar literally means "to turn into smoke," and a different word is used for destructive fire (*saraph*). Besides, the wages of sin is death, and the animal is already dead and cut into pieces before it is placed on the altar. Forget the picture in your children's story book that shows a whole lamb tied to the horns of the altar. It never happens that way. The animal is dead long before its flesh is put on the altar. And if it's already dead, why does it have to suffer the punishment of hell?

Fire destroys, but here the fire destroys the animal to change it into something new. Passing through the fire, the animal is purified, transformed, and glorified.[7] The animal is burned and becomes part of the cloud that represents God's presence over the altar. The fire consumes or "eats" the animal into the Lord's cloud. Further, the fire shows that the substitute is acceptable to God. Though the worshiper is defiled by sin, God has accepted him and his works through substitutionary death and the blood of an animal. He accepts the worshiper as a sweet-smelling savor in his nostrils. As a sign that the worshiper is accepted by God, God's fire eats the animal that represents the worshiper. God agrees to have a covenant meal, and the worshiper is the main course.

Finally, the rite for animal offering ends, in most cases, with a communion meal. Priests and sometimes the worshiper receive a portion of "God's bread" to eat. Eating together is a way to make a covenant or have fellowship. Throughout the Bible, when people conclude treaties, they eat a meal together to show that they are now friends. Jacob and Laban ate together after they had made a treaty of peace between them (Genesis 31:44–55). So also, when men draw near to God, they eat with Him. The elders of Israel eat and drink in God's presence, and He does not stretch out His hand against them (Exodus 24:9–11). The end—the goal and the conclusion—of Israelite worship is a fellowship meal with God, and this renews the covenant. Our worship in the church is the same: After we have confessed our sins, heard God's word, and praised Him, He invites us to His table to share a meal. We don't eat the flesh of an animal, but the flesh and blood of the perfect sacrifice, Jesus.

To summarize, we find a five-part rite in each of the animal offerings:[8]

Action	Meaning
Laying hands	*substitution*—sinner draws near through another
Slaughter	*penalty for sin*—sinner must die
Presentation of blood	*evidence of penalty*—Passover
Burning	*transformation to smoke*—becomes food for God
Meal	*fellowship*—renewal of covenant

So far, we have been looking at the basic rite of animal sacrifice, which can be summarized in five actions. Most of these five actions are done every time a worshiper brings an offering. But there are four distinct animal sacrifices, and each one is slightly different. There are many complicated details, but again, the basics are easy. Each of the animal offerings emphasizes one of the steps of the basic sacrificial ritual. One type of offering emphasizes the blood rite, another the burning, and another expands on the meal.

In Leviticus 1–7, the first offering is the so-called "whole burnt offering." This is a bad mistranslation. The Hebrew word (*olah*) means neither "whole" nor "burnt" nor "offering." Instead, the word means "to go up" or "to ascend," and this offering should be called an "ascension offering."[9] This offering highlights the burning of the animal, since the entire animal is dismembered and placed on the altar to be burned (with the exception of the skin, which goes to the priest). With the other animal offerings, only the fat and some of the internal organs are turned to smoke.

The second animal offering listed in Leviticus is the "peace offering" (Leviticus 3). Here, the meal is highlighted, since this is the one offering that the worshiper is allowed to eat. No one eats the flesh of the ascension offering (except Yahweh), and only priests are allowed to eat flesh from some sin and guilt offerings. By contrast, meat from the peace offering is divided into four shares. Yahweh receives the innermost parts. Then the priest who offers the sacrifice receives the right thigh, the priesthood as a whole receives the breast, and the worshiper keeps the rest (Leviticus 7:11–34). When there is reference to "sacrifice" in the Old Testament, it usually means a "peace offering."

Third among the animal offerings is the "sin" or purification offering (Leviticus 4). The distinctive thing about the purification offering is the sprinkling of blood. With the ascension offering, the blood is sprinkled or dashed on the sides of the altar of ascension, and the same is true of the blood of the peace offering. By contrast, the blood rite for the purification offering is very complicated. For one thing, the placement of the blood changes depending on who is bringing the offering. If a priest offers a purification offering, blood is taken into the Holy Place and smeared on the horns of the golden altar of incense. If a common Israelite sins, the blood of the purification is smeared on the horns of the bronze altar.

While the patriarchs offer ascension and peace offerings, the purification offering doesn't exist until Israel builds the tabernacle at Sinai. This helps us to understand what the blood of the purification is doing. It cleans the areas of the tabernacle that the worshiper defiles. A priest works in the Holy Place, so his sin defiles that room of the house. The blood of a priest's sin offering has to clean the golden altar, the main piece of furniture in the Holy Place. A common Israelite worships in the tabernacle courtyard, and therefore his sin dirties only the bronze altar. So only the bronze altar has to be smeared with blood.

The last of the animal offerings is "guilt," "reparation," or "trespass" offering. There is nothing unique about the ritual of a guilt offering (Leviticus 7:1–10). It does not have the complicated blood rite of the purification offering. Blood from the guilt offering is simply dashed on the sides of the bronze altar, like the peace offering. It doesn't have a meal for the worshiper as the peace offering does. Only priests are allowed to eat meat from the guilt offering, since its flesh is most holy. What makes the guilt offering different is the sin that it deals with (Leviticus 5:14–6:7). Purification offerings clean an unclean person of his uncleanness or a sinner of his sin, but guilt offerings turn a person who is holy back to the status of a commoner. If someone touches the flesh of an animal offering, he becomes holy (Leviticus 6:27). That means he has become God's special possession. But if he is not a priest, becoming consecrated is dangerous. He has come near to God without being prepared for it. Therefore, he needs to offer a guilt offering to "de-sanctify" himself. Guilt offerings are also brought when a worshiper sins against God's holy things (Leviticus 5:15).

The distinctive aspects of each offering are summarized in this chart:

Basic Rite	*Specific Offering*	*Action Done*
Blood sprinkled/ poured	Purification offering	Blood on horns of altar
Burning	Ascension	Whole animal burned
Meal	Peace offering	Worshipers eat

The guilt offering is not included in the chart, since there is nothing distinct about its ritual. We learn the meaning of the guilt offering by studying when it is offered, not by studying the rite itself.

All the offerings make it possible for Israel to live safely with the house of Yahweh in their midst. With Yahweh living just next door, sins and uncleanness became very dangerous. According to Leviticus 15:31, Israel is to separate from uncleanness "lest they die in their uncleanness by their defiling my tabernacle that is among them." Because the tabernacle is a picture of Israel, Israel's sins and uncleanness make the tent dirty. If this uncleanness is ignored, Yahweh will leave Israel and His house. Israel needs to clean up the house continually to make sure that her Husband keeps living with her.

Servants of the Lord's House, Exodus 28–29; Leviticus 8–9

Yahweh is a great King, and the tabernacle is His palace. Like every great king, the Lord has palace servants. The Lord's palace servants are called "priests."[10] According to the books of Moses, the priests have a number of duties as the "household servants" of God. Priests alone may enter the sanctuary, and only the High Priest enters the Most Holy Place on the Day of Atonement to sprinkle blood before the ark (Leviticus 16). In the Holy Place, priests offer incense and trim the wicks of the lamps every morning and evening (Exodus 30:7–8; Leviticus 24:1–4). Each Sabbath, the priests remove and eat the old shewbread and put out new loaves on the golden table (Leviticus 24:5–9). In the courtyard, priests offer sacrifices every morning and evening and at feast days (Numbers 28–29) and help lay Israelites with their offerings. Priests, along with the Levite clans, guard the tabernacle (Numbers 3:8, 38) and take in firstfruits, tithes, and votive offerings (Leviticus 27; Numbers 18). They decide when someone is unclean and do some of the rites for cleansing (Leviticus 12–15). In return for their service at the sanctuary, they receives tithes and some portions of the sacrifices (Leviticus 7–8; Numbers 18).

Priests also have duties that are more like the duties of Christian pastors. The High Priest wears a "breastpiece" on his robe. Inside the breastpiece are Urim and Thummim, which are used to ask God questions (Exodus 28:30; Numbers 27:21). Priests teach the law (Deuteronomy 33:10), especially the differences between clean and unclean, sacred and profane (Leviticus 10:8–11; cf. Jeremiah 18:18; Hosea 4:4–6; Malachi 2:1–9), and in certain cases, they serve as judges (Deuteronomy 17:9).

Though the priests have many different duties, they are all different parts of serving the Lord's house. Israel's priests are supposed to keep the house of God clean by sprinkling the blood of the animal offerings on the furniture of the tabernacle. Sprinkling blood at the altars is a form of "housecleaning." Offering God's bread on the altar is serving God His "meals." Standing at the doorway of the tabernacle, the priests are personal "bodyguards" to Israel's king. In these ways, Israel's priests "stand and serve" in Yahweh's house (Deuteronomy 18:5; Joel 1:13).

Aaron's High Priestly clothing shows that he is a servant in the Lord's house. Exodus 28 says that the robes are given to Aaron "that he may be priest to Me" (vv. 3, 4; my translation). He wears the breastpiece over his heart when he serves in the house (Exodus 28:29). He puts on the robe of the ephod, which has bells and pomegranates on its border, so that he may enter the tent without dying (Exodus 28:35). Both he and his sons wear linen breeches to ascend the altar without exposing their nakedness (Exodus 28:42; cf. 20:26). Dressed in these robes, the priests are welcome in the Lord's tent.

But the priests' clothing does not just picture the priests' "standing" in the tabernacle. The clothing also shows that priests are servants in the "house" of Israel. Aaron carries the names of the tribes on the stones that are over his heart and on his shoulders (Exodus 28:9–12, 29). Urim and Thummim, which help to guide Israel, are in the pouch of the breastpiece (Exodus 28:30; Leviticus 8:8). The "flower" of gold on the front of Aaron's turban is for "bearing the iniquity of the holy things" consecrated by Israel (Exodus 28:36–39). Dressed as a priest, Aaron is ready to serve Israel as well as God.

Service to Yahweh in the sanctuary is service for and among Israel, and the priest's work among the people is ministry in Yahweh's "house." Priests guard and protect Israel by teaching the law as well as by serving as guards at the sanctuary gates. Priests cleanse Israel as much by leading sinners to repentance as by sprinkling blood. They perform Yahweh's table service as much by conducting worship as by turning flesh and grain to smoke. Even when the priests move out of the holy place to stand and serve among the people, they are serving Yahweh by "housekeeping."

Review Questions.

1. What is a *qorban*? How does an offering renew fellowship between God and the worshiper?
2. In what sense are the animal offerings "bread for God"?
3. What are the five basic steps of the animal offerings?
4. What is the meaning of laying hands on the animal's head?
5. Why does the priest put the blood on the tabernacle furniture after the animal has died?
6. What is the meaning of burning the animal?
7. How is the meal after an offering connected with the covenant?
8. How is the "ascension offering" different from the other offerings? The peace offering? The purification offering?
9. What is the difference between the purification offering and the reparation offering?
10. What is a priest? What does a priest do?

Thought Questions.

1. Leviticus 2:2 says that a priest puts a "memorial" of the grain offering on the altar. Who receives this memorial portion? Jesus uses a similar word when instituting the Lord's Supper, saying that the Supper is His "memorial." In light of Leviticus 2:2, who is "receiving" the memorial in the Supper?

2. In Leviticus 6:1–5, a man who steals something has to pay back what he stole and add a fifth of the value. In Exodus 22:4, he has to pay back twice as much as he stole. Why the difference?

3. What is done with the "sin offering" on the Day of Atonement? (Leviticus 16:11–22). How is this different from other sin offerings?

4. What kinds of defects disqualify a descendant of Aaron from serving as priest? (Leviticus 21:16–24). Compare Leviticus 22:17–25. What do these passages suggest about what it means to be a priest?

5. How many bulls are offered as burnt offerings during the course of the Feast of Booths? (Numbers 29:12–38). What does this tell us about the meaning of the Feast of Booths?

[1] Nahum M. Sarna calls the tabernacle a "living extension of Mount Sinai" (*Exploring Exodus: The Origins of Biblical Israel* [New York: Schocken, 1996]).

[2] This is evident from the way that the book of Exodus describes the construction of the tabernacle and its furnishings. Exodus 25–31, which describes the tabernacle, is divided into seven speeches, that recall the seven days of creation. This becomes clearest in the seventh speech, which is a reminder to keep the Sabbath (31:12–17). But the sixth speech also parallels the sixth day of creation: the Spirit of Yahweh is given to Bezalel and Oholiab so that they can build the Lord's house with skill, as the Spirit enlivened Adam to dress and guard the Garden. In Exodus 25–31, in short, a new world is made by the word of the Lord.

[3] We can fill out the meaning of offerings as *qorban* further yet. Etymologically, *qorban* is related to *qereb*, which means "in the midst of," and *qarab*, a verb meaning "to draw near, to bring near, or to approach." In its verb form, the word is used for the approaching of priesthood to the Holy

Place and altar (Exodus 40:32; Leviticus 9:7; 16:1; 21:17; 22:3). From this we might suggest that the *qorban* is that which is brought near, into the presence of God. This suggestion is confirmed and expanded by a careful study of the text of Leviticus 1:1–2, the introductory verses to the whole Levitical system. In the space of a few verses, in addition to the uses of *qorban* itself, related words are used five times. In Leviticus 1:2, the verb is used twice (translated as "bring"); in 1:3, the verb is again used twice (translated as "offer"); and in 1:5, the verb is used again and translated as offer. This clustering of forms of the same word is significant; the text is hammering home the point: This is what you do with *qorban*: you "bring it near" to "offer" it.

[4] According to Gordon Wenham and others, the word translated as "fire offering" throughout Leviticus (*'isheh*) really has the sense of "food offering." In some places, the verbs used to describe the burning of an offering; according to Leviticus 6:10, the fire on the altar "eats" the burnt offering. See Wenham, *The Book of Leviticus* (NICOT; Grands Rapids: Eerdmans, 1979), p. 56 n. 8.

[5] The act of laying a hand or hands has a number of different uses in the Old Testament. Sometimes it involves the transfer of something to the one who receives the hands, as when the High Priest laid the sins of Israel on the head of the scapegoat on the Day of Atonement (Leviticus 16). Laying hands might also be an act of blessing (Genesis 48:13–14).

[6] In all this, an important part of the sprinkling is what Paul calls the "justification of God." God's justice has to be vindicated and defended against charges of laxity and sloppiness. God is the justifier of His people, but He must also be just. Blood publicly presented shows that God does not pass over sin but carries out the penalty against a substitute.

[7] The fire on the altar leaves a residue of ashes, and these are taken away. Thus, the fire both "sanctifies" by burning off the "flesh" and glorifies by turning the animal to smoke. For an extensive discussion of the meaning of burning, see J. H. Kurtz, *Offerings, Sacrifices and Worship in the Old Testament* (trans. James Martin; Peabody, MA: Hendrickson, [1863] 1998), pp. 150–162.

[8] Two other dimensions to the sacrificial rite should be noted. First, the actions of the worshiper in offering a sacrifice closely parallel the actions of God in creation. He takes hold of the world, tears it in pieces, distributes it, tests it, and enjoys it. So also, the worshipper lays hands on the animal, slaughters it, the priest distributes the blood and flesh, and the Lord "eats" the substitutionary animal into His presence. Sacrifice is a rite of recreation; the world is made new through faithful, sacrificial worship. Second, the rite of sacrifice is a rite of transition or a passage from one condition to another. A sinner approaches the Lord's house in a condition of alienation from God, but through the rite of sacrifice, the Lord restores fellowship with His people. Covenant is made through sacrifice (Psalm 50).

[9] Everett Fox translates the word as "going-up offering" in his *Five Books of Moses* (The Schocken Bible; New York: Schocken, 1995).

[10] A more rigorous version of the following can be found in my article, "Attendants of Yahweh's House: Priesthood in the Old Testament," *Journal for the Study of the Old Testament* 85 (1999) 3–24.

3
From Sinai to Shiloh

At the beginning of the Bible, God creates a world and puts Adam and Eve in it. Right away, Adam sins and spoils God's world. But Adam is only the first man in the Bible to sin and ruin things; all through the Old Testament, this same story happens over and over again. The Lord does something to make the world new. He raises up a new Adam in the new world, and more often than not, these new Adams, like the first, make a mess of things.

Rebellion in the Wilderness, Numbers 1–7; 13–14

The book of Numbers tells this story. Here, the story is not about the sin of one man but about the sins of the nation of Israel. The Lord saves Israel out of Egypt to bring them into the land of Canaan. He wants them to conquer Canaan, build His house, and serve Him. God is making the world new and putting Israel in it so they can be a nation of new Adams and Eves. But before they ever get to the land, they prove they are more like the old Adam and Eve.

God begins to make a new world while Israel is still in the wilderness. For many readers, the first ten chapters of Numbers are boring, with long lists and lots of numbers. What these chapters tell us is how God is organizing His people at Sinai. One part of this is the way that Israel camps around the tabernacle. At the end of the book of Exodus,

Yahweh comes down in His glory-cloud, the same glory-cloud that hovers over the original creation (Genesis 1:2), to sit on the throne in the Most Holy Place. With God ruling as King in their midst, Israel is called together, and each tribe is told where it should camp. Aaron and his sons, the priests, along with the Levites, camp closest to the tabernacle, and the other tribes camp in groups of three further from the Lord's tent (Numbers 3). Then, the leaders of each tribe appear before the Lord to bring Him gifts (Numbers 7). The house of Israel is camped around the house of their King.

In the Hebrew Bible, the name for the book of Numbers is "in the wilderness." This reminds us that the book is about Israel's journey through the wilderness to the land. One of the important contrasts in the Bible is the contrast of wilderness and garden. Wilderness is a place of death and drought and also a place of testing and temptation. In Numbers and the following books, Israel moves through the wilderness to the garden-like land. But the English name of this book is a good title too since twice in the book the fighting men of Israel are counted (Numbers 1 and 26), and these two censuses are the "bookends" that hold the book of Numbers together. The numbers in the first counting show that God has fulfilled His promise to Abraham. God promises Abraham that he will have a seed like the sand on the seashore. When Moses counts, he finds that the fighting men number 600,000, and that means that there are perhaps as many as two million if you include women and children. Even though Pharaoh has tried to kill off all the Israelites, Israel has been fruitful in Egypt. God is not only keeping His promise to Abraham. These numbers also show us that Israel is doing what Adam was told to do: being fruitful and multiplying (Genesis 1:26-28).

Right away, though, the people sin. When Israel sets out from the camp, Moses prays that God will defend Israel against her enemies:

> Rise up, O Yahweh!
> And let Thine enemies be scattered,
> And let those who hate Thee flee before Thee. (10:35)

When they set up camp again, Moses calls on God to return to His place among them: "Return Thou, O Yahweh, to the myriad thousands of Israel" (10:36). These two brief songs of Moses are reminders that Yahweh, the King of Israel and the universe, lives right in the middle of Israel's camp.

But the very next verse says:

> Now the people became like those who complain of adversity in the hearing of the Lord; and when the Lord heard it, His anger was kindled, and the fire of the Lord burned among them and consumed some of the outskirts of the camp. (11:1)

Moses sings that the Lord comes to live among the armies of Israel. Sometimes, though, that is not a blessing. For a complaining people, having God close is dangerous, for God is a consuming fire.

This is only the first of many sins. Miriam and Aaron complain about Moses (Numbers 12); Korah, Dathan, and Abiram rebel against Aaron (Numbers 16–17); and the men of Israel have immoral sexual relations with the women of Moab (Numbers 25).[1] By the time we get halfway through the book, Israel has rebelled against Yahweh ten times (Numbers 14:22), and the punishments they suffer remind us of the ten plagues in Egypt. The people long to return to Egypt, and the Lord says, "Let me remind you what it's like to live in Egypt. For people who harden their hearts like Egyptians, life is not going to be pleasant."

Complaining and fornication are bad enough, but the big sin of Israel comes a little later, when Israel arrives at Kadesh.[2] From Kadesh, Moses sends twelve spies into the land, and all but two, Joshua and Caleb, come back saying that Israel cannot conquer the Canaanites (Numbers 13). The land is good, we admit, but the people who live in the land are strong, and the cities are fortified and very large; and moreover, the seed of Anak [a race of giants] are there. We are not able to go up against the people, for they are too strong for us (Numbers 13:28, 31).

Kadesh means "holy place," and an earlier name for Kadesh is *En-mishpat*, which means *well of judgment.* Kadesh, a well-watered place in the wilderness, is a small sample of what Israel will enjoy if they trust the Lord. But they sin in the "garden-sanctuary" by refusing to enter the new Eden-land.

If only they would remember Abram when they spy out Hebron (Numbers 13:22). They should remember that Abram camps in Hebron right after the Lord promises him the land (Genesis 13:17-18). Chedorlaomer, one of the kings that Abram conquers, fights at En-mishpat or Kadesh (Genesis 14:7), and this is the same place where Israel rebels (Numbers 13:26). During that same war, Abram set out to fight Chedorlaomer from a place that belonged to Mamre, brother of Eshcol (Genesis 13:18; 14:13); Eshcol is also the name of one of the places the spies visit (Numbers 13:24). Abram, with 318 fighting men, conquers the land. Israel, with over 600,000 fighting men, is afraid and doesn't even try. Israel is Abram's seed, but they don't have the faith of Abram.

When God punishes Israel, His punishments are always just. They always fit the crime. The false spies accuse the land of murder (Numbers 13:32), and they are killed as false witnesses against the land (Numbers 14:36-37; cf. Deuteronomy 19:16-19). The people want to die in the wilderness, (14:2) so God lets them die in the wilderness. Because this generation refuses to enter the garden-land, they are not allowed to enter the garden-land. They get everything they want, but when they get it, they don't want it anymore.

Numbers might well have the title, "Rebellion in the Wilderness." But where Israel's sin increases, God's patience and mercy increase all the more. Even though Israel refuses to go into the land, Yahweh promises to give them what He's promised. But the Israel that gets to enter the land will not be the old Israel, the Israel that rebelled in the "garden" at Kadesh. It will be a new Israel. During the nearly forty years in the wilderness, the old Israel gradually dies off, and a new Israel takes its place. This is why there is a second counting of the people at the end of the book. And the numbers are nearly the same: At the beginning of Numbers, there are 603,550 men who are twenty and older, and at the end, there are 601,730. Israel has died, but Israel has risen again.

Dead Israel begins to rise again when the High Priest Aaron dies (Numbers 20:22-29).

Aaron is part of the older generation that is dying in the wilderness, and Aaron himself is not entirely faithful to the Lord (Exodus 32:1–6; Numbers 12; 20:1–13). But right after Aaron dies, Israel wins its first victory over the Canaanites (21:1–3, 21–35) and begins to conquer the area known as the Transjordan, to the West of Canaan. The death of a High Priest is also important in the law. A man who accidentally kills his neighbor may flee to a city of refuge and live there in safety. When the High Priest dies, the blood he shed on the land is cleansed and he may return home (Numbers 35:22–34). For forty years, the wilderness has been a "city of refuge" for all Israel. When Aaron dies, they are allowed to enter the land of promise.

Aaron is not a perfect High Priest, but his death points ahead to the death of another Priest, Jesus, whose death and resurrection means the death and resurrection of Israel. Because of the death of Jesus, we may move out of the wilderness and enter the land of our inheritance.

Review Questions.

1. What are the first ten chapters of Numbers about? Why is this important?
2. Why are the numbers in Numbers important?
3. What is the title for Numbers in the Hebrew Bible?
4. How does Israel behave in the wilderness? How does God punish them?

5. What happens at Kadesh? Why is this such a serious sin?

6. What does "Kadesh" mean? Why is this significant?

7. Explain the connections between Abram's war and the events at Kadesh.

8. Explain how God's punishment of the ten spies fits the crime.

9. How is the book of Numbers a story of the "death and resurrection" of Israel?

10. What happens after the death of Aaron? Why is this important?

Thought Questions.

1. Numbers 5:1–4 says that certain groups of people have to be removed from the camp. Who are they? Why are they removed? What does this say about the camp?

2. What is the test for an adulterous woman in Numbers 5:11–31? How does this relate to Moses' actions in Exodus 32:19–20?

3. The Hebrew word for "almond" sounds a lot like the Hebrew word for "watcher." How does this help us understand Aaron's budding rod in Numbers 17?

4. Who is Balaam (Numbers 22:5–14)? Why is it funny that his donkey sees the angel of the Lord before he does?

5. Why does Moses get angry at the tribes of Reuben and Gad (Numbers 32:1–27)?

***War and Rest,* Deuteronomy 12; Joshua 1–12**

The Pentateuch ends with Israel camped in the plains of Moab, east of Canaan. They are still "east of Eden," but they are now preparing to cross the Jordan to receive their land. While they are camped in Moab, Moses preaches to them, and his sermons make up the book of Deuteronomy. Since this is a new Israel, the covenant that God made at Sinai is renewed. Moses repeats the Ten Commandments (Deuteronomy 5:1–21) and tells the people that they have a choice between life and death:

> See, I have set before you today life and good, and death and evil, in that I command you today to love the Lord your God, to walk in His ways and to keep His commandments and His statutes and His judgments, that you may live and multiply, and that the Lord your God may bless you in the land where you are entering to possess it. But if your heart turns away and you will not obey, but are drawn away and worship other gods and serve them, I declare to you today that you will surely perish. (Deuteronomy 30:15–18)

In Deuteronomy, Moses focuses on what Israel is supposed to do when they enter the land. Yahweh is giving Israel the land, but Israel has to follow and obey Him if they want to hold onto it. In Deuteronomy 28, he describes the blessings that Israel will enjoy if they are faithful and the punishments they will suffer if they don't follow the Lord. If Israel turns away from the Lord and serves the idols of the Canaanites, they will be treated like Canaanites: "You shall be torn from the land where you are entering to possess it" (28:63).

Israel's main job is to utterly destroy all the places where "the nations whom you shall dispossess serve their gods, on the high mountains and on the hills and under every green tree. And you shall tear down their altars and smash their sacred pillars and burn their Asherim with fire, and you shall cut down the engraved images of their gods, and you shall obliterate their name from that place" (Deuteronomy 12:2–3).

After all Canaanite altars and sanctuaries are destroyed, Israel is to build the Lord's house at the place He chooses and worship Him there.

For Israel to do this, they have to trust the Lord and remember what He has done for them. One of the key words in Deuteronomy is "remember." At Kadesh, the people forgot about Abram and about how the Lord had fought for them in Egypt. Moses doesn't want the same thing to happen again. So he tells them to "remember" what Yahweh has done to the Egyptians, because He is going to do the same kinds of things to the Canaanites (7:18). When Israel celebrates feasts to the Lord, they are to remember the Exodus (16:3). At the end of Deuteronomy, Moses composes a song that will help Israel to remember the covenant that God has made with them (32). If Israel remembers, they will trust the Lord to stretch out His right arm and give them Canaan.

When the book of Joshua opens, Moses is dead. In fact, the book of Joshua begins with the death of Moses and ends with the death of the leaders of the conquest, Joshua and Eleazar, the priest. Throughout the Old Testament, the death of a leader brings a crisis. Will the new leaders continue in the footsteps of those who have gone before? This was a real problem for the Israelites. After the death of Joshua, Israel falls into idolatry, and throughout the book of Judges, the people fall into idolatry every time a judge dies. At the beginning of Joshua, the question is, "With Moses gone, will Israel be able to conquer the land? Is the Lord also with Joshua?"

The early chapters of Joshua answer this question by showing that Joshua is a new Moses. He leads the people across the Jordan River on dry ground, just as Moses led the people through the Red Sea (Joshua 3:1–17; see 4:23). When the people see Joshua perform the same miracle as Moses, they fear him as they feared Moses (4:14). This second "passing through the waters" is important for other reasons too. Israel left Egypt by passing through the Red Sea, and here they enter the land by passing through the Jordan. In a sense, these are different parts of the same "crossing." The Exodus from Egypt is not really finished until Israel enters the land. Water, as we saw in chapter one, is often a picture of the nations that threaten Israel. But with the Lord's power, Joshua divides the waters, just as he will conquer the nations of Canaan.

Once they enter the land, all the men are circumcised, and this reminds us of Moses too. Moses has to circumcise his son when he reenters the land of Egypt after sojourning in Midian (Exodus 4:24–26), and in the same way, Joshua has the people circumcise themselves as they cross from the wilderness into the land. Once they recover from the wound of circumcision, they celebrate the Passover (Joshua 5:10–11), a feast instituted under Moses commemorating their deliverance from Egypt. Passover is not only a reminder of their escape from Egypt, but also a sign of their entrance into the land of promise. Before Joshua goes out to war against Jericho, he meets the angel of the Lord, who tells him to remove his shoes because he is standing on holy ground (Joshua 5:13–15), like Moses at the burning bush (Exodus 3:1–5). Like Moses, Joshua sends spies into the land. Unlike the spies that Moses sent, these spies are faithful. They return with an encouraging report: "Surely the Lord has given all the land into our hands; and all the inhabitants of the land, moreover, have melted away before us" (Joshua 2:24). Old, rebellious Israel is surely dead, but Israel lives. Moses too has died, but a new Moses leads Israel.

The conquest takes place in three main stages. First, Israel conquers Jericho and then moves north and conquers Ai. These victories give Israel control of central territory in the land, especially the roads leading north and south. After renewing the covenant at Mounts Gerazim and Ebal (Joshua 8:30–35), there are two main campaigns. In the South, Joshua fights to save the city of Gibeon from an attack led by the king of Jerusalem. The Northern campaign begins when kings from the North, led by Jabin, king of Hazor, attack Israel, and a battle occurs at the waters of Merom. Joshua defeats them, hamstrings their horses, and burns their chariots. Hazor is devoted to Yahweh, being burned as a "whole burnt offering." At the other cities, all the men are killed, but the cattle, women, and children are taken as plunder (Joshua 11:10–15).

It is interesting that Canaanites start the battles both in the North and the South. The king of Jerusalem attacks the city of Gibeon because of Gibeon's alliance with Israel, and the king of Hazor gathers the Northern kings to fight against Joshua. According to Joshua 11:19–20, only the Gibeonites make peace. The rest harden their hearts, like Pharaoh, and they are wiped out as he was. In a sense, the conquest finishes what the Exodus started. But in another sense, the conquest is like a replay of the Exodus. As Pharaoh refuses to repent in spite of the plagues, so the Canaanites refuse to submit to Yahweh, in spite of Israel's miraculous victories at Jericho and elsewhere. As in Egypt, some Canaanites see what is happening and join with Israel. Israel comes out of Egypt as a "mixed multitude," with many Egyptians among them (Exodus 12:38). Besides the Gibeonites, there is Rahab, a Canaanite and a prostitute who switches sides and helps the Israelite spies (Joshua 2). Like a greater Joshua after him, Joshua the son of Nun not only conquers the wicked but offers salvation to the Gentiles.

Reading Joshua makes it seem that the conquest is very short, but it actually takes seven years.[3] At the end of seven years, the land is at "rest" (Joshua 11:23). After a "week" of purging the land and making it new, Joshua brings Sabbath. But Joshua also makes it clear that there is still much land to conquer. Israel has taken the main cities and crushed the head of the Canaanites, but the various tribes still have to finish off the work in their own areas.

Joshua is a book of warfare, but it is not like other ancient books that describe war. The *Iliad* tells about the great acts of Greek heroes. The book of Joshua describes little about actual warfare, and in Joshua, Israel doesn't win because her army has great warriors. Instead, what is important is to trust in God, who is the Warrior of Israel. The goal of the conquest is to set up God's house in the land and to worship Him, and even the battles sometimes look more like a service of worship. Think of the most famous battle of the conquest: Jericho. Instead of organizing the army, Joshua focuses on what the priests are going to do. Priests carry the ark, the throne of God, to proclaim that Yahweh is the new King of the land and also that He is claiming Jericho for Himself. Trumpets announce the coming of this new King. These ram's horn trumpets are mentioned in Leviticus 25:9, where they announce the Day of Atonement, a day of solemn assembly.

Everything at the battle of Jericho is organized by sevens. Jericho falls on a *Sabbath* day, the last day of the *week* of the siege. The battle at Jericho sends a clear message: When Israel worships God, He brings the walls down.

Israel's defeat at Ai shows that Israel wins only if they remain holy (Joshua 7). Israel is called to be a holy people, and they lose when one of their members sins. When they are defeated at Ai, the Lord tells them there is sin in the camp. All the plunder of Jericho belongs to the Lord, but Achan (whose name means "troubler") takes some of the plunder for himself. He steals holy things, things that belong to the Lord. Israel can win at Ai only after they have cleaned this sacrilege out of the camp.

Joshua conquers the land through faithful worship, and his conquest is based on Abram's worship. Long before Joshua, Abram moves through the land, setting up altars in various places. The Lord appears to him at Shechem, and he builds an altar (Genesis 12:7). Then he moves to a place between Bethel and Ai and builds another altar there (Genesis 12:8) before continuing into the Southern region, the Negev. Abram divides the land by setting up altars, and he establishes his claim to the land by worshiping the Lord in these places. Two generations later, Jacob moves through the land setting up pillars and altars (Genesis 28:18–22; 35:1, 16–22). When Joshua enters the land, he first conquers Jericho and then moves on to Ai, which is not far from Bethel (Joshua 7:2). When he sets up the ambush for Ai, the armies are between Bethel and Ai, to the west of Ai (Joshua 8:9). This is very close to the place where Abraham worshiped God centuries before. Abram's and Jacob's worship is a "pre-conquest" of the land. Once the land is consecrated to the Lord by worship, eventually the land will be conquered. It may take centuries, but the Lord will establish His house in the land.

After the land is under Joshua's control, it is divided among the tribes. First Caleb, the faithful spy, is given his land (Joshua 14:6–15). Then Judah (15:1–63) and Joseph, the two main tribes of Israel, receive their land (16:1–17:18). Later, the Northern Kingdom will be dominated by the tribes of Joseph and the Southern Kingdom by the tribes of Judah. Other tribes are given their inheritance, but before the other tribes receive their land, Israel sets up the tabernacle at Shiloh (Joshua 18:1).[4] As Moses had said, when the land is given rest, Israel sets up the Lord's house. This makes the land a holy land, a land that contains Yahweh's palace. Joshua, in obedience to Moses, also sets up forty-eight cities throughout the land as Levitical cities, places where the Law of God is studied and taught (Joshua 21).

The main task of the conquest is finished. But Canaanites and Canaanite shrines remain. If Israel is going to hold onto the land, she has to worship faithfully at Shiloh and listen to the Law of God as it is taught throughout the land. Israel's future depends on her faithfulness to the Lord's word, and this depends a great deal on the faithfulness of her priests and Levites. But it will be priests and Levites who fail most miserably.

Review Questions.

1. What is in the book of Deuteronomy?
2. According to Deuteronomy 12, what is Israel's mission?
3. What is Israel supposed to remember? Why?
4. How is Joshua like Moses? Why does the book of Joshua show these similarities?
5. Give a summary of the conquest.
6. What is unusual about Israel's strategy at Jericho? What kind of warfare is this?
7. What happened at the first battle of Ai? What did Israel learn from this?
8. How is Joshua's movement through the land like Abraham's? Why is this important?
9. What is the last half of the book of Joshua about?
10. What happens in the middle of dividing up the land? Why is this important?

Thought Questions.

1. What does Rahab have to put in her window in order to save her house from destruction (Joshua 2:17–18)? Why? Compare Exodus 12:7, 13.
2. What effect does Israel's crossing of the Jordan have on the Canaanites (Joshua 5:1)? Explain the connection of this verse with Exodus 15:14–16. Compare Genesis 35.
3. In Joshua 9, Joshua agrees to make peace with the Gibeonites. Discuss how this passage serves as background for what happens in 2 Samuel 21.
4. What are cities of refuge used for (Joshua 20:1–9)?
5. Why does Joshua get angry with the tribes of Reuben and Gad (Joshua 22)?

***No King in Israel,* Judges 8–9, 17–21**

When Judges begins, the Lord tells the tribes to continue the conquest in their own areas.

Judah goes up first and begins well, but the story quickly changes into a story of defeat. Seven tribes are listed in chapter one, and as the chapter goes on, things get worse and worse. Judah is a more successful tribe, but the next few tribes "did not drive out the Canaanites" (1:21, 27, 29, 30, 31, 33). When we get to the end of the list, it's even worse. Dan, the northernmost tribe, is the least successful. Not only do they fail to "drive out" the Amorites, but they themselves are driven out "into the hill country" (1:34–36).

Why has this happened? Why has the nation of Moses and Joshua failed to conquer the land? Has the Lord's promise failed? The angel of Yahweh comes to Israel to answer these questions:

> I brought you up out of Egypt and led you into the land which I have sworn to your fathers; and I said, "I will never break My covenant with you, and as for you, you shall make no covenant with the inhabitants of this land; you shall tear down their altars." But you have not obeyed Me; what is this you have done? Therefore I also said, "I will not drive them out before you." (Judges 2:1–3)

Israel has not destroyed the Canaanite altars and shrines as the Lord commanded. And soon we'll see that Israel even joins in Canaanite worship. The book of Judges includes many exciting stories about biblical heroes: Ehud killing Eglon in a surprise attack; Gideon defeating the Midianites with a mere three hundred men; Samson killing Philistines with any weapon that he can lay his hands on. But the big point in the book of Judges is this: If Israel worships the Lord, they will win their battles and enjoy blessings, but if Israel turns to idols, their enemies will defeat and enslave them.

Judges 2:6-19 is a summary of the whole book. In verse ten, we learn that a generation arises in Israel that does not know the Lord. Because they do not "remember" the Lord or what He has done for Israel, they begin to worship other gods, the gods of the nations. So, the Lord gives them into the hands of the nations they are so keen to imitate. They want to worship like Canaanites, so God gives them a taste of what it's like to be a Canaanite. And it's not pleasant. In fact, it's like a return to slavery in Egypt. But, as in Egypt, when the people cry out, the Lord raises up a "new Moses," a judge to deliver Israel from her enemies (see 1 Samuel 12:8-9). Once the judge dies, Israel turns right back to the gods of the Canaanites, and the whole thing starts over again.

How is Israel supposed to fix this? Late in the book we read this statement: "There was no king in Israel; every man did what was right in his own eyes" (17:6; 18:1; 19:1). Does this mean that having a king would have kept Israel from idolatry? When Israel does have kings, many of them lead Israel into idolatry instead of protecting them from idols. So it doesn't seem that having a king is much help. Even in Judges, having a king isn't much help. The Canaanites, after all, have kings, but they are idolaters, and their kings are harsh and cruel. The first king we meet in the book is Adoni-bezek, who boasts, "Seventy kings with their thumbs and their big toes cut off used to gather up scraps under my table" (Judges 1:7). Here is a king, but he treats people like dogs.[5]

Israel too gets a king in the book of Judges, and his story

is right at the center. Judges tells about seven major judges:[6]

1. Othniel, 3:7–11
2. Ehud, 3:12–30
3. Deborah and Barak, 4:1–5:31
4. Gideon, 6:1–8:32
5. Abimelech, 8:33–9:57
6. Jephthah, 10:6–12:7
7. Samson, 13:1–16:31

At the center of the book is Gideon, a great hero of the faith. He destroys the altar of Baal in his own hometown, saves the people from the Midianites, and renews Israel. Gideon's spiritual effect on Israel is apparent from the story of the fleece (Judges 6:36–40). Gideon wants a sign that the Lord has chosen him to deliver Israel. First, he sets out a fleece on a threshing floor and asks the Lord to make the fleece wet but leave the floor dry. Then, he asks the Lord to make the floor wet but keep the fleece dry. God does both, and so Gideon knows that the Lord has chosen him.

What does this sign mean?[7] The sign is showing Gideon that the Lord will deliver Israel through him. That's the question he's trying to answer: "Will Yahweh deliver Israel through *me*?" (v. 36). In some way, the sign must confirm that Gideon is Israel's savior. The fleece represents Gideon himself. Plus, the first time we see Gideon, he is threshing wheat in a wine press (6:11). The "fleece on the threshing floor" is like "Gideon threshing in the wine vat." If Gideon is the fleece, then when the fleece is wet with dew, it is a picture of Gideon being "sopping wet" with God's blessing. In verse thirty-four, we are told that the Spirit of Yahweh "clothes" Gideon to prepare him for battle, and the dew is a picture of the Spirit poured out on Gideon (see Psalm 133). The first sign tells Gideon that he is the dew-drenched fleece, a lamb of God filled by the Spirit.

Gideon is drenched with dew, but Israel is like the dry threshing floor. Because Israel has gone after Baal, the Lord has withdrawn His Spirit and blessing. But the Lord promises to make Israel "wet" again through Gideon. The second sign follows from the first. First Gideon is filled with the Spirit, and then through his work as judge, the Spirit is poured out on the dry ground of Israel. First the head of Israel is renewed, then the body follows. By challenging Baal (6:25–32) and summoning Israel to battle (6:34–35), Gideon gives the Spirit to the whole people. Gideon, a Spirit-clothed judge, heads a Spirit-filled army. It is no accident that Israel defeats the Midianites by reproducing the sight and sound of Yahweh's glory-cloud, for Gideon's army is filled with the Spirit-glory.[8] Because of Gideon's faithfulness, Israel is no longer Ichabod—without glory (cf. 1 Samuel 4:21).

So, Gideon not only delivers Israel from the Midianites, he also renews Israel spiritually. And he is a hero later on when the people offer to make him king. Gideon replies: "I will not rule over you, nor shall my son rule over you; Yahweh shall rule over you" (8:23). This is exactly what he should say. But in the next breath, he is asking for contributions of gold. Acting in a similar way to Aaron (see Exodus 32), he uses the gold to make an ephod that leads Israel astray (8:28). Gideon is known as Jerubbaal because he attacked Baal, but he ends his life leading Israel into idolatry. Before the story of Gideon closes, we learn that he "had seventy sons who were his direct descendants, for he had many wives" (8:30). Gideon refuses the kingdom, but he is acting like a two-bit oriental despot, complete with a harem.

Gideon must have been thinking a lot about becoming king, because his son is named "Abimelech," which means "My father is king." Abimelech doesn't care whether Yahweh is king or not. He wants to become king, and he is the first king of Israel. To secure his throne, he kills the other sons of Gideon. There are seventy of them, and this number reminds us of the seventy kings that Adoni-bezek dismembered (9:5). Abimelech may be the son of Gideon, but he is more like a Canaanite king. Jotham, the one son of Gideon who escapes, calls him a "bramble," a thorn bush growing from the ground of Israel. Abimelech, the bramble king, will harshly punish anyone who resists him: "If in truth you are anointing me as king over you," Jotham has the bramble say, "come and take refuge in my shade; but if not, may fire come out from the bramble and consume the cedars of Lebanon" (9:15). Later, Abimelech's friends from Shechem turn against him, and fire comes from the bramble king to destroy them (9:49). Whatever the writer of Judges means when he says "There was no king in Israel," he doesn't mean that having a king will help. Abimelech, the only king Israel has ever had, is a serpent whose life ends with his head crushed by a stone (9:53).

One reason Israel keeps turning to idols is that the Levites and priests are being unfaithful. In the first six books of the Bible, we see priests a lot: Aaron and his sons, Phinehas, Eleazar. But in Judges there are almost no priests at all. Where are they? The book of Judges doesn't tell us much about priests because the priests aren't doing much. And when they are doing something, it is often bad. At the end of Judges, there are two long stories about Levites, and in both cases, they are unfaithful. Micah hires a Levite to work in his idolatrous shrine (Judges 17:7–13). The Levite is willing to serve idols, but his real god is money (18:14–20). In Hebrew, the phrase that means "to ordain a priest" is literally "to fill his hands." This Levite has his hands filled too. But his hands aren't filled because he is a good priest; his hands are filled because he's willing to work for any idol, provided he gets paid (Judges 17:12). His hands are filled with cash. With Levites like this, is it any wonder that Israel follows after other gods?

Throughout the period of the judges, there *is* a King in Israel, with His palace set up at Shiloh. The problem is not that Israel doesn't have a king. The problem is that they won't follow the King they have. Instead, Israel wants to serve other kings, and so the Lord lets her have her way. Judges places the blame for this situation on the Levites, who are supposed to teach and lead Israel. When the book of Judges says that "every man did what is right in his own eyes," it is not talking about Israel's disobedience in general. It is talking about Israel's failure to worship Yahweh faithfully (see Deuteronomy 12:8). Only one King can fix the problems that Israel faces, and His name is Yahweh. But before things are fixed, the broken things have to be utterly destroyed.

Review Questions.

1. Why are the tribes of Israel unable to conquer the Canaanites?

2. Explain the "cycle" of the book of Judges from Judges 2.

3. What is the sentence repeated three times at the end of Judges? What does it mean?

4. How is the book of Judges arranged? What story is at the center of the book?

5. What does the sign of the fleece mean? What does this say about Gideon's effect on Israel?

6. What happens when the Israelites want Gideon to be king? What does he do right after that?

7. Who is Abimelech? What does his name mean? How does he die?

8. What is the story of Micah about?

Thought Questions.

1. How does Sisera die (Judges 4:17–22)? Why is this significant?

2. Jael is said to be "most blessed of women in the tent" (Judges 5:24). Compare Luke 1:42. Explain the connection between the two passages.

3. Is Samson in sin when he finds a woman among the Philistines (Judges 14:1)? Notice the context with 13:24–25 and see 14:4.

4. What does the behavior of the men of Gibeah remind us of (Judges 19:10–26)? What does this say about the condition of Israel?

5. Look at Judges 20:28 and answer this question: During which part of the period of the judges did these events in Gibeah take place? Why is this story placed here in Judges?

Mercy for Widows, Ruth

The time of the judges is a bad time for Israel. Priests and Levites are unfaithful, the people turn to idols, and the judges cannot keep Israel from lapsing back into sin. Because of her sins, the garden of Israel has become a place of death, strife, and slavery. But the story of Ruth shows us that the Lord will restore all that Israel lacks. Naomi is a picture of Israel, and the Lord's mercy to Naomi is a promise of mercy to His people. Israel is God's bride, but Israel has not been paying attention to her Husband. She has been looking for other husbands. So, the Lord has left Israel a widow. When Ruth begins, Naomi's family has suffered one shock after another. Elimelech leaves the land because of a famine, but he and his sons die while in Moab, and Naomi is left without husband or sons. Her only help comes from two Gentile women who, like Naomi, are helpless widows. Every one of these "lacks"—food, husbands, sons—is reversed by the end of the story. The message of Ruth is a message of hope for widowed Israel.[9]

The story begins with famine. It is a famine in Bethlehem, which means "house of bread." But soon God visits His people to provide bread (1:6), and Boaz, the redeemer, later gives abundant food to Ruth and Naomi (2:17; 3:17). The first chapter is an exodus story: Elimelech and Naomi leave the land, and Naomi returns with Ruth. But it is a strange exodus. Instead of prospering when they are out of the land, as Jacob did in Haran and as Israel did in Egypt, Elimelech and his sons die, leaving Naomi with no seed. Jacob flees from Esau with only a staff and comes back with two companies; he goes out empty and comes back full. Naomi goes out full and comes back empty (1:21). At the end of chapter one, there has been no real exodus, no redemption, but at the end of the book, the exodus is complete as Ruth and Naomi find rest in the land.[10]

The story begins with the deaths of Elimelech and his two sons. Moab, east of the garden-land, is a place of death. Naomi is literally past childbearing years; Ruth is not barren, but she has no husband. At the end of the book, the seed is born. Obed is described as Naomi's redeemer (4:14), and so barren and aged Naomi is made a mother of children. All this reminds us of the stories in Genesis where the wives of the patriarchs are barren. As in Genesis, God provides the seed in a miraculous way. God sends the "redeemer," the seed who will eventually produce the Seed who will crush the serpent's head. There is a move from death to life at the center of Ruth, and this is a promise that barren Israel will come alive and bear a son.

Ruth is a very well-written book, and the writer uses words skillfully to make his point. Some important words are used only twice but are used at key moments in the story.[11] The word "lads," for example, is used in 1:5, where Naomi loses her two "lads." The other use of the word comes in 4:16, where Naomi takes the "lad" and becomes his guardian or nurse. Naomi's lost "lads" are now restored in the "lad" Obed. The word "empty" is also used twice. Naomi complains against the Lord that she has been emptied (1:21). She is an empty vessel in every sense: She will no longer bear children, and she has lost her husband, sons, and land. After his midnight meeting with Ruth, Boaz measures out barley, telling Ruth that she ought not return to Naomi with "empty" hands (3:17). Naomi complains of her emptiness, but Boaz makes sure that she gets filled.

The word "wings" occurs twice also. Boaz prays that the Lord will reward Ruth, who has come under the wings of Yahweh (2:12). This means that Ruth has come under the protection of the Lord's covenant and become a sojourner in the Lord's land among the Lord's people. When Ruth visits Boaz at night, she asks him to spread his wing over her (3:19), a sign that he intends to marry her. Married men and women are covered with a single garment because they are one flesh, so spreading a "wing" of a garment over a woman is a sign of marriage. Ruth places her trust in Yahweh and is thus protected by His "wings." And the Lord provides Boaz to spread his "wing" over Ruth.

All these changes in the fortunes of Naomi and Ruth are from the Lord and show the Lord's *hesed*. This Hebrew word is translated as "lovingkindness," "mercy," or "kindness" and has the basic sense of loyalty to covenant. God displays His *hesed* in fulfilling the promises He has made to His people. But the way He fulfills His promises is often startling and surprising. The book of Ruth shows the surprising *hesed* of God by emphasizing things that happen by "chance." Ruth "chances" to go to the field of Boaz, and Naomi sees that this "chance" shows that the Lord has not withdrawn His *hesed* from the living and dead (2:20). The Lord's *hesed* is seen especially in hopeless situations. Embittered widows, barren women, sojourners in the land—these are the special objects of God's care.

The Lord displays His *hesed*, His kindness and loyalty to His promises, through the *hesed* of Boaz. Boaz shows mercy by doing what is required of a "near relative," the "kinsman-redeemer." Near relatives redeem land and slaves and take care of a brother's widow. Boaz fulfills all these obligations. But Boaz goes beyond the strict letter of the law. He not only lets Ruth glean in his field but gives special instructions to his men not to bother her. He tells them to leave some extra grain behind for Ruth. He invites her to sit with him and share his meal (2:14–16). Later, he gives Ruth an abundance of grain for her to take back to Naomi. His kindness, like the kindness of his Lord, overflows.

Another change occurs in the book of Ruth: The story begins in the time of the judges, a time when there is "no king in Israel." It ends with a genealogy of David and the beginning of the time of the kings. This too shows the Lord's *hesed*. Though Israel serves idols, Yahweh does not abandon her. He is at work to fulfill His promises by giving food, land,

and freedom to Israel. And His promises move ahead into a new phase of Israel's history. He is preparing to raise up a King to be her Husband.

Review Questions.

1. How is Ruth a story for all Israel?
2. What kind of story do we have in Ruth 1? What's odd about it?
3. What does Naomi "lack" at the beginning of the book? How is this reversed at the end?
4. Explain the use of key words in Ruth.
5. What is *hesed*?
6. What are the duties of a "near relative"? How does Boaz fulfill these? In what ways does he go beyond them?
7. How does Ruth reflect the change from the time of judges to the time of kings?

Thought Questions.

1. Many Jewish commentators believe that Elimelech sins when he leaves the land. Is this a good interpretation? Note what kind of place Bethlehem is during the period of the judges (Judges 17:7, 9; 19:1).
2. Boaz is a type of Christ, saving Ruth and Naomi. In light of this, why is it important that Ruth is a Moabitess?
3. Ruth meets with Boaz at night on the "threshing floor" (Ruth 3:6). What light does this shed on 2 Chronicles 3:1?
4. How many generations are there from Judah to David (Ruth 4:18–22)? Explain the significance of this, referring to Genesis 38 and Deuteronomy 23:2.

***"The Glory Departs,"* 1 Samuel 1–3**

Toward the end of the period of the judges, the Lord visits Israel with both judgment and mercy. Judgment falls on the sanctuary established at Shiloh, but at the same time, the Lord is raising up Samuel as priest and prophet and judge to prepare the way for the coming of a new order of things. We shall look in more detail at the ministry of Samuel in the next chapter, but here we shall examine some early chapters in 1 Samuel to see what leads up to the devastating judgment at Shiloh.

1 Samuel 2:11–3:21 is one connected story, that shows the judgment and severity of the Lord of Israel. On the one hand, the passage is held together by the repeated sentence about Samuel's growth and his youthful ministry before the Lord (2:11b, 18, 21, 26; 3:1, 19). On the other hand, Samuel's faithfulness is contrasted with that of the priests, Eli's sons, Hophni and Phinehas.[12] Samuel is "adopted" into the house of Eli (see 3:6, 16) and serves at the house of his heavenly Father. Eli's natural sons, though, don't serve Yahweh and don't even listen to their earthly father. Samuel ministers to the Lord (2:11b), but Eli's sons despise the offering of the Lord (2:17). Samuel is growing, and the word here means "becoming great." It refers not only to his growth from a boy to a man but also to his growing importance in Israel. Meanwhile, the sins of Eli's sons are "very great" (2:17). Hophni and Phinehas are growing great—in wickedness.

There is also a contrast of two "houses." Despite Elkanah's bigamy, Samuel's parents are generally faithful worshipers of God. They come up to Shiloh for annual sacrifices, and Hannah makes a robe for Samuel when she comes, a robe that shows the position that Samuel holds and will hold. And the Lord blesses their house. Hannah, the barren woman, gives birth not to seven (cf. 2:5), but to five more children. Like Samuel himself, his father's house is becoming "great." Hannah not only sings that the barren woman becomes fruitful but also that the one who has children languishes. This alludes to the house of Eli, which languishes and is dying. The house of Eli, being "great" in wickedness, will be destroyed.

Two sins of Hophni and Phinehas are mentioned. First, they sin against the sacrifices. Instead of taking the portions of meat that God commands (Leviticus 7:28–34; Deuteronomy 18:1–5), they grab whatever they can get

(1 Samuel 2:14). And they don't wait to burn the fat before grabbing their meal. Fat is the Lord's portion, the portion known as Yahweh's "bread." Eli's sons do not give the Lord His portion first; they serve the Lord only after serving themselves. They are like waiters who eat their own meals before serving the people in the restaurant, or like a butler who doesn't serve his master until he's well-fed. Hophni and Phinehas insult the Lord, and their insult is a "very great" one.

The second area of sin is adultery with the women who serve the tabernacle (2:22). Exodus 38:8 refers to these women who do various kinds of chores at the Lord's tent. Adultery is a picture of the priests' unfaithfulness. In Leviticus 18, sexual sins are described as "uncovering nakedness," and Leviticus draws a parallel between approaching a woman to commit adultery and approaching the tabernacle wrongly. "Drawing near" to "uncover nakedness" is like a stranger "drawing near" to enter the tabernacle. Here, the women around the tabernacle are being violated, and this is a sign that the tabernacle itself is being violated. It is interesting that "Phinehas" is involved in sexual sins. Earlier another Phinehas with a spear pierced through a man and woman who were fornicating in the camp, and by doing this, he stopped the spread of a plague (Numbers 25). Phinehas the son of Eli is an anti-Phinehas who fornicates in the area of the tabernacle without a second thought. Instead of ending a plague, he is the cause of one.

At the end of chapter two, a man of God comes to bring charges against Eli and his sons. He tells Eli that the Lord is going to judge his house because Eli and his sons have broken the covenant. Like many other prophets in the Bible, he begins by reminding Eli of all the good things the Lord has done for him. The Lord revealed Himself to the house of Aaron (v. 27) and chose Eli's house to do priestly duties—to offer incense, consult the Lord using the ephod, and to share in Yahweh's "food offerings." Verse twenty-nine states the charges against Eli. But why does the man of God condemn

Eli? In chapter two, Eli has not been doing anything wrong with the offerings, and he even attempts to restrain his sons (vv. 23–25). Yet the Lord holds Eli responsible for their sins, because Eli honors his sons above God, and Eli has received benefits from his sons' wickedness (1 Samuel 2:30). Instead of making sure that the Lord receives the fat, Eli has become "fat" from the meat of offerings. When he dies, we are told that he is "very heavy" (4:18). In the Hebrew, there is a pun on the "honor" that Eli shows to his sons and his "heaviness." Both are based on the Hebrew word *kabad*, which often means "glorify." Eli treats God "lightly" and gives "weight" to his sons. By giving weight to his sons, he makes himself "weighty" with the fat of the Lord's offerings, but this very "weightiness" will mean his death.

God's judgment falls on the "house," a word used eight times in 1 Samuel 2:30–36 (not to mention "dwelling" in v. 32). The house of Eli is going to be cut off from the altar so that they will no longer do altar service or share the sacrifices. Eli's house is not completely eliminated, but no one from his house will live to old age. Thus Yahweh will "shatter the arms" of Eli's house (2:31) as he later does to the Philistine god Dagon (5:4). On the other hand, the Lord promises to raise up a faithful priest who will lead an "enduring house." Though Samuel functions as religious leader of Israel throughout his life, he is not that priest, since he is not a descendant of Aaron. The "faithful priest" is Zadok, the priest who replaces Abiathar, the last priest in the line of Eli (1 Kings 2:26–27).

The man of God also predicts that Eli will see the distress of Yahweh's dwelling. The tabernacle at Shiloh will be devastated by the Philistines, and the ark will be captured. After this, the ark is never put back into the tabernacle of Moses. The end of the Shiloh sanctuary is a disaster for Israel. As bad as the period of the judges has been, nothing like this has happened since Israel entered the land. Nothing like this happens again until Nebuchadnezzar destroys Solomon's temple and takes the people into captivity. But if it is a terrible judgment, it also means that God is preparing to makes things new. As so often seen before, the Lord brings a flood of judgment, but on the other side of the flood, a new world awaits.

Review Questions.

1. Who is being contrasted in 1 Samuel 2? How are they contrasted?

2. What are the sins of Eli's sons?

3. What does the man of God say will happen to Eli's house? To the tabernacle at Shiloh?

4. Why does the man of God talk to Eli instead of Hophni and Phinehas?

5. Explain the play on the words "weight" and "honor" in 1 Samuel 3–4.

Thought Questions.

1. What is Hannah promising in 1 Samuel 1:11? Compare Judges 13:1–7.

2. Hannah is a barren woman who gives birth to a son. Yet, her song of celebration talks about the Lord overthrowing the rich and powerful and raising up the poor and weak. Why?

3. How is Hannah's song connected to the man of God's prophecy to Eli? Compare 2:5, 36.

[1] This incident is parallel to the sin of intermarriage committed by the sons of God with the daughters of men in Genesis 6:1–4. In Genesis, this is the climactic sin that leads to the flood; the world is wiped out and a new world emerges. In Numbers, the sin with the daughters of Moab leads to a plague that kills 24,000, and this is the climactic rebellion of Israel in the wilderness. Immediately after, Moses takes another census, a census of a "new Israel."

[2] David Dorsey (*Literary Structure of the Old Testament: A Commentary on Genesis–Malachi* [Grand Rapids: Baker, 1999], p. 85) has suggested that the journey of Israel from Sinai is organized by a chiasm centering on the rebellion against Aaron and the subsequent confirmation of Aaron's status as priest:

A. Journey begins from Sinai (10:11–36)
 B. Complaints about hardship, manna, no food (11:1–35)
  C. Miriam punished for her sin (12:1–16)
   D. Rebellion at Kadesh (13:1–14:45)
    E. Ritual regulations (15:1–36)
     F. Rebellion against Aaron (15:37–16:50)
      G. Aaron's rod (17:1–13)
     F´. Duties and privileges of priests (18:1–32)
    E´. Ritual regulations (19:1–22)
   D´. Rebellion of Moses and Aaron (20:1–21)
  C´. Aaron dies (20:22–29)
 B´. Complaints about hardship, manna, no food (21:4–9)
A´. Journey ends; camped on plains of Moab (21:10–20)

[3]We can calculate this by comparing Joshua 14:7–10 with Deuteronomy 2:14. The latter passage tells us that Caleb was forty when he was sent from Kadesh to spy out the land. Caleb, unlike the other spies, lived through the entire thirty-eight years of wandering and thus was seventy-eight when Israel entered the land. In Joshua 14, we are told that Caleb is eighty-five. Thus, there were seven years between the end of the wandering and the end of the conquest. This suggests that there were many battles of which we have no record.

[4]Dorsey organizes Joshua 13–24 in a way that highlights the centrality of the establishment of the sanctuary at Shiloh (*Literary Structure*, p. 94):

A. Instructions to Joshua, 13:1–7
 B. Transjordan tribes, 13:8–33
  C. Levites, 14:1–5
   D. Caleb, 14:6–15
    E. Judah, 15:1–63
     F. Joseph, 16:1–17:17
      G. Tabernacle at Shiloh, 18:1–10
     F´. Benjamin, 18:11–28
    E´. Simeon and others, 19:1–48
   D´. Joshua, 19:49–50
  C´. Levitical cities, 20:1–21:45
 B´. TransJordan tribes, 22:1–34
A´. Joshua's farewell, 23:1–24:33

[5]John Hamlin (*Judges: At Risk in the Promised Land* [ITC; Grand Rapids: Eerdmans, 1990]) points out several "bookends" that frame Judges as a whole. The book begins with a story of Acsah, who lights from her donkey to request springs of water. Near the end of the book, another woman on a donkey appears: the Levite's concubine, who died after a night of abuse from the men of Gibeah. The book is also framed by instances of *herem* warfare: Judah and Simeon turned Zephath into Hormah (1:17), and toward the end, Jabesh-Gilead is utterly destroyed (21:11).

[6] I have taken this over from Dorsey, *Literary Structure*, p. 107.

[7] For various options, see James B. Jordan, *Judges: God's War Against Humanism* (Eugene, OR: Wipf and Stock, [1985] 1999), pp. 128, 131–132.

[8] See Jordan for the idea that Gideon's strategy involves replicating the sight and sound of the glory-cloud. Hamlin develops an interesting symbolic interpretation of Gideon's warfare against the Midianites: While the trumpets sound the beginning of the year of release, the empty jars (worthless Canaanites) are broken and the light of salvation will shine in the world.

[9] The chronological indicator in 1:1, especially when combined with the references to David in 4:17 and 22, shows that the author was concerned with God's dealings with Israel as a whole and not just with the individual characters of the story. Ruth is redemptive history, not merely an ancient short story.

[10] James B. Jordan suggests that the story can be read as follows: Bethlehem starts out as "Egypt," and Naomi's experience in Moab is a "wilderness" experience during which a generation dies. The return to Bethlehem is a conquest with Bethlehem now transformed from Egypt into Canaan (personal communication, February 2000).

[11] For further discussion of the repetition of key words, see Edward F. Campbell, *Ruth*, The Anchor Bible (Garden City, NY: Doubleday, 1975).

[12] Thus, the passage breaks down into several subsections:

a. Sins of Eli's sons, 2:11b–17 ("Samuel ministered" at beginning and end)
    b. Samuel's parents, 2:18–21 ("ministered" and "grew")
a′. Sins of Eli's sons, 2:22–26 ("grew" at beginning and end)
        c. Two prophecies of judgment against the house of Eli:
            i) an unnamed man of God, 2:27–36
            ii) Samuel, 3:1–21

4
The House of David and the House of Yahweh

The books we know as 1 and 2 Samuel are actually two parts of one book and two stages of one story. The story is about the end of one house of God and the beginning of a new house. At the beginning of 1 Samuel, we learn about the sins of Eli's sons. Because of their sins, the Lord takes the priesthood away from Eli's family, gives it to a priest after God's own heart (2:35), and brings distress to his own dwelling. Over the next few chapters, this threat is carried out. At the battle of Aphek, the ark is taken captive by the Philistines (4:11), and on the same day, Eli and his sons die. This marks the end of the Mosaic tabernacle and the beginning of the end for the house of Eli. Phinehas's wife gives birth to a son on the day of the battle, but she doesn't rejoice in his birth. She realizes that he is "Ichabod"; she knows that the glory (*kabod*) has departed (4:21–22).

The Distress of My Dwelling, 1 Samuel 3–6

When the Philistines capture the ark, it begins another exodus story. During the battle of Aphek, Israel shouts as the ark is brought into the camp, and the Philistines remember that "These are the gods who smote the Egyptians with all kinds of plagues in the wilderness" (1 Samuel 4:7-8). But the Philistines haven't really learned much from the Exodus. They take the ark to Philistia, but the Lord sends plagues (5:6–12).

It is not a surprise that Philistines get treated like Egyptians, since according to Genesis 10:13–14, they come from the family of "Mizraim," the Hebrew name for Egypt. The Lord can handle the Philistines; long ago, He won a great war with their relatives, the Egyptians. As in the Exodus, Yahweh wars not only against a nation but against the gods of the nation. Yahweh's throne is put in the temple of Dagon, because the Philistines think Dagon has defeated Yahweh. In the morning, the image of Dagon is fallen before the ark, and the next day, he is broken in pieces (1 Samuel 5:1–5). The Lord judges the gods of Philistia as He had judged the gods of Egypt (Exodus 12:12).

The story of the ark is like the story of the Exodus in a number of ways. But there is also an important difference. In the exodus, Israel was in captivity in Egypt. Back in Deuteronomy 28:64–68, Moses warns Israel that they will be driven from the land if they do not obey the Lord. For a couple of centuries, Israel has been worshiping idols, and Eli's sons are guilty of "very great" sins. Yet Israel is not being driven from the land. Instead, the ark, the symbol of the Lord's presence in Israel, leaves. The Lord Himself takes on the curse of the covenant: He goes into exile in place of His sinful people. And while He is in exile, He defeats Israel's enemies. This is a picture of the gospel: As Jesus defeated Satan and sin by His humiliation, so Yahweh defeats Dagon and Philistia by suffering "defeat" and exile. But Yahweh proves that the defeat of God is greater than the victory of men.

Though the ark returns to the land, it is never put back into the Mosaic tabernacle (1 Samuel 7:1–2). The battle of Aphek ends the Mosaic house and the Mosaic covenant. That is the beginning of the story of 1–2 Samuel. 2 Samuel tells how the Lord begins to put things back together again. When David conquers Jerusalem in 2 Samuel 5, he brings the ark up into the city and makes plans to build a house for the Lord. But the Lord promises to build a house for David, a royal family that will include the Messiah (2 Samuel 7). Then, this "house of David" is going to build and keep the "house of

God." Throughout 2 Samuel, David is gathering plunder from his wars and giving it to the Lord. This plunder, like the plunder of Egypt, will be used to construct the Lord's house.[1]

After all the threats to the promise that the Lord would build His human temple, build David's dynasty, and permit David's son to build His house, the book of Samuel ends with David buying the threshing floor of Araunah (2 Samuel 24). This seems to be an odd end to the book of Samuel. After all the wars and excitement, the book ends with a land deal. But the ending is fitting, since the threshing floor of Araunah becomes the temple site (2 Chronicles 3:1). 1–2 Samuel tell about the end of the tabernacle and the beginning of the temple. The story moves from one old and destroyed house to a new house.

Between Eli and David is a time of transition, of labor pains, as a new world is being born, and the midwife of this new Israel is Samuel. As the mediator of a "new covenant," Samuel is in many ways like Moses. Like Moses, Samuel has a number of different jobs in Israel. He serves as something like a priest when he is with Eli. Though 1 Samuel 1:1 tells us that Samuel is from Ephraim, in 1 Chronicles 6:27–28 we learn that Samuel is from the clan of Kohath, a subdivision of the tribe of Levi. Of the three subtribes of Levi, the Kohathites have the greatest privileges, since they are the Levites who carry the ark and furniture of the tabernacle (Numbers 4:1–20).[2] As we saw in the last chapter, Samuel is not like Eli's sons but is a faithful Kohathite who cares for the tabernacle and the ark (see 2:11–12, 22–26; 2:12 with 3:1–21).

Like Moses, Samuel is also a prophet. He delivers the Word of the Lord, especially the Word of judgment, to Eli's house and to all Israel. In his induction into prophetic ministry in 1 Samuel 3:19–20, there is again a contrast between Samuel and Eli's sons. Hophni and Phinehas don't know the Lord (2:12), and in their time, the Lord rarely speaks to Israel (3:1). But the Lord reveals Himself to Samuel and does not let His words fall (3:19). Eli, the High Priest, is going blind (3:2; 4:15), but Samuel is called a "seer" (9:19). As prophet, Samuel begins to build a new world in Israel—a new form of government and a new order of worship. Throughout the Bible, prophets begin new periods of Israel's history with their words.

Like Moses, Samuel is a military leader. The structure of 1 Samuel 4–7 shows this:

A. Israel defeated by Philistines at Battle of Aphek, 4:1–10
  B. Ark taken and Eli's house destroyed, 4:11–22
    C. Yahweh fights Dagon in Philistia, 5:1–12[3]
  B´. Ark returned, 6:1–7:2
A´. Israel victorious over the Philistines at Battle of Ebenezer, 7:3–14

Notice that the stories at the beginning and end are both about battles between Israel and the Philistines. But the two battles are very different. In the first battle, the priests bring out the ark as if it were some kind of magic box that will defeat the Philistines. Instead, the ark is captured and the priests are killed. As at Ai, Israel is defeated because of an "Achan"—a troubler—in their midst. This time, the "Achans" are actually carrying the ark. Before the battle of Ebenezer, with Samuel now the leader of Israel, the people turn to Yahweh in repentance. They put away their idols, confess their sins, listen to Samuel's rebukes (7:3–4), and then gather for covenant-renewal at Mizpah. While they offer sacrifices, the Lord thunders against the Philistines and confuses them so that Israel wins a rout. Led by a true "priest," Israel is victorious. As at Jericho, Israel wins when they worship the Lord rightly.

Samuel is also a judge (7:15–17), just as Moses was the supreme judge of Israel. Samuel is also compared to the faithful judges from the book of Judges. Like Samson, he is born to a barren woman, consecrated as a Nazirite throughout his life, and fights the Philistines.[4] In his farewell speech, Samuel refers to Gideon, Jephthah, and himself as deliverers of Israel (12:11). Samuel is the last and greatest of the judges.

Despite his greatness, Samuel, like Eli, has unfaithful sons (8:1–3). When Samuel grows old, the elders of Israel ask for a king like the other nations have. Samuel is not pleased by this, but having a king is not wrong in itself. Jacob speaks of the "scepter" of the tribe of Judah (Genesis 49:10), and Moses tells Israel what kind of king they are to have (Deuteronomy 17:14–20). The king is not to be a tyrant who does whatever he pleases. He should remember that he rules as king under a greater King, Yahweh. Yahweh lays down three rules to the kings. First, Israel's king is not allowed to multiply horses and chariots, which are used to conquer other nations (v. 16). The best kings of Israel trade with other nations, but they are not to establish an empire beyond the land that the Lord had promised. Multiplying horses and chariots is like returning to Egypt, and the Lord does not want Israel to become another Egypt. Secondly, the king is not allowed to multiply wives because foreign wives will tempt him to follow after other gods (v. 17a). Finally, he is not to multiply gold and silver or live in luxury (v. 17b). Above all, the king is to have the Word of the Lord before him to remind him that he is not above his countrymen. Israel's king is under the law of God as much as anyone. These laws show that God approves the idea of kingship in itself. Adam was created to rule, and as the new Adamic race, it is fitting for Israel to have a king.

Though it is not wrong for Israel to have a king, Israel sins in asking for a king in this particular way and at this particular time. In 1 Samuel 8:7, the Lord reveals to Samuel that Israel has asked for a king because they reject the Lord as their king. As Gideon knew, some human kings try to compete with Yahweh. 1 Samuel 8:19–20 highlights the wickedness of Israel's request. The elders claim that they want a king to "judge us" and to "go out before us and fight our battles." Specifically, they are fearful of the Ammonites, who are advancing into Israel, led by King Nahash (1 Samuel 12:12). Yet just a chapter before they ask for a king, Yahweh wins a great victory over the Philistines at Ebenezer. The message is the same as in the book of Judges: Israel has a king, and His name is Yahweh.[5] He will fight for them, if they will but serve Him faithfully. But they don't want this One to be king over them.

Though the Lord is displeased with the request, He tells Samuel to give the people what they ask for, but he also tells Samuel to warn the people about the "ordinance" or "custom" of the king (1 Samuel 8:11). The Hebrew word is *mishpat*, which normally means "judgment," and Samuel's use of this word is interesting. When he tells the elders that he is going to discuss the "judgment" of the king, the elders expect him to talk about the king's justice: the laws and procedures of the kingdom. But Samuel is actually talking about the "habits" of the king, not about his "justice," and the king's habits are very unjust. As the speech moves on, it becomes clear that the king *is* a judgment upon the people for rejecting Yahweh and His messenger, Samuel. Israel's elders ask for a king "who may judge us." Samuel tells them that is exactly what they will get: a king who will bring judgment.

Israel gets what they ask for in another way too. Samuel delivers one basic message: "You want a king like the nations, so you will get a king like the nations." Yahweh judges the people's sin by giving them exactly what they sinfully request—that is, the *mishpat* of the king. Throughout Samuel's speech, the key word is "take," which is repeated six times (vv. 11, 13, 14, 15, 16, 17).[6] Like the kings of the nations, Israel's king will take everything productive from the Israelites: sons for his army and to work on his lands, daughters to serve in his household, fields to reward his favorites, servants and work animals. The king will exalt himself to be equal with God, demanding, as God does, a tenth of Israel's increase (v. 17). Samuel is telling the elders that rejecting Yahweh as their king is like trying to turn back the clock. Israel might as well go back to Egypt, for their king will treat them no differently than Pharaoh. But it is worse than that: When Israel cries out in her bondage in Egypt, when Israel cries out throughout the period of the judges, the Lord sends deliverers. But when the kings of Israel oppress the people, the people will cry out to the Lord, and He will not answer (8:18). That bond has been broken by the request for a king, and the Lord will send no deliverers. Because the people refuse to hear Him, He will not hear them.[7]

Review Questions.

1. Explain how the books of Samuel follow the story of the Lord's house.
2. How is the story of the capture of the ark like the Exodus from Egypt? How is it different?
3. In what ways is Samuel like Moses?
4. Explain the structure of 1 Samuel 4–7. What is important about it?
5. What are the rules for Israel's king in Deuteronomy?
6. What is wrong with the elders' request for a king?
7. Explain the changing meaning of "judgment" in Samuel's speech.
8. According to Samuel, what is Israel's king going to do?

Thought Questions.

1. When the Israelites bring the ark into the camp at the battle of Aphek, it is called the "ark of the covenant of Yahweh of hosts who sits above the cherubim" (4:4). Why is this elaborate description used here?
2. Why is it significant that Eli dies by falling from his seat(4:13–18)?
3. The ark of God goes into "exile" in Philistia, and when it returns it is filled with gold (6:4). How does this fit with other "exile" or "exodus" stories?
4. What happens to the men of Beth-shemesh when the ark returns there (6:19–21)? What does this tell us about the righteousness of Israel at the time? Are they any better than the Philistines?
5. When the elders of Israel ask for a king, the Lord says that this is "like all the deeds which they have done since the

day that I brought them up from Egypt to this day—in that they have forsaken Me and served other gods" (8:8). How is the request for a king an act of idolatry?

'Tis Like Another Fall of Man, 1 Samuel 9–15

After Samuel's speech, we expect the chosen king to be a horrible person. Surprisingly, this is not the case. Saul, the first king, begins as an ideal choice to lead and judge Israel. Despite the sin of Israel, the Lord is merciful and gives them a good ruler. When Saul first appears, he's out looking for his father's donkeys (1 Samuel 9:3ff). Saul cares for his father's animals (as did Joseph and Moses, and as David will), and he is a dutiful son. The relation of fathers and sons has already been an issue in 1 Samuel. Eli's sons don't listen to their father, and Samuel's sons don't walk in his ways. Saul is a faithful son, more like Samuel than like Hophni and Phinehas, and this is a hopeful sign for Israel.

Saul is a handsome man and a head taller than any Israelite (9:2). The Bible doesn't describe people very often. Even when it does, it does not tell us enough so that we could draw a picture. Lots of people besides Saul are tall and handsome. When the Bible does describe how a person looks, it is important to the story. Esau is hairy because he is a beast and only interested in hunting and getting his next meal. Hair is associated with glory in the Bible (see Psalms 68:21; Proverbs 20:29), so Esau's hairiness shows that he has outward glory, though he is a wicked man. Unfortunately, all that Isaac can see is Esau's outward glory. Absalom, David's hairy son, is handsome, but that makes him proud and vain. Here, Saul's size and good looks mean that he looks like a king. He is like another handsome Joseph (Genesis 39:6), and David is described in the same way (1 Samuel 16:12).

Unlike the handsome Absalom, Saul is a humble man. He is not itching to be king. When Samuel praises Saul's family, Saul wonders why Samuel thinks so much of a small household in the smallest tribe of Israel, Benjamin (9:21). When

Israel gathers to choose Saul as king, he is hiding in the baggage (10:22). Saul is also humble after his first victory in battle, when he saves the town of Jabesh-gilead from the Ammonites. At this battle, Saul crushes Nahash, whose name means "serpent." Before this, some people say they don't want Saul to be king (10:27). After Saul wins the battle, some of his supporters want to kill Saul's opponents, but Saul won't let them (1 Samuel 11:12–13). He is following the example of Moses, who is meek when attacked by Aaron and Miriam (Numbers 12:3). Saul does not return evil for evil; despised and rejected, he does not open his mouth.

Saul's humility reminds us of Gideon, who is also surprised that Yahweh chooses him to save Israel (Judges 6:15; cf. Exodus 3:11). Gideon and Saul both receive signs that show the Lord has chosen them to lead Israel. Gideon uses his famous fleece, and the Lord gives Saul three signs as he returns home after being anointed as king (1 Samuel 10:1–7). When Saul goes to fight against the Ammonites, the battle reminds us of Gideon's triumph over the Midianites. In both battles, the number three is prominent. Gideon fights with 300 men (Judges 7:6), and Saul has 330,000 (1 Samuel 11:8). Both divide their armies into 3 companies (1 Samuel 11:11; Judges 7:16), and both launch nighttime attacks and win great victories. After the battle, both show humility. Gideon refuses to become king, and Saul refuses to put the sons of Belial to death. Comparing Saul to Gideon shows what a good king Saul is when he begins.

But Gideon, as we saw in the last chapter, falls into sin. Comparing Saul to Gideon makes us wonder whether Saul will end up like one of the kings of the nations after all. Right away, that question is answered. In 1 Samuel 13–15, Saul commits three sins. First he sins by not waiting for Samuel to sacrifice. Samuel has told him to wait seven days (10:8), but when Saul sees the army scattering, he offers an ascension offering by himself. Worse, when Samuel rebukes him for his sin, he blames the people (13:11–12), like when Aaron blamed the people for the golden calf. Saul's sin perhaps seems small, but it strikes at the heart of what a king in Israel is supposed to be. The kings of Israel are to be directed by the Word of the Lord, which comes through prophet and priest, but Saul wants to sacrifice and head into battle without the blessing of Samuel. He is acting like any old king, not like a king of Israel. He is becoming a king like the kings of the nations.

Saul's second sin is a sin against his army and against his son Jonathan (1 Samuel 14). While the Philistines are camped at Michmash, Jonathan and his armor bearer go up to engage the enemy. They kill twenty Philistines, and the rest of the Philistine camp begins to panic. Israel wins, but they don't beat the Philistines as badly as they could have because Saul has told his men not to eat during the battle. Jonathan, who didn't hear his father's command, eats some honey, and at the end of the battle, Saul is ready to kill his son for violating his command. This is not the same Saul who didn't want anyone put to death after his victory over the Ammonites. Now he's ready to kill his heroic son. By mistreating his army—which is really the Lord's army—he is again becoming more like the kings of the nations.

1 Samuel 14 continues the comparison of Saul and Gideon, but now the comparison is not favorable to Saul. The battle with the Philistines at Michmash is like Gideon's battle against the Midianites. Israelites hide in caves for fear of the Midianites (Judges 6:2), and they do the same when they see the Philistine force (1 Samuel 13:6). In both battles, the Lord sets Israel's enemies against one another (Judges 7:22; 1 Samuel 14:20). Both Midianites and Philistines are like the sand on the seashore (Judges 7:12; 1 Samuel 13:5), false Israels. Another battle where Israel's enemies are like the sand is Joshua's battle against the kings led by Jabin of Hazor (Joshua 11:1–9). These are the only places in the Old Testament where enemies of Israel are described this way, and in each case, the Lord gives Israel a great victory against enormous armies.

But Saul doesn't remember Gideon's battle or the battle

of Hazor. The situation he faces is like Gideon's, but Saul isn't acting like Gideon anymore. Gideon fought with only three hundred men, trusting the Lord to fight for him, while Saul is concerned because his forces have dwindled to six hundred (1 Samuel 13:15). The only person acting with the boldness of a Gideon is Saul's son Jonathan. Jonathan knows that the Lord does not need great numbers to win a victory (1 Samuel 14:6). But Saul wants to kill Jonathan, as he will later want to kill another Israelite war hero, David. Instead of acting like Gideon, Saul begins to act more like Abimelech, the bramble king who was the son of Gideon.

Saul's last fall occurs in 1 Samuel 15 when he doesn't carry out the ban of holy war that God has decreed against Amalek (see Exodus 17:8–16; Deuteronomy 25:17–19). When the Lord places a nation under the "ban," all the people and animals are supposed to be destroyed. In his battle with the Amalekites, Saul spares the best of the flocks and herds, and also saves King Agag of the Amalekites. Saul sees Agag as another king like himself; Saul is again thinking of himself as a king like the kings of the nations. When Samuel tells him he has sinned, Saul blames the people (1 Samuel 15:15, 20–21, 24). Like Adam, he blames the "bride," Israel, rather than taking responsibility for his sin. Samuel pronounces the Lord's judgment: "Because you have rejected the word of the Lord, He has also rejected you from being king" (1 Samuel 15:23). As Samuel leaves, Samuel tears Saul's robe.[8] Since the robe is a sign of office, tearing the robe is a sign that the kingdom will be torn from Saul (1 Samuel 15:27–28). After these sins, Saul goes into a long downward spiral: God's Spirit leaves him, an evil spirit torments him, the Lord no longer talks to him, he consults a medium, and finally he ends up falling on his own sword during the battle of Gilboa.

In our study of Genesis, we saw that the earth is divided into three areas: garden, land, and world. Saul sins in each area. He sins in the "garden" when he sacrifices without waiting for Samuel. He sins in the "land" when he makes his men fast during a battle and then seeks to kill Jonathan. He sins in the world when he spares Agag and the plunder of the Amalekites. Saul is another Adam, another Cain; and, he is like the sons of God. Because of his sins, his house will be wiped out.

Saul is especially wicked in his treatment of David. He is envious of David's success and wants to protect his rights as king. He spends most of his time as king worrying about David. Comparisons between Saul and Abimelech are sprinkled through the story. Saul massacres the priests of the town of Nob because they help David (chapter 22). Only one escapes, just as only one of Abimelech's brothers survives a similar slaughter (Judges 9).[9] At the battle of Mount Gilboa, Saul is wounded by the Philistine archers and asks his armor-bearer to run him through so that the "uncircumcised" will not be able to kill him and mock him. Abimelech made a similar request when wounded during an attack on the fortress of Thebez. With his head crushed by a millstone, he is still concerned with his honor and asks his armor-bearer to run him through so it won't be said that he has been killed by a woman (Judges 9:54).

Saul starts out as a Gideon but ends up an Abimelech. The monarchy in Israel is not off to a good start. But it's the Lord's business to give new starts.

Review Questions.

1. What is Saul doing when he first appears in 1 Samuel? What does that tell us about Saul?
2. What does Saul look like? What does that tell us about him?
3. In what ways is Saul like Gideon?
4. What is Saul's first sin? How does this sin make Saul like a king of the nations?
5. What is Saul's second sin?
6. Explain the connections between Gideon's battle with the Midianites and Saul's battle at Michmash.
7. What is Saul's third sin?

8. How are Saul's sins like the sins of Genesis 3–6?
9. Explain how Saul becomes like Abimelech.

Thought Questions.

1. As Saul goes to meet Samuel, he comes across some young women at a well (1 Samuel 9:11–13). How is this similar to scenes in Genesis 24 and 29? How is it different? Why is it different?

2. What is Samuel going to do when Saul first meets him (1 Samuel 9:11–14)? In the light of Deuteronomy 12, is this a lawful thing for Samuel to do?

3. What is Saul's hometown (1 Samuel 10:26)? What happened in this town before Saul's time (Judges 19–20)? Why does the Lord choose a man from this town as the first king?

4. Saul receives the Spirit and becomes a new man (1 Samuel 10:6–13). Was he saved? See 1 Samuel 16:14.

5. How does Samuel's statement in 1 Samuel 15:23 foreshadow Saul's future (see 1 Samuel 28)? How is rebellion like "divination"?

***Humility Before Honor,* 1 Samuel 25; 2 Samuel 6, 11–12**

First the priesthood, and now the kingdom. The Lord is tearing Israel apart. But God is also busy laying the ground for a new world. A priest is rising to take Eli's place, and the Lord has chosen a man to take Saul's throne. After Saul sins, the Lord directs Samuel to anoint David. When Adam falls, there is another Adam waiting in the wings to become king over the Lord's people.

David's life can be divided in two. After Samuel anoints him, David spends ten years or more fleeing from Saul before he becomes king (1 Samuel 16–31).[10] Throughout this decade, David is the crown prince, already anointed as Saul's replacement (1 Samuel 16:12–13), yet he suffers years of wandering, flight, danger, persecution, and outlawry before ascending to his throne. Like his greater Son, David undergoes humiliation before being exalted. The other big part of

David's life is his reign as king, which lasts forty years (2 Samuel).

David is, like Saul, an ideal choice to be king. When Samuel goes to anoint a son of Jesse, he first thinks that Eliab, Jesse's oldest son, is the chosen king (1 Samuel 16:6–7). The Lord tells Samuel that He does not look on the outward appearance but on the heart. This reminds us that Saul was handsome and tall yet lost the kingdom. Yet David is handsome and has beautiful eyes, and as with Saul, this description is a picture of his character. Also like Saul, David receives the Spirit of God after his anointing (1 Samuel 16:13). The Spirit is given so that David can be a faithful king, fighting the Lord's battles and ruling with wisdom. When David receives the Spirit, it is a sign that the kingdom is being given to him. Saul, plagued by an evil spirit, becomes a wicked ruler. David does not yet rule the kingdom, but he has the Spirit, and that's the earnest of his inheritance.

Though David is like Saul in some ways, David is very different from Saul in other more important ways. The story of David and Goliath shows that David is more ready to be king than the king. In some ways, David's triumph over Goliath reminds us of the early reign of Saul. Goliath wears "scale armor," dressing himself like a serpent (1 Samuel 17:5). In his first battle, Saul too faced a "serpent," Nahash, king of the Ammonites, whose name means "serpent." David faces his serpent and passes his test by crushing Goliath's head (17:49). David is a head-crusher, like the judges, and once the head is broken, the Israelite army wins a great victory.

Mostly, though, David's fight with Goliath shows that David is a better man than Saul. Saul is a giant of a man, yet he's afraid of the Philistine giant, Goliath. David, though only a youth, is not afraid but angry that the Lord and His armies are being mocked (1 Samuel 17:26). Saul is a Benjamite, and Benjamites are known for their skill with the sling (Judges 20:16). But David shows that he is the true "son of the right hand" by using a sling to defeat Goliath. David is a better

Benjamite than Saul the Benjamite. Benjamin's original name, Ben-oni, "Son of my sorrow," is a better description of Saul (Genesis 35:18). Saul tries to put his own armor on David, but David refuses (1 Samuel 17:38–39) and arms himself with trust in Yahweh's strength. Jonathan sees clearly what is going on. Following the battle with Goliath, Jonathan strips off his armor and robe and gives them to David (1 Samuel 18:1–5). Jonathan knows that David is the crown prince, the true son and heir of Saul's kingdom.

David's later exploits also contrast with Saul. Every time David goes out to battle, he asks the Lord if he should go (23:2–12; 30:8; 2 Samuel 5:19). Meanwhile, Saul ignores the Lord, and eventually the Lord stops speaking to him altogether (28:6). Abandoned by the Spirit, Saul inquires of a medium who consults with the dead. David also begins to finish battles that Saul left unfinished. Saul is the king and should be bringing rest to the land, but he uses his spear against David instead. While David is based in Ziklag in Philistine territory, he goes out to fight against the Geshurites, Girzites, and, more importantly, the Amalekites (1 Samuel 27:8). While David marches to battle in the company of Achish of Philistia, the Amalekites attack Ziklag. After he inquires of the Lord, David goes out and defeats the Amalekites, and only four hundred escape (1 Samuel 30). Saul was deprived of the kingdom for his failure to carry out the ban against the Amalekites; David's last battle before receiving the kingdom is with the Amalekites.

Saul loses the kingdom partly because of his impatience. David wins the kingdom by showing patience. David is crown prince, but he does not rebel in order to take the throne. He does not kill Saul, despite two chances to do so. These two incidents where David refuses to strike Saul are near the center of this portion of the book of Samuel:[11]

- A. Saul kills Yahweh's priests, 21:1–22:23
  - B. David saves Keilah from Philistines, 23:1–18
    - C. Ziphites betray David; David spares Saul's life, 23:19–24:22

D. David and Abigail, 25:1–44
C´. Ziphites betray David; David spares Saul's life, 26:1–25
B´. David protects Judean towns, 27:1–12
A´. Yahweh kills Saul, 28:1–31:13

In 1 Samuel 24, Saul goes into a cave to go to the bathroom. David and his men are in the cave, and the men encourage David to attack Saul while he can be beaten easily. David instead cuts the edge of Saul's robe, a symbol of Saul's office and authority. Even this slight act of rebellion, this attack on the sign of Saul's position as king, troubles David's conscience, and David confesses to Saul (24:4–5). Two chapters later, David and Abishai sneak into Saul's camp and take the spear and jug that are beside Saul's head. Again, Abishai urges David to kill Saul, but David rebukes him: "who can stretch out his hand against the Lord's anointed and be without guilt?" and "the Lord will strike him down" (26:9–10). David is destined for the throne and mistreated by Saul, but he does not seize the kingdom by force and does not rebel against the Lord's king. Like David's later Son, Jesus, he entrusts himself to the Lord, who will raise him in due time.

At the center of this section is the story of Abigail and Nabal (1 Samuel 25). It does not deal with Saul directly, but it does reflect David's relation with Saul. When Nabal ("Fool") refuses to help David, David gathers some soldiers to attack Nabal (v. 13). Abigail, a wise and beautiful woman, intercedes for her wicked husband, and David changes his mind. His patience is rewarded, for Nabal dies soon after, and David inherits his lands and wife (vv. 39–42). This episode shows that David's patience toward Saul will be rewarded too. The Lord will remove the king as he removed Nabal, and David will inherit his crown.

David's patience does pay off. In the end, the Lord deals with Saul and with Saul's entire household. Saul's death is recorded at the end of 1 Samuel. The opening chapters of 2 Samuel show the Lord eliminating the rest of Saul's house. At the age of thirty, David is anointed as king over Judah

(2 Samuel 2:4), but Saul's son Ish-bosheth, "man of shame" continues to rule the other tribes of Israel.[12] After seven and a half years, Ish-bosheth is assassinated in his bed by Baanah and Rechab (2 Samuel 4). David says that he has nothing to do with the murder, and he even puts the assassins to death, just as he had put to death the Amalekite who claimed to have killed Saul (2 Samuel 4:9–12; see 1:11–16). Later David brings the ark to Jerusalem. David dances before the Lord's throne, acting like a fool before the King. Michal, Saul's daughter and David's wife, sees him and despises him. The Lord punishes her by making her barren, and this brings an end to all hope that the house of Saul will have a share of the kingdom (2 Samuel 6:20–23). David never lifts a hand against the house of Saul. On the contrary, he seeks out members of Jonathan's family to show kindness to. Mephibosheth, the lame son of Jonathan, sits at his table, and David restores all Saul's lands to him (2 Samuel 9). David doesn't have to lift a hand against Saul, because the Lord is wiping out the house of Saul as he wiped out the house of Eli.

After David becomes king over all Israel, one of his first acts is to conquer the capital city of Jerusalem (2 Samuel 5:6–10). Once he has taken the city, he decides to set up the throne of Israel's king there, the ark-throne of Yahweh. This is an important moment in restoring the house of God that was ruined by the sins of Eli's sons. The story of the end of the Mosaic tabernacle, given in 1 Samuel, can be outlined this way:

A. Ark taken (house of Eli eliminated), 4:1–22
 B. Ark in exile in Philistia, 5:1–6:9
  C. Ark returns on cart (sin regarding ark), 6:10–21
   D. Ark with Abinadab, 7:1–2

When David restores the ark in 2 Samuel by taking it into Jerusalem, the series of events happens in reverse order:

  C′. Ark returns on cart (sin regarding ark), 6:1–9
 B′. Ark in the house of Obed-edom, 6:10–11
A′. Restoration of the ark to a tabernacle, 6:12–19[13]

A new stage of Israel's history begins here with the building of a new "house" in Jerusalem—the "tabernacle of David."

Let's look at some of the details of this story. Obed-edom, who keeps the ark for several months, is a "Gittite," a convert from the Philistine city of Gath. Just as the ark is exiled among the Philistines for seven months (1 Samuel 6:1), so during its return the ark remains in the house of a Philistine for three months. But the Lord's treatment of the Philistines is very different in the two cases. When the ark is in Philistine territory, Egyptian plagues devastate the land, but when the ark is in the house of the Gittite Obed-edom, the Lord blesses him. David takes this as a sign that it is safe to carry the ark to Mount Zion. Blessings on Obed-edom make David confident that Yahweh is not going to break out with plagues upon the city of David as He did upon the Philistine cities. The Lord's blessing on a Gentile "provokes David to jealousy" (Deuteronomy 32:19–22; cf. Romans 9–11).

The blessing of Obed-edom and his house shows that the Davidic period will bring blessing to the Gentiles, something promised to Abraham. This is fulfilled especially during Solomon's reign, when the nations come to learn wisdom from Israel's king (1 Kings 10:24). It is also interesting that an "Obed-edom" appears in the list of singers who worship before the ark of Yahweh in the tabernacle of David. This is perhaps a sign that the Gentiles will be blessed through the house of David and made part of the choir that praises the Lord in His house (cf. 1 Chronicles 15:18, 21, 24; 16:37–38). Of course, even under the Mosaic order, Israel is to be a light to the nations. Yet, under the Mosaic economy, Egypt is judged, the Canaanites conquered, foreign invaders assassinated by judges, and Philistines judged with plagues. Now, for the first time, the ark of God is placed among Gentiles and finds a home. In this way, the "tabernacle of David" points to the inclusion of the Gentiles in the New Covenant church, as the elder James points out at the Council of Jerusalem (Acts 15:16–18; Amos 9:11–12).

When David puts the ark in Jerusalem, he also reorganizes the priests and Levites. The clearest difference between the Mosaic worship described in Leviticus and the Davidic worship set up in 1 Chronicles is the role of music and song. From what we see in Leviticus, almost nothing is said during worship at the Mosaic tabernacle. Priests who are descendants of Zadok still burn animal offerings at the Davidic tent (1 Chronicles 16:39–40), but the main thing is the Levitical orchestra and Psalm-singing.[14] David's tabernacle is the place of worship found in most of the Psalms. Psalm 122 is called a Psalm of Ascents, of David. It describes going up to the *house of God* (v. 9). Yet the temple is not yet built. Psalm 27 is a Psalm of David, yet David wants to meditate in the Lord's temple all his days, and this cannot be the temple of Solomon. Another Psalm of David says, "blessed is the one whom Thou dost choose, and bring near to Thee, to dwell in Thy courts. We will be satisfied with the goodness of thy house, thy holy temple" (Psalm 65:4). All the references to "temple" and "house of God" in David's Psalms refer to the tabernacle of David and to the "people house" that worships in music and song.

Once David has brought the ark into Jerusalem, he wants to build a more permanent house for the Lord. It makes sense for David to do this. Whenever God wins a victory over his enemies, He builds a house with the spoils, a place for Him to rest on his throne. After the Exodus, the spoils of Egypt build the tabernacle. In Ezekiel 38–39, there is a great battle, and then chapters 40–48 describe a new temple for the Lord to live in. All of this points to Jesus, the greater David, who wins a victory on the Cross and in His resurrection. After winning this victory, Jesus goes to a throne at the right hand of the Father and begins plundering Satan and building a new temple, the Christian Church.

Though building a house seems like a good idea, the Lord tells David he may not do it. According to 1 Chronicles 22:8 and 28:3, David is not allowed to build the house of the Lord because he is a man of war who has shed much blood. The reason given in 2 Samuel 7, however, is different. The Lord does not permit David to build Him a house because He intends first to build a house for David. To understand 2 Samuel 7, we need to remember that the true temple of God is not a building but a people. We have already seen in this book that God always builds up His human house before He puts His people to work building a house for Him. So also here, the Lord tells David that He will establish David's royal house over Israel, so that the kingdom will not move from family to family and tribe to tribe. Once He has built the house for David, David's son will build a house for Him.

The promises to David in 2 Samuel 7 are an important event in Israel's history and in the history of the world. In one sense, these promises are like promises that God has made from the beginning. God has never changed His original plan to give thrones and crowns to His sons and daughters, the sons of Adam and daughters of Eve. The promises to Abraham point forward to this, and the promises to David build on the promises to Abraham. David, like Abraham, will have a great name; David's son too will have a great name, for he will build a temple that connects heaven and earth, the true tower of Babel. David, like Abraham, is given a land for Israel to rest in (2 Samuel 7:11). As Abraham is promised that those who bless him would be blessed and those who curse him would be cursed, so David is promised victory over and peace with his enemies. God tells Abraham that his seed will bless the nations, and now David learns that this seed will come from him. All the promises of God to Abraham are now delivered to David, so that the future of Israel is bound up with David's household.

But the covenant with David does not merely repeat the covenant with Abraham. There is progress in the plan of God. Israel has been wandering since they entered the land, but now the Lord promises to plant them so that they will be stable and secure (7:10). Israel has never had a permanent dynasty, but now Israel will have a Davidic dynasty. David's son will finally bring peace to the land. He will not be a man of war but a man of peace, "Shalom," a fact reflected in his very name, "Shlomo." And because rest has come to the land, it will become possible to build a house for the Lord. Israel will have a central, permanent temple.

None of God's promises are given to Israel for her own sake. Abraham's seed is a blessing to the nations, and the promises to David also include all humanity. When the Lord reveals His plan to David, David says, "This is the charter of humanity" (7:19).[15] David sees that the future history of the world, not just of Israel, is bound up with the Davidic dynasty. Yahweh says his program, his purpose for the creation, will be fulfilled through David's house, and particularly through the Son of David, Jesus Christ.

The Lord has promised that David's dynasty will continue, that his son will build a temple for the Lord, and that the Seed of David will reign forever. Right away, something happens that almost ruins the promise: David's sin with Bathsheba (2 Samuel 11–12). As before, when God places a new Adam on the throne, he sins. David's sin is like Adam's and Saul's. Like Adam, David has been set upon the throne, to rule the land. Like Adam, David sins in a relationship with a woman, though as with Adam the sin is David's, not the woman's. The sin of Adam was spiritual adultery, while the sin of David is literal adultery. Like Adam, David's sin involves taking of forbidden fruit. Like Potiphar with Joseph, the Lord has given all He possesses into the hand of his steward, David. But unlike Joseph, David cannot keep his hands off a woman. After waiting patiently to receive the kingdom from the Lord and now established as a king, David begins to seize things. He begins to act like a king of the nations. Just as Samuel warned, he begins to "take." He begins to act like Saul.

David's sin, like Saul's, is not just his own sin but a threat to the whole kingdom. If David does not repent of this sin, his robe will be torn from him, as Saul's was. This is clear when we look at the whole story of David's sin in 2 Samuel 11–12:

A. Joab is on the field besieging Rabbah, but David has stayed behind in Jerusalem, 11:1
  B. David sleeps with Bathsheba and she becomes pregnant, 11:2–5
    C. David arranges for Uriah's death, 11:6–25
      D. Bathsheba mourns for Uriah, 11:26–27
        E. Nathan confronts David's sin, 12:1–15a
      D´. David mourns for his infant son, 12:15b–17
    C´. David's son dies, 12:18–23
  B´. David sleeps with Bathsheba and she becomes pregnant, 12:24–25
A´. David goes to Rabbah and finishes the siege, then returns to Jerusalem, 12:26–31

First, notice what is at the center of the story: Nathan the prophet comes to charge David with sin. Up to that point, David has sinned and tried to cover it up. Nathan uncovers the sin and tells David what the punishment will be. In the rest of the story, we see Nathan's prophecy beginning to come true. Fortunately, David does not respond like Saul. He does not blame Bathsheba or the people or God. He confesses his sin, and because of that, he keeps the kingdom. What turns things around is the Word of God. The Word of Yahweh delivered by the prophet is a sharp sword, dividing joints and marrow (Hebrews 4:12–13).

The first part of the punishment is that Bathsheba's son dies. David mourns for the boy until he knows the child is dead, and then "David arose from the ground, washed, anointed himself and changed his clothes; and he came into the house of Yahweh and worshiped. Then he came to his own house, and when he requested, they set food before him and he ate" (12:20). David rises from the dust and moves from fasting to feasting. Notice too that after he "rises" from mourning, he and Bathsheba have another child. David's adultery with Bathsheba brings forth death, but after he repents, he becomes the father of a "son of God" (see 2 Samuel 7:14).

But what an odd way to mourn! While the child lives,

David mourns, but when the child dies, David gets up (12:21). Bathsheba's mourning is more normal; she mourns after her husband dies. We can understand this when we see that the death of David's child is the punishment for David's sin of murder. If the Lord were just with David, David would die for killing Uriah. But the Lord preserves David, and David's son dies for his father's crime. When the child has died, David rises up to new life. This points to the death of another "Son of David," whose death brings us up from the dust so that we may feast at His table.

The threat to the kingdom is emphasized by the references to the siege of Rabbah at the beginning and end of the story. In 11:1, David remains behind in Jerusalem while Joab leads the army. This happened "when kings go out." The phrases "going in" and "going out" are sometimes used to describe a king's duties (1 Samuel 8:20; 1 Kings 3:7; 2 Chronicles 1:10). A king who does not "go out" is failing to act like a king. Uriah doesn't go to his house and to his wife when called in from Rabbah, and this makes David's failure even more clear (11:11). David does not act like a king at the beginning, and this leads to an even worse violation of his duties as king. Instead of "coming in" to protect the brides of Jerusalem, he stays behind and "takes" one of them; instead of "going out" to lead his men into battle, he arranges for the death of one of his mighty men. But after Nathan corrects him, he "goes out" (12:29) to capture Rabbah, receive its crown, and pile up the spoils. The passage ends with David "coming in" to Jerusalem, leading the victorious procession back to his throne. Because his son has born his punishment, David not only rises from the dust but is set on a throne.

Though David retains his throne, he is punished for his abuse of power, and the punishment for David's sin fits the crime. David raises the sword against Uriah, and because of his sin, the sword doesn't depart from his house. The most obvious example of this is Absalom's revolt, which is like David's sin on a huge scale. As David seized Bathsheba, so Absalom seizes the kingdom by deceit and trickery. As

David seized a woman, so Absalom seizes David's concubines after David had fled from Jerusalem (2 Samuel 16:20–23). As David ordered the murder of Uriah, Bathsheba's husband, so Absalom murders his brother Amnon because Amnon has raped Absalom's sister, Tamar.

As long as David is patient and faithful, the kingdom is secure. When he begins to "take," the promises that God will build David a dynastic house and that his son would build a temple for the Lord are in danger. David's own house is divided, and the promise that his son will sit upon his throne is under threat, as one by one, David's sons are dying: first, his son by Bathsheba, then Amnon, then Absalom, later Adonijah (1 Kings 2:19–25). There is also a threat to the promise of the land. When David returns to Jerusalem after Absalom's revolt, he is met with another revolt, from Sheba. This is a revolt of the tribes of Israel against the tribe of Judah. Already the kingdom is breaking into pieces, and in another generation, it is divided. God promises David rest from enemies, but because of his sin, there are enemies on every side. As the Lord said of Solomon: if he sins, he will be chastened. But the Lord promised not to remove his love from him. So also with David, the Lord chastens him by men, but the Lord does not utterly forsake him. And so the kingdom of David limps into a second generation ruled by David's great son, Solomon.

Review Questions.

1. How is David like Saul? How does David's battle with Goliath show that he is superior to Saul?
2. How does David treat Saul when Saul is persecuting him?
3. What is the significance of the incident with Nabal and Abigail?
4. What does David do after he conquers Jerusalem?
5. What is the difference between the worship of the Mosaic tabernacle and the worship of the Davidic tabernacle?

6. How is the covenant with David like the covenant with Abraham? In what ways is it different?

7. Explain the structure of the story of David and Bathsheba. How does this show that David's sin threatens the kingdom?

8. What is odd about David's mourning for his son? Why does he mourn this way?

Thought Questions.

1. When David is going out with the Philistines to fight Saul, they suspect he will turn and fight against them (1 Samuel 29:1–5). Are they right?

2. What kind of men are the "sons of Zeruiah" (2 Samuel 3:39)? Who are they? Why doesn't David just get rid of them? Look at 1 Chronicles 2:16.

3. 2 Samuel 10 records David's victory over the Ammonites. Why is this story placed here? Compare 1 Samuel 11 in context.

4. During the rebellion of Absalom, David leaves the land and returns when Absalom is defeated. How is this "exodus" similar to and different from other exodus stories?

5. 2 Samuel 20:23–26 lists the officials of David's court, but they have already been listed in 2 Samuel 8:15–18. Why are they listed again?

Son of David, 1 Kings 1–11

Like David, Solomon is a new and improved Adam. Solomon is known as the king who is wiser than any man on earth: "Solomon's wisdom surpassed the wisdom of all the sons of the east and all the wisdom of Egypt. . . . He also spoke 3,000 proverbs, and his songs were 1005" (1 Kings 4:30, 32). Solomon wants wisdom mainly so he can rule well as a king. As Lady Wisdom says in Proverbs 8:

> By me kings reign
> And rulers decree justice.

> By me princes rule, and nobles,
> All who judge rightly. (vv. 15–16)

This is the kind of wisdom that Solomon asks for when the Lord appears to him. He prays, "Give Thy servant an understanding heart to judge Thy people and to know good and evil" (1 Kings 3:9). "Knowing good and evil" reminds us of the tree in the garden of Eden. Adam, who hasn't learned to know good and evil, is not allowed to eat from the tree of judgment. Solomon has moved beyond Adam, and God allows him, as it were, to eat from the tree of knowledge.

During Solomon's reign, God keeps His promises to Abraham and David. Solomon is a blessing to the nations. Gentile rulers visit Solomon and confess their faith in the God of Israel. Hiram, the king of Tyre, sends wood and woodcutters to Israel to help build the temple, and Hiram praises the Lord because He "has given to David a wise son over this great people" (1 Kings 5:7). The queen of Sheba later comes to learn wisdom, and she too blesses Yahweh: "Blessed be the Lord your God who delighted in you to set you on the throne of Israel; because the Lord loved Israel forever, therefore He made you king, to do justice and righteousness" (10:9). All the nations of the earth seek Solomon to learn wisdom; they bring gifts of silver and gold to honor Israel's king (10:23–25). For Solomon, the fear of Yahweh is the beginning of wisdom, so the Gentiles, in learning wisdom, are learning about the God of Israel and His ways. As Israel shines as a light among the Gentiles, the treasures of the Gentiles are flowing to Israel and are used to build the Lord's house.

God promises to give Abraham and his seed the land where they may live in peace and safety, rejoicing in the Lord's goodness. This too happens in Solomon's reign (4:20, 25). The borders of Solomon's kingdom are the borders promised to Abraham (4:21), from the River (Euphrates) to the border of Egypt (see Genesis 15:18). God promises Abraham that his seed will be like the sand and like the stars, and this occurs under Solomon (1 Kings 3:8; 4:20, 29). So far in the Bible, this promise to Israel has not been fulfilled. Prior to this, only the Lord's enemies have been described as "sand on the seashore" (Joshua 11:4; Judges 7:12; 1 Samuel 13:5; 2 Samuel 17:11). Under Solomon, Israel's many enemies are subdued, and Israel herself multiplies like the sand and stars.

God promises Abraham that He will be God to him and his descendants and will live among them. To keep this promise, God tells Solomon to build the temple so that He can dwell in a permanent house among His people. Building a temple takes as much "wisdom" as ruling a nation. When the tabernacle is built, the Lord gives "wisdom" to Bezalel and Oholiab to make the curtains and furniture of God's house (Exodus 31:1–11). Solomon is a new Bezalel, and the temple he builds restores the tabernacle that had been broken up during the time of the judges.

But Solomon's temple is not exactly like the tabernacle. On the inside, Moses' tabernacle is a glorious place. It has wooden walls covered over with gold, and along the walls hang blue, purple, and scarlet hangings that have cherubim woven into them. The furniture inside the tabernacle is gold or gold-plated, and the "mercy seat," with cherubim at either end, and the lampstand are pure gold. These are expensive and beautiful materials. Though the tabernacle is beautiful, the temple is more beautiful still. And with the temple, the beauty outward. Someone looking at the tabernacle from the outside would only see the goat-hair covering. But the glory of the temple is obvious to everyone. The tabernacle has a bronze laver in the courtyard, but the temple has a bronze "sea," decorated with gourds and resting on the backs of twelve oxen, along with ten water stands of bronze set up in the courtyard, with five on each side (7:27–39). On either side of the door are two huge bronze pillars, Jachin and Boaz (7:15–22), with capitals formed like lilies and a collar of chains and pomegranates around the base of the capital.

Inside, the temple is also a glorified house. The walls of

the Holy Place and Most Holy Place are covered with cedar wood, and gourds, flowers, cherubim, and palm trees are carved into it (1 Kings 6:29). Gold covers over the cedar (vv. 21–22), and even the floor of the temple is gold (v. 30), replacing the dirt floor of the tabernacle. In place of the veils of the tabernacle, Solomon makes doors for the two rooms of the temple. The door of the Most Holy Place is olive wood carved with cherubim, palm trees, and flowers, overlaid with gold and set on two pentagonal doorposts (vv. 31–32). The doors of the Holy Place are made of cypress wood, also covered with gold and carved with figures. In the Most Holy Place, Solomon places two giant cherubim of olive wood. Ten cubits (fifteen feet) tall, they are overlaid with gold (vv. 23–28). The tabernacle has a single golden lampstand, but Solomon's temple has ten golden lampstands, five on each side of the Holy Place, all of pure gold (7:49). Solomon, fulfilling the promises to Abraham and David, makes a name for himself by building a building that reaches to the heavens, the true "tower of Babel." This is the connection point of heaven and earth.

One of the main differences between the tabernacle and the temple is that the king's house is part of the temple area. 1 Kings 6:1 begins the record of the building of the Lord's house, and this does not end until 7:51, which says that "all the work that King Solomon performed in the house of the Lord was finished." Between 6:1 and 7:51, though, the writer tells not only about the temple but about Solomon's palace and other buildings that Solomon built for himself (7:1–8). The description of Solomon's palace comes right in the middle of the passage talking about building the "house of Yahweh." This means that Solomon's house and the temple are both parts of something called the "house of Yahweh." Nothing like this has happened in Israel before. Before this, the Lord has never shared His house. Priests serve in the tabernacle, but there is no king's tent beside the tent of King Yahweh. But Solomon lives "in" the Lord's house, as prince over Israel.

Like all the Old Testament kings, Solomon is far from perfect. The promises to Abraham are fulfilled to a large extent, but Solomon sins and the blessings turn to curses. In Deuteronomy 17, the Lord commands kings not to multiple horses, wives, or gold. Solomon sins in all three of these areas. Solomon collects 666 talents of gold each year, a huge amount of money for a small nation like Israel (1 Kings 10:14). Solomon gathers a large number of horses and chariots (10:26) and even brings in horses from Egypt (10:28). Just as Deuteronomy 17 warns, collecting horses and chariots takes Israel back to Egypt. Finally, Solomon, like the sons of God in Genesis 6, marries foreign women, and these women turn Solomon to other gods (11:1–8). Despite his wisdom, Solomon acts very foolishly.

Because of his sin, the Lord punishes Solomon by tearing the kingdom in two (11:9–13; 11:26–40). Even during his lifetime, he faces several enemies: Hadad of Edom, Rezon of Zobah, and finally Jeroboam, one of Solomon's own officials from the tribe of Ephraim. For the sake of David and Jerusalem, the Lord leaves Solomon part of the land. He cuts back the house of David, but He does not completely forsake it.

Any faithful Israelite living during the period of Solomon and David could see that God has not yet fulfilled His promises. David and Solomon are great, but there must be some greater King coming, a King who will sit on David's throne forever ruling in faithfulness, a King who will truly bring rest to His people, and a King who will build a temple that would never be destroyed. Both in his glory and in his failures, Solomon points us to the greater Son of David, Jesus Christ.

Review Questions.

1. Why does Solomon ask for wisdom?
2. How is Solomon's wisdom connected to Adam?
3. In what ways is Solomon's reign a fulfillment of promises to Abraham?
4. How is the temple different from the tabernacle?

5. What three sins does Solomon commit?
6. What happens to Israel because of Solomon's sins?

Thought Questions.

1. Explain the location of the story about the two harlots and the child (1 Kings 3:16–28). Why is it here?

2. How does Solomon reorganize Israel (1 Kings 4:7–19)?

3. Compare the two dreams of Solomon (3:1–15 and 9:1–9). Compare the two encounters with Hiram of Tyre (5:1–15 and 9:10–14). How are these similar scenes different? What does this say about Solomon's reign?

4. The account of the building of the temple is at the center of 1–2 Chronicles. This differs in a marked way from 1–2 Kings. What does this suggest about the purpose of those books? Note especially 2 Chronicles 36:22–23.

5. The center of Solomon's prayer in 1 Kings 8 is about plagues in the land (vv. 37–40). Why is this central? As a clue, notice how 6:1 dates the construction of the temple.

[1] 1 Chronicles 23–28 tells us that David also reorganized the priesthood, creating Levitical orders of singers, gatekeepers, and treasurers in anticipation of the building of the temple.

[2] 1 Samuel 1:1 indicates that Samuel is an "Ephraimite," but this can be harmonized with the Levitical genealogy in 1 Chronicles 6. Following the conquest, priests and Levites scattered all over the land of Israel, and many Levites lived in the towns and served as "pastors" of local synagogues (Deuteronomy 14:27; 16:11). Samuel's ancestors were evidently among those Levites who lived and labored away from the sanctuary. Thus, Elkanah was geographically an "Ephraimite" but tribally a Levite, as I am geographically an "Ohioan" but ancestrally German.

[3] In the exile of the ark, as we have seen, Yahweh suffers exile as a substitute for Israel. Significantly, because Yahweh has borne the curse for Israel's sins, Israel is victorious in her next battle.

[4] In fact, Samuel and Samson were contemporaries.

[5] Chronologically, there is a gap of perhaps several decades between the end of chapter seven and the beginning of chapter eight; in the interim, Samuel "grew old" (8:1). But the writer deliberately puts the request for a king immediately after the battle scene, to highlight the rebelliousness of the request.

[6]In the Hebrew, the verb "take" is placed at the beginning of each phrase, giving it an emphatic prominence.

[7]The words "ask" and "hear" are used frequently in the first chapters of 1 Samuel. Samuel is "asked" of the Lord, and the Lord hears (see 1:20). He is the one that Israel should be "asking" for. But Israel is not satisfied and asks for another leader. They get what they "ask" for; Saul's name means "asked." Because Israel is asking for a king and ignoring the one they should ask for help, the Lord refuses to "hear" when "asked" for help.

[8]The Hebrew is ambiguous about whose robe is torn. Since Saul's robe, not Samuel's, represents the kingdom, it seems more likely that Saul's robe is being torn. This also linked this event up with David's later assault on Saul's robe (1 Samuel 24:4).

[9]When Saul asks for a volunteer to slaughter the priests of Nob, none of the Israelites want to help. Suspecting them of loyalty to David, he asks whether or not they can expect favors from David, a son of Judah, since they are Benjamites (22:7). This exchange implies that Saul has been bestowing favors on his fellow Benjamites, and this may explain the enduring loyalty to Saul's house among the Benjamites. It also serves as another indication that Saul has become precisely the kind of king that Samuel warned about, one who takes fields and vineyards.

[10]Acts 13:21 informs us that Saul reigned for forty years, and we learn from 2 Samuel 5:4 that David was thirty when he became king. Thus, David was born in the tenth year of Saul's reign. When he fought Goliath, he was either too young to be part of the army (therefore, under twenty, cf. Numbers 1:3) or old enough to be in the army but kept behind to take care of the flocks of his father. If he was under twenty at the time, he was only slightly so, for he was very quickly promoted to be a captain of a thousand (1 Samuel 18:13). Thus, the time between his anointing and his ascension to the throne stretches from the time he was near twenty until the time he became king at thirty.

[11]David A. Dorsey, *The Literary Structure of the Old Testament: A Commentary on Genesis–Malachi* (Grand Rapids: Baker, 1999), p. 132.

[12]Why would Saul give this kind of name to his son? The answer is he didn't. His original name was "Ish-Baal" or "Eshbaal," which means "man of Baal" (1 Chronicles 8:33; 9:39). "Bosheth" is also a name for Baal in some passages (see Jeremiah 11:13). So, why would Saul have named his son after Baal? There is no evidence that Saul worshiped Baal, so the answer to this question is likely that "Baal" is being used here in its generic sense of "lord" or "master." In this sense, Baal is sometimes used as a designation for God (see Hosea 2:16). See Ronald F. Youngblood, *1–2 Samuel* in *The Expositor's Bible Commentary* (Frank E. Gaebelein, ed.; Grand Rapids: Zondervan, 1992), 3.822–823.

[13]The two A sections in the outline are linked not only because of the "ark taken—ark returned" dynamic but because each section records the end of a dynasty. On the same day that the ark is taken into captivity, Eli and his

sons die, definitively ending the house of Eli as a priestly house (though this is not finally carried out until the time of Solomon, 1 Kings 2:26–27). When the ark is returned, a royal dynasty comes to an end—the dynasty of Saul. Michal, as noted above, sees David rejoicing before the ark, despises him in her heart, and is punished with barrenness, a barrenness that reflects the withered tree that Saul has become. Saul's blood will never run in the veins of Davidic kings. With the closing of the Mosaic tabernacle, a priesthood ends; with the erection of David's tent, a royal house is cast down.

[14]This provides a strong line of argument against Reformed liturgists who would reject the use of instruments in worship. Instrumental music does not fall in the category of "forbidden" nor even in the category of "adiaphora." On the contrary, it should be a central part of Christian worship. According to the very first church council, we do not worship at a silent Mosaic tent; we worship at the restored tent of David, and our praise in Psalms should be accompanied by an orchestra at least as robust as that of the Levites (1 Chronicles 15:16–24).

[15]The phrase is difficult and debated, but Walter Kaiser has argued persuasively that it means "a charter for humanity" and that it is a statement rather than a question (*Toward an Old Testament Theology* (Grand Rapids: Zondervan, 1978), pp. 152–155.

5
Walking in the Customs of the Nations

Solomon begins a new and wonderful time in Israel's history. God has kept His promises to Abraham, and now He lives among the people in a permanent house. But Israel's time of greatness does not last long. Solomon sins against the laws for kings, multiplying gold, horses and chariots, and wives (1 Kings 10:14, 26; 11:1–8). Because of Solomon's sin, Yahweh divides the nation into the Northern Kingdom of Israel and the Southern Kingdom of Judah. During the next three centuries, both kingdoms go back to Canaanite and Egyptian worship, and eventually the Lord drives both Israel and Judah out of the land. In 722 B.C., the Assyrians conquer Samaria, the capital of the Northern kingdom, and 150 years later, Nebuchadnezzar king of Babylon captures Jerusalem, destroys the temple, and takes many from Judah to Babylon.

The books of Kings tell this story, and the books of Chronicles tell the same story, though Chronicles focuses on the Southern Kingdom. Like the books of Samuel, the books of Kings are two parts of one story. It begins with Solomon building the temple, and it ends with Nebuchadnezzar destroying the temple. Kings is like Samuel in reverse: 1–2 Samuel moves from a distressed tabernacle to a new house, while Kings moves from the building of Solomon's temple to its destruction.[1] The books end with a little glimmer of hope, when Evil-merodach, king of Babylon, raises King Jehoiachin of Judah from prison and gives him a place at his table (2 Kings

25:27–30). This is a sign that Judah will someday leave Babylon and be fed in the land of milk and honey, though even then they will be under the authority of "Babylon."

In the first part of this chapter, we will look at the Northern Kingdom, and in the second part, we will focus on the South. This is known as the time of the "divided kingdom," which ends when the Northern Kingdom is taken over by Assyria. In the next chapter, we'll look at Judah in the time after the Northern Kingdom fell.

1–2 Kings opens the history of the Northern Kingdom by talking about a group of seven kings and ends the story with another group of seven kings. In between these two groups is the work of Elijah and Elisha:[2]

A. First Seven Kings
1. Jeroboam, 1 Kings 12:1–14:20
2. Nadab, 15:25–32
3. Baasha, 15:33–16:7
4. Elah, 16:8–10
5. Zimri, 16:11–20
6. Omri, 16:21–28
7. Ahab, 16:29–34

B. Ministries of Elijah and Elisha in the Northern Kingdom, 1 Kings 17:1– 2 Kings 13:21

A′. Last Seven Kings
1. Jeroboam II, 14:23–29
2. Zechariah, 15:8–12
3. Shallum, 15:13–16
4. Menahem, 15:17–22
5. Pekahiah, 15:23–26
6. Pekah, 15:27–31
7. Hoshea, 17:1–41

Notice how balanced this history is. Both groups of seven kings begin with a "Jeroboam," and both end with a king whose reign is a terrible disaster for Israel. The first group ends with Ahab, the worst king Israel ever has, and the second group ends with Hoshea, who is king when Samaria, the capital of Israel, falls to the Assyrians. A "Sabbath" judgment comes on the seventh king in each sequence. Notice too that Elijah and Elisha are in the center of the book. Jews do not think of the books of Kings as "history" books, but as "Books of the Former Prophets." One reason for this is that Elijah and Elisha have such an important place in the story.

A lot of things go on in the books of Kings, and we cannot look at everything. Instead, we'll look at three events: the first king of the Northern Kingdom, Jeroboam; the work of Elijah and Elisha during the reign of Ahab; and the fall of Samaria under Hoshea.

The Garment Torn, 1 Kings 11–12

Long before Solomon's time, the Northern tribes and Southern tribes have trouble getting along. When Saul calls together the tribes to fight the Ammonites, Judah and Israel are counted separately (1 Samuel 11:8; see 1 Samuel 15:4). Absalom wins over the people to his plot against David by telling them that different tribes are treated differently. He claims that David is treating people from Judah, his own tribe, better than people from other tribes. Absalom says that anyone in one of the "tribes of Israel" should come to him for help, not to David (2 Samuel 15:1–6). After the reign of Solomon, the problems among the tribes get worse, and David's kingdom is torn into two separate kingdoms.

North and South separate because of the foolishness of Rehoboam, Solomon's son. Solomon has made the "yoke" of the people very heavy, ruling over them harshly (1 Kings 12:3), so the people ask Rehoboam to lighten the yoke. But Rehoboam takes the advice of his young foolish friends and says he will make the yoke even heavier (1 Kings 12:12–15). Rehoboam acts foolishly, but the blame for the division of the kingdom goes to Solomon. During Solomon's reign, the prophet Ahijah meets Jeroboam, one of Solomon's important officials. Ahijah is wearing a robe, and he tears it in twelve pieces and then gives ten pieces to Jeroboam (1 Kings 11:26–40). The robe represents the kingdom (as it did in Saul's time), and giving ten pieces to Jeroboam means he will rule ten tribes of Israel. Ahijah tells Jeroboam why the robe of the kingdom is being torn: "Because [the tribes of Israel] have forsaken Me, and worshiped Ashtoreth the goddess of the Sidonians, Chemosh the god of Moab, and Milcom the god of the sons of Ammon" (11:33). Ahijah is blaming the people for worshiping idols, but mainly he's blaming Solomon. These are the very same gods that Solomon has been worshiping (11:5, 7). As in the period of the judges, the nation of Israel suffers because she worships idols.

Ahijah's prophecy of a torn kingdom comes true. This is one of the early examples of how 1–2 Kings shows the power of the word of the prophet. When Solomon dismisses Abiathar from serving as priest, it fulfills the Word of Yahweh spoken against Eli, because Abiathar is a descendant of Eli (1 Kings 2:27). Solomon sees that building the temple fulfills promises made to David (1 Kings 8:20). The Lord hardens the heart of Rehoboam so that he does not listen to the people, fulfilling the words of Ahijah (12:15). Sometimes, the prophet's word doesn't come true for centuries. During the reign of Ahab, "Hiel the Bethelite built Jericho." When he does this, his firstborn and youngest sons die, and this fulfills the curse that Joshua has spoken centuries before against anyone who rebuilds Jericho (1 Kings 16:34; see Joshua 6:26). Many prophets warn that Israel and Judah will be driven from the land unless they repent, and this also comes true (2 Kings 24:2). These examples of the power of the Word of the Lord that comes through the prophets are another reason why the Jews think of Kings as a "prophetic" book.

Ahijah's words come to pass almost immediately. Jeroboam leads the group of men who ask Rehoboam to lighten the yoke of Solomon (1 Kings 12:1–5). When Rehoboam won't listen, Jeroboam seems like a good choice to lead the tribes that separate from the house of David. One of the first things Jeroboam does is set up idols for the Northern tribes. He does this because he is afraid of what will happen if he lets the Northern tribes go to Jerusalem to worship. If they go to Jerusalem for feasts every year, they might "return to the house of David" (12:26). To protect his power and to keep people from moving to Judah, Jeroboam wants to make sure that the Northern tribes worship in the Northern Kingdom. And so he sets up golden calves at Dan (in the far North) and Bethel (at the southern edge of the Northern Kingdom). This reminds us of Aaron's sin at Mount Sinai when he helps the people set up golden calves (Exodus 32). Jeroboam says that the calves are the "gods that brought you up from the land of Egypt" (1 Kings 12:28), and this is almost exactly what Aaron says at Sinai (Exodus 32:4, 8). Instead of going to Jerusalem for the Feast of Booths in the seventh month (Leviticus 23), the Northern tribes celebrate a feast in the eighth month (1 Kings 12:32). Like the Feast of Booths, Jeroboam's feast begins on the fifteenth day of the month.

Jeroboam chooses Bethel for one of the places of worship, and this is an important choice. Bethel is a holy place long before Solomon builds his temple, even before Moses leads Israel from Egypt. Jeroboam can say to his people: "I'm not doing anything new. We're worshiping the way Israel worshiped a long, long time ago. We worship golden calves like Aaron did, and we worship at Bethel, like Jacob did. We're the true sons of Jacob. Those people in the South are doing something new with their temple and all." Jeroboam even names his sons Nadab and Abijah (14:1; 15:25), after the sons of Aaron, Nadab and Abihu, who perished when they offered "strange fire" before the Lord (Leviticus 10).

Jeroboam says that Israel is worshiping the God who brought Israel from Egypt. He says they're worshiping the God of the Exodus, though he is worshiping Yahweh through golden calves. He is not breaking the first commandment, which tells us that we must not worship any other gods. He is breaking the second commandment, which says that we are not to worship even the true God by using images or statues. The people of Israel don't worship the calves themselves, but they do worship "before" the calves (12:29–30). The Northern Kingdom continues in this sin for its whole history. Many of the kings of Israel "walk in the way of Jeroboam" and commit the "sin of Jeroboam the son of Nebat" (cf. 15:29–30; 15:34; 16:19; 16:26)—the sin of worshiping through golden calves.

The second commandment warns that those who hate God by worshiping Him through images will be punished to the third or fourth generations. This is what happens to the kings of Israel. They break the second commandment, and only one family rules the North for more than four generations. Most of them rule for only a couple of generations:

Dynasty	*Kings*
Jeroboam I	Jeroboam, Nadab
Baasha	Baasha, Elah
Zimri	Zimri
Omri	Omri, Ahab, Ahaziah, Jehoram
Jehu	Jehu, Jehoahaz, Jehoash, Jeroboam II, Zechariah
Shallum	Shallum
Menahem	Menahem, Pekahiah
Pekah	Pekah
Hoshea	Hoshea

Only Jehu's dynasty lasts longer than four generations, and Zechariah, the last king in that house, rules for only six months (2 Kings 15:8). Meanwhile, a single house—the house of David—rules in the South (with one interruption). Because the kings sin against the second commandment, the Northern Kingdom has a series of houses that are eventually "swept clean" (see 1 Kings 14:10; 21:21).

The sins of Jeroboam the son of Nebat are bad enough. But something even worse begins with the dynasty of Omri. We'll look at that dynasty in the next section.

Review Questions.

1. How are the books of Kings a "reverse" of the books of Samuel?
2. Explain the order of the story of the Northern Kingdom in 1–2 Kings.
3. Why is the kingdom of Solomon divided?
4. Give some examples of the power of a prophet's word in 1–2 Kings.
5. Why does Jeroboam set up golden calves?
6. What commandment does Jeroboam break?
7. Why does Jeroboam choose Bethel for one of his shrines?
8. How is the punishment for breaking the second commandment seen in the books of Kings?

Thought Questions.

1. The prophet Ahijah is called a "Shilonite" (1 Kings 11:29; 14:2). Why is this significant?
2. A "man of God from Judah" prophesies that Jeroboam's altar in Bethel will be defiled by Josiah (1 Kings 13:1–2). This is fulfilled in 2 Kings 23:15–16. How does this fit with the larger themes of the books of Kings?
3. Why is the man of God from Judah eaten by a lion (1 Kings 13:20–25)?
4. Jeroboam's son Abijah gets sick in 1 Kings 14:1. What does the sickness of the king's son represent? What does the boy's death represent (14:6–16)?
5. Yahweh tells Baasha that he raised him from the "dust" to be king (1 Kings 16:2). Discuss this in light of Genesis 2:7.

***Return to Canaan,* 1 Kings 17–2 Kings 4**

After Jeroboam, the second strong family in the Northern Kingdom is Omri's. 1 Kings skips Omri's reign without saying much (1 Kings 16:15–28), but in his time, Omri was an important king. Years after his death, the Northern Kingdom is still being called "Omriland" by other nations. The writer of Kings mentions that Ahab, the son of Omri, builds Samaria as the capital of the Northern Kingdom. Mainly the Bible focuses on the fact that Omri "did evil in the sight of Yahweh, and acted more wickedly than all who were before him" (16:25). But Omri's evil is nothing compared to the evil done by Ahab. The opening words about Ahab's reign tell us that he is the worst of Israel's kings:

> Ahab the son of Omri did evil in the sight of Yahweh more than all who were before him. And it came about, as though it had been a trivial thing for him to walk in the sins of Jeroboam the son of Nebat, that he married Jezebel the daughter of Ethbaal king of the Sidonians, and went to serve Baal and worshiped him. So he erected an altar for Baal in the house of Baal which he built in Samaria. And Ahab also made the Asherah. (1 Kings 16:30–33)

Ahab has planned his actions carefully. He aims to revive Canaanite worship in the land. Under Joshua, Israel destroyed the altars and shrines of the Canaanites, but Ahab is building them again. He marries Jezebel, a Sidonian princess. Tyre and Sidon are the twin cities of Phoenicia, and the man Sidon is the firstborn son of Canaan (Genesis 10:15). Jezebel is thoroughly Canaanite, and Ahab is jumping into bed with her. During Ahab's reign, Hiel rebuilds Jericho, as if he's trying to turn back the conquest. Trying to reverse the conquest is foolish. Ahab and his kingdom are in the land only because of Joshua's conquest. When Ahab permits the conquest to be reversed, he's giving up his own right to be king. And his plan to revive Canaanite worship is suicide for Israel. Canaanites get driven from the land, and if Israel acts like the Canaanites, the Lord will force Israel from the land too. The threat of exile is looming in the background already.

Ahab is not satisfied with just restoring Canaanite worship. He also wants to reunite the Northern and Southern Kingdoms. But he doesn't want them united under the house of David, and he doesn't want Solomon's temple to be at the center. Ahab wants to reunite the kingdoms under the house of Omri, with a temple of Baal at the center. Jehoshaphat of Judah, though righteous, works with Ahab, and Jehoshaphat's son, Jehoram of Judah, marries Athaliah, the daughter of Ahab and Jezebel (2 Kings 8:18, 26). North and South get all mixed up during this period, and this is why these chapters of Kings are so confusing to read. Kings of Judah and kings of Israel both act wickedly, and several of them even have the same names. There is an Ahaziah of Israel and there is one in Judah; there is a Jehoram of Israel and there is a Jehoram of Judah. David's family is in danger of being swallowed up by the dynasty of Omri and Ahab. Worship of Baal is seeping into the Southern Kingdom.

Ahab's plan almost succeeds. For a short time, a descendant of Ahab, Athaliah, sits on the throne of David and Solomon (2 Kings 11), and during her reign, there is even a temple of Baal in Jerusalem (11:18). Ahab's plan almost succeeds, but it doesn't—because of Elijah and Elisha, two prophets of God.[3] Like Moses and Joshua, they lead the people out of "Egypt," renew the covenant, and conquer the land, driving out Ahab's "Canaanites."

Elijah's life follows the story of Israel very closely. Like Jacob and his sons, Elijah is driven out of the land by a famine (1 Kings 17:1–4). In exile, Elijah receives food from ravens and then from a Gentile widow, just as Israel is given the fruitful land of Goshen. In a Passover scene, he raises the widow's son from the dead (vv. 8–24). Finally, in the middle of a week of years (see Luke 4:25), Elijah returns to the land to fight against the prophets of Baal (1 Kings 18). Elijah's life is an exodus, return, and conquest.

Elijah also follows closely in the footsteps of Moses. He first appears telling Ahab that a plague of drought is coming to the land. Ahab is hostile to him, so Elijah has to flee, as Moses flees from Egypt to Midian because of the hatred of Pharaoh (Exodus 2:11–15). While fleeing, both Elijah and Moses encounter women (1 Kings 17:8–16; Exodus 2:16–22), and in both cases, the women are associated with water. Moses meets the daughters of Reuel at a well, and Elijah asks the widow of Zarephath for water. Moses marries Zipporah, who bears his son in a strange land (Exodus 2:23). While Elijah does not marry the widow, he does "give" her a son by restoring him to life (1 Kings 17:17–24). After forty years in Midian, Moses returns to Egypt to confront Pharaoh and lead Israel out of bondage (Exodus 3:1–4:17). Similarly, "after many days," the Lord sends Elijah to confront the "Pharaoh" of Israel (1 Kings 18:1). Before his first meeting with Pharaoh, Moses speaks to Aaron and the assembled elders of Israel (Exodus 4:27–31), and Elijah first meets with his ally, Obadiah (1 Kings 18:7–16).

Elijah's battle with the prophets of Baal at Mount Carmel mixes together a number of events from the life of Moses. On the one hand, the events at Carmel reflect the plagues and Passover in Exodus. At Carmel, the gods of Ahab are mocked and humiliated, which reminds us of the Lord's defeat of the gods of Egypt (1 Kings 18:27; see Exodus 12:12). On the other hand, Carmel is a mountain like Sinai, and the event at Carmel renews the Sinai covenant. After the Lord's display of power, the people agree that Yahweh is God and promise to follow Him and obey His voice. As at Sinai, idolaters are slaughtered by the command of the Lord's prophet (1 Kings 18:40; Exodus 32:27).

After Israel's fall into idolatry with the golden calves, Moses asks the Lord to remove his name from the book of life in order to save Israel (Exodus 32:31–32). After Carmel, Elijah flees again into the wilderness and asks the Lord to take his life (1 Kings 19:4). Refreshed with food from an angel, Elijah travels for forty days and nights to Horeb. He stays in "*the* cave" (1 Kings 19:8–9), where the Lord's glory appears to Him (vv. 11–14). This is precisely the place where Moses is allowed to see the passing glory of the Lord while spending forty days on the mountain (Exodus 33:17–34:9; 34:28).

The departure of Elijah resembles the death of Moses. Both Elijah and Moses are outside the land to the east when they leave the earth. No one knows where Moses is buried

(Deuteronomy 34:6), and a party searches for Elijah for three days but cannot find him (2 Kings 2:15–18). In both cases, the Lord's prophet passes on his authority to a "disciple." Before Moses dies, Joshua is named his successor (Numbers 27:15–23). By laying hands on Joshua, Moses confers some of his "glory" (Numbers 27:20). In Deuteronomy 34:9, Joshua is said to receive the "spirit of wisdom" through the laying on of Moses' hands. Similarly, Elisha is Elijah's successor, and he receives a "double portion" of Elijah's spirit. This enables him to perform the same miracles that Elijah performs, and he follows the path of Elijah back to Samaria (2 Kings 2:9–14, 23–25; cf. vv. 1–6).[4]

These links between Elijah and Moses are not just there to help us enjoy the story. The point is that Elijah's ministry is like Moses'. Moses is the great prophet who sets up the tabernacle and sacrificial system. In Elijah's day, worship has been corrupted, especially in the Northern Kingdom. Elijah's mission is to call Israel back and to rebuild the foundations for the worship and life of Israel. Elijah's mission is to call Israel to renew the covenant.

Elijah's life is itself a message to the Northern Kingdom, and to Ahab in particular. Elijah's experience is connected to other earlier events in the Bible. Yahweh directs Elijah to move to the east of the Jordan (1 Kings 17:3, 5). This connects his exodus with the exile of Adam, Eve, and Cain from Eden (Genesis 3:24; 4:16), and also with the eastward direction of the tabernacle (Numbers 3:38). But Elijah is driven out of the sanctuary-land not by his own sin but because of the sins of Ahab and Jezebel. Elijah's exile east of the land points to Israel's capture and exile by Assyria. For the time being, the prophet, like the ark in 1 Samuel 4–6, is taking the sin of exile onto himself. But Elijah's exile is a sign telling Israel that the whole nation will go into exile if they do not repent.

While camping at the brook Cherith, Elijah is fed bread and meat by ravens (1 Kings 17:4, 6). Ravens are unclean birds (Leviticus 11:15) and picture the nations around Israel.

The unclean ravens that provide food are like the widow of Zarephath, who also provides food for Elijah. In 17:4, the Lord says, "I have commanded the ravens to provide for you," and in verse nine, He says "I have commanded a widow there to provide for you." The fact that Elijah is fed by ravens is a sign that, in exile, he will be sustained by Gentiles. Later, Israel will be sustained by Gentiles while in exile (see 2 Kings 25:27–30).[5]

Elijah's sojourn among the Gentiles has another meaning as well. The prophet of the Lord, who bears the life-giving Word, is rejected by Israel and goes to bring God's blessing to the Gentiles. Jesus later says that Elijah's ministry to the widow of Zarephath is a picture of the Jews' rejection of the Messiah and of the Messiah's turning to the Gentiles (Luke 4:25–26). The widow, moreover, lives close to Sidon. Her self-sacrificial kindness toward Elijah is the opposite of the hatred shown by the other woman of Sidon, Jezebel (16:31; 19:2). The Sidonian queen of the land seeks to kill the prophet, while the poor Sidonian widow offers him food and drink. Again, there is a sharp contrast between the spiritual condition of the nation of Israel and that of the Gentiles.

The fact that the woman of Zarephath is a widow is also important. In part, her widowhood makes the contrast with Jezebel even stronger. The weak and poor widow, not the wealthy queen, provides for the prophet. Plus, Israel is sometimes pictured as a widow (Isaiah 54:4–8; Lamentations 1:1). When Israel turns from her Husband and offers herself to Baal and Asherah (16:28–34), her Husband threatens to abandon her, to leave her a "widow," and to seek another bride among the Gentiles. This is the "sign of Jonah," as we'll see shortly.

If Elijah is a new Moses, Elisha is a new Joshua. He is a servant to Elijah, as Joshua was to Moses. When Elijah leaves in 2 Kings 2, Elisha receives a double portion of his spirit, the portion of the firstborn, and continues Elijah's ministry. His first stop when he reenters the land is Jericho, where he restores the water that has become bad and unfruitful. Elisha's role as "Joshua" is best seen, though, in 2 Kings 2:23–25, in the story of the bears killing the forty-two "lads" at Bethel. This story is often misunderstood.[6] Remember that this is right after Elijah's third and last "exodus" from the land. Elijah and Elisha leave the land (through the parted waters of Jordan, just as Israel left Egypt through the Red Sea), Elijah ascends and cannot be found (like Moses), and Elisha returns through the parted Jordan, just as Israel entered Canaan under the leadership of Joshua. Elisha is a new Joshua who enters the land to purge it of Canaanites. He meets the "young lads" at Bethel, one of the places where Jeroboam set up his golden calves (1 Kings 12:25–33). Cursing the forty-two "lads" is part of the new Joshua's conquest of the land.[7]

But who are the "lads"? The Hebrew word (*na'ar*) sometimes means "official" or "steward" and sometimes doesn't say anything about age. Mephibosheth's servant Ziba is a *na'ar* of Saul's house (2 Samuel 16:1), but he is clearly not a boy since he has fifteen sons of his own (2 Samuel 19:17). Boaz would have been a fool to put a "boy" in charge of his reapers, but his foreman is called a *na'ar* in Ruth 2:5–6.[8] The forty-two killed by bears are servants at the shrine at Bethel, the shrine devoted to golden calves. Elisha does not slaughter babies or infants or little children but instead calls down curses on the "officials" of the idolatrous shrine of Bethel. As the new Joshua, he is beginning his holy war against the shrines of the "Canaanites" who dominate the Northern Kingdom.

But the "conquest" of this Joshua is quite different from the first Joshua's. Elisha does call on God to destroy the "lads" at Bethel; his conquest is mainly a conquest of mercy, not destruction. This is evident from the chiastic order of 2 Kings 3–7:

- A. War with Moab, 3:1–27
  - B. Elisha provides for indebted widow, 4:1–7
    - C. Elisha raises the Shunammite's son, 4:8–37
      - D. Elisha heals the poison stew, 4:38–41

D´. Elisha feeds 100 men, 4:42–44
C´. Elisha heals Naaman the leper, 5:1–27
B´. Elisha recovers a borrowed axe head, 6:1–7
A´. War with Aram, 6:8–7:20

Elisha's ministry does not center on destroying God's enemies (D and D´). He is more like the greater Elisha, Jesus, who does miracles of food and gives life rather than take it.

Aftershocks in Judah

Elisha doesn't carry out this conquest all on his own. Instead, he anoints Jehu as the avenger against the house of Ahab. Jehu's job is to "cut off from Ahab every male person both bond and free in Israel," and to execute Jezebel as well (2 Kings 9:1–13). He is going to destroy all the Canaanites in the house of Ahab and restore the land. Jehu's attack is primarily against the Northern Kingdom, and he becomes the king of Israel. He kills Joram of Israel, then goes into Samaria and has Jezebel killed. He then kills the seventy sons of the king (10:11). Then he gathers the worshipers of Baal into the temple in Samaria and slaughters them all. By the end of 2 Kings 10, all of Ahab's immediate family and many of his supporters have been killed.

Jehu's conquest also brings trouble to the Southern Kingdom. The problem for the Southern Kingdom is that Israel and Judah are almost the same. When Jehu wipes out Ahab's family, that includes members of the Davidic house. Jehu kills Ahaziah, the king of Judah (9:27), and then forty-two members of Ahaziah's household (10:12-14). Jehu provides a good lesson for kings of Judah: If you are too close to the Northern Kingdom, you'll be punished in the same way.

After killing Ahaziah, Jehu is finished in the South and goes back to the Northern Kingdom. But Judah needs a Jehu, because a member of Ahab's house, Athaliah, is ruling in Jerusalem. As a daughter of Ahab, she is a Southern version of Jezebel. But 2 Kings does not treat her as a real queen.

Throughout 1–2 Kings, the story of a king's reign begins by telling the king's name, his father's name, the year he began to rule, and his faithfulness or lack of faithfulness to the Lord (see 1 Kings 15:1–6). But sometimes the stories in Kings don't begin in this typical way. Elijah bursts on the scene without any introduction (1 Kings 17:1). He interrupts the pattern of the story just as he interrupts the course of Ahab's reign. Athaliah's reign does not begin in the normal way either; she is an interruption of the normal course of history, just as Elijah is. Elijah interrupts history to call the people to repentance; Athaliah interrupts the story of David's kingdom and leads Judah further astray.

Once Athaliah has become queen, "she rose and destroyed all the royal seed" (2 Kings 11:1). She sees that her family is being wiped out by Jehu and that Baal worship is being purged from the land. If the family of Omri is going to continue and if Baal worship is going to flourish, Athaliah is the last, best hope. She needs to destroy all the royal seed to protect herself. If she leaves any of the seed of David, he might later try to take the kingdom back. Athaliah's murder of the royal seed is not only a terrible act of mass murder. It also threatens the promises to David. If all the royal seed is killed, then none is left to continue the line of David. If that's true, the Lord's promise has failed: David's lamp has gone out, and "Jezebel" and Baal have triumphed over David and Yahweh.

But Yahweh is a God who brings life from the dead. So far as Athaliah is concerned, "all the royal seed" has been killed. But in fact, the Lord has saved a new Moses from this female Pharaoh, and he will rise to lead Israel out of "Egypt," renew the covenant, and rebuild the house of God. Putting Joash on the throne is a renewal of the covenant with David. The story is filled with covenant language (cf. 2 Kings 12:4). The guards take an oath, making a covenant that they will be loyal to Joash. Then, in verse twelve, the coronation is a covenant-ceremony. One of the things that Joash receives is the *testimony,* another term connected with covenant. Verse seventeen describes a covenant among the people, the king, and the Lord. Joash swears to walk in the Lord's ways, the people swear that they will be the Lord's—instead of Baal's —and the people also agree to submit to the king's rule, as he rules according to the law.

To make a new beginning in Judah, the remnants of Ahab's house have to be swept clean. In the North, Jehu has violently destroyed the house of Ahab and the worshipers of Baal. Though the priest Jehoiada, who helps Joash regain the throne, does not act so violently, he is just as thorough. Athaliah is killed (2 Kings 11:15-16). She won't join in praising the new king and cries instead that Jehoiada has committed treason. She is the treasonous one, the false bride and false queen who destroys rather than gives life. Not only the queen, but the institutions for Baal are destroyed. All the people of Jerusalem help destroy Baal's house. The priest of Baal, Mattan, is put to death (11:18). Jehoiada in the South, like Jehu in the North, is reconquering the land and destroying the Canaanites. He is continuing the ministry of the prophet Elisha.

Jehoiada's work to renew Judah begins and ends with the house of Yahweh. Athaliah comes from the house of Baal, and her whole reign is guided by Baalism. The movement to restore Joash, the Davidic dynasty, and the worship of Yahweh flows from the house of the Lord. Joash is hidden in the house of the Lord (v. 3). Jehoiada gives instructions while the guards are gathered in the house of Yahweh (v. 4), and Joash is crowned in the temple (vv. 9-11). After the people make a covenant, they stream out from the temple to destroy the house of Baal (vv. 17–19). Life and prosperity come from Yahweh's house.

The story of Joash is full of "sevens." Jehoiada begins to organize the coup when Joash is seven years old (v. 4), and Joash receives his crown and his throne on a Sabbath. There is a good reason for doing this on the Sabbath. On the Sabbath, when one group of guards is ending a shift and another is beginning, Jehoiada has a chance to act without making anyone suspicious. But the "sevens" are important for other reasons too. The seventh year in Israel is a Sabbath year, when debts are canceled and slaves released, a time of freedom and new beginnings. The phrase in verse four "now in the seventh year" is also found in Leviticus 25:4, which describes the beginning of the Jubilee, a year when the land is given rest. After six years of the ruthless reign of the Southern Jezebel, the people of the land are hungry for rest, for a restoration of peace and blessing. And so they rejoice when the city is quiet (v. 20; see 2 Chronicles 14:1, 5; 20:30). Like another Joshua, Jehoiada brings rest to the land.

The story of Joash is written to show the similarities between Joash and Solomon. Both become king only after overcoming an opponent. Adonijah, one of David's sons, challenges Solomon (1 Kings 1), and Athaliah tries to kill Joash. In both cases, a wise advisor makes a bold plan to put the king on the throne. Nathan and Bathsheba work together to convince David to put Solomon on the throne, and Jehoiada leads the effort to crown Joash. Both Solomon and Joash reign for forty years. The descriptions of the coronation ceremony for the two kings are very similar (compare 1 Kings 1:38–40 with 2 Kings 11:9–12). This connection with Solomon explains why Joash is called the "king's son" (2 Kings 11:4, 12). Calling Joash the "king's son" shows that he is the true heir. But Joash is "king's son" in another sense too. From his infancy, Joash's true "home" is the temple, and this means that his true father is Yahweh. "King's son" means that he is both David's son and the "son of God," a title that God promised to give to Solomon (2 Samuel 7:14).

With all these parallels with Solomon, it is not surprising to find that once he becomes king, Joash turns his attention to the temple. He does not build a new house but works to repair the house that Solomon built. Like Solomon, he tells the priests how they are supposed to care for the temple and hires craftsmen similar those who worked on the temple in Solomon's time (2 Kings 12:11–12; cf 1 Kings 5:13–18; 6:7). A restored covenant means a restoration of the house of

Israel and the house of Yahweh. The "exodus" and "conquest" that began with Elijah and Elisha are now complete. The house of the Lord has been rebuilt.[9]

Joash, like Solomon, is the high point of an important period of history. But like Solomon, he sins and the kingdom again is threatened. Hazael, king of Aram, comes up against Jerusalem. To keep Hazael from attacking the city, Joash takes money from the temple, and not just the treasures he put there but the treasures of four generations (2 Kings 12:17–18). At the dedication of the temple, Solomon asks the Lord to save Israel from her enemies when they pray toward the temple. Instead of praying toward the temple, Joash plunders it. Though he spends much of his reign repairing the house, at the end he attacks it. Chronicles tells us about a different event but shows again that Joash fell into sin. According to Chronicles, after Jehoiada dies, Joash begins to worship the gods of his mother (2 Chronicles 24:18). When Zechariah, the son of Jehoiada, rebukes him for this, Joash puts Zechariah to death. Shortly after, a small army of Arameans defeats a much larger force from Judah (2 Chronicles 24:24).

In the reign of Joash, we see a picture of the whole history of Judah: After attention to the house of Yahweh, Judah falls into idolatry, persecutes the prophets, and is attacked by other nations. In Joash's reign, the attack comes from Aram. But soon, a much more serious attack will come from Assyria. And then the Northern Kingdom will be no more.

Review Questions.

1. What does the Bible tell us about the reign of Omri?
2. What made Ahab's reign worse than any other?
3. What was Ahab trying to do? How can you tell?
4. Explain how Elijah and Elisha are like Moses and Joshua.
5. Who is Jehu? What did he do?
6. What effect does Jehu's attack on Ahab's house have on Judah?

7. Who is Athaliah? What makes her reign different?

8. How is the family of David restored to the throne of Judah?

9. How is Joash like Solomon?

10. What does Joash do after Jehoiada's death?

Thought Questions.

1. At Carmel, Elijah sets up an altar of twelve stones, which is consumed by fire from heaven (1 Kings 18:30–40). What does this signify?

2. Ahab fights a battle against the Arameans, but he spares the Aramean king, Ben-hadad (1 Kings 20:26–34). Compare to 1 Samuel 15. What does this suggest about Ahab? See also 1 Kings 22:34 and 1 Samuel 31:3.

3. How does the Lord entice Ahab to his death (1 Kings 22:13–23)? Is this fair?

4. Remember Elijah's exile among the Gentiles. How does Elisha's aid to Naaman fit with this (2 Kings 5)? Who is Naaman? What effect will his recovery have on Israel?

5. 2 Kings 8:1–6 is a story about the woman whose son Elisha has raised from the dead. How does this story fit with the rest of the story about this woman?

***Assyrian Threat*, 2 Kings 17; Jonah 1–2**

While the Lord is restoring the Southern Kingdom through men such as Jehoiada and Joash, and later Hezekiah and Josiah, the Northern Kingdom is on the edge of collapse. To the East, the Assyrians are getting more powerful and beginning to threaten Israel. This is happening during the time of Jonah. Looking at Jonah will help us understand what is going on in Israel at this time.

The opening verses of Jonah set us up for a shock. Jonah 1:1 is not surprising: "The word of the Lord came to Jonah." We have read this countless times in books of the prophets; the same word comes to Isaiah, Jeremiah, Ezekiel, Elijah, and many others. Verse two brings a small surprise. Instead of sending the prophet to preach to Samaria, the Word of the Lord sends Jonah to Nineveh, the capital city of the Assyrians. This is not quite what we expect, but other prophets have preached to Gentile nations. Verse three is a real shock. Unlike Elijah, Elisha, Isaiah, and all the other prophets we know of, Jonah doesn't go where the Lord sends him. He goes in the other direction, toward Tarshish. Instead of Isaiah's "Here I am, send me," Jonah says, "I'm outta here."

Why does Jonah act this way? Two things help to explain why Jonah flees to Tarshish rather than going to Nineveh. These reasons do not excuse Jonah's actions. He sins by disobeying the Word of the Lord. But we should still try to understand exactly what his sin is. The first reason for Jonah's actions has to do with Jonah's time in history. Jonah is a prophet in the Northern Kingdom during the reign of Jeroboam II (2 Kings 14:25). Jeroboam is an evil king, leading the people in the same sins as Jeroboam I, the son of Nebat. In spite of his sins, the Lord is merciful to Israel and restores some of the land that other kings lost. This fulfills the Word of the Lord through Jonah (2 Kings 14:24, 26). This is the same Jonah in the book of Jonah.

With Jeroboam II as king, Israel is spared. Jeroboam even looks like a prosperous king. But Israel is doomed. Within a few years, the Assyrians begin to invade (2 Kings 15), and within a few generations of Jonah's time, Samaria has been destroyed and the Northern Kingdom no longer exists. Jonah is a prophet during the last period of Israel's history, living among an idolatrous people devoted to worshiping golden calves. Already in Jonah's day, wise men see that the Lord will not put up with Israel forever. This helps us understand what Jonah is thinking about when the Lord tells him to preach in Nineveh. At first, Jonah may have been pleased that the Lord was preparing to destroy Nineveh and Assyria. If Assyria is destroyed, Israel will be much safer. But the more he thinks about it, the more he realizes that the Lord has other plans. After all, if He simply wanted to wipe out Nineveh, why send a prophet? Why not just send a couple of angels to check things out and see if there are more than ten righteous men? Jonah knows that when God warns people about their sins, it is an act of mercy because it gives sinners a chance to repent.

Jonah knows what kind of God he serves. He knows that the Lord is compassionate and slow to anger (Jonah 4:2). And he knows that if the Lord has compassion on Assyria, Israel is in bigger trouble than ever. Above all, Jonah loves his country, in spite of her sins. For the sake of Israel, he wants Assyria to be destroyed without any warnings. He does not want to have a part in helping a mortal enemy of his people prosper. Jonah knows that God will show mercy, and that makes him afraid and angry.[10]

There is another factor that helps explain Jonah's actions. Other prophets have prophesied against the nations. Elijah anoints Hazael as king over Syria, for example. But no other prophet has been sent personally to preach to another nation. This is new, and Jonah knows the law well enough to know it can only mean one thing. In Deuteronomy, Moses warns Israel about what will happen if she turns from Yahweh:

> Jeshurun [Israel] grew fat and kicked—
> You are grown fat, thick, and sleek—
> Then he forsook God who made him,
> And scorned the Rock of our salvation.
> They made Him jealous with strange gods;
>
> With abominations they provoked Him to anger....
> And the Lord saw this, and spurned them
> Because of the provocation of His sons and daughters.
> Then He said, "I will hide My face from them,
> For they are a perverse generation.
> Sons in whom is no faithfulness.
> They have made Me jealous with what is not God;
> They have provoked Me to anger with their idols.
> So I will make them jealous with those who are not a people;
> I will provoke them to anger with a foolish nation."
> (Deuteronomy 32:15–21)

The Lord's punishment fits the crime. If Israel provokes Him to jealousy, He will provoke *them* to jealousy. And He will do this by turning His attention to another nation. In the long run, this is an act of mercy to Israel, a part of the Lord's way of bringing back His wayward bride. Once Israel sees how the Lord has blessed the Gentiles, she will be stirred up to return to her true Husband. But in the meantime, the Lord will be seeking out a new bride.

The "Song of Moses" in Deuteronomy 32 is quoted dozens of times in the Old Testament. Jonah knows this song and perhaps has even sung it. When the Word of the Lord comes to Jonah and tells him to go to another nation to preach, Jonah sees what is happening. The Lord is turning His attention to a new people. Like Israel, Jonah is provoked to jealousy and anger when the Lord showers his attention and blessing upon another nation. Jonah does not want to help Assyria repent, and he does not want to help the Lord turn from Israel to another nation.

So Jonah runs away. But it's a useless flight. The whole time he is going "down." He goes "down" to Joppa to catch the boat (1:3), goes "down" into the boat (1:3), and then he goes below into the hold and falls asleep (1:5). When the Lord stirs up the storm, he is thrown overboard and plunges down to the bottom of the sea and cries to the Lord from "the depths of Sheol" (2:2). Fleeing from the Lord always takes you "downhill." Jonah's flight brings him to the gates of death. But even when he finds himself at the gates of Sheol, he cannot escape from God. God is the "Hound of Heaven" who will not let his quarry get away. The Lord hurls a great wind (1:4) and appoints a fish (1:17), and from the deep, Jonah says that the Lord is the one who had cast him down (2:3). Even if he makes his bed in hell, behold the Lord is there (see Psalm 139).

Jonah knows this all along. He knows that the Lord is the God of heaven, Maker of sea and land (1:9). Why is he running, then? He's not running to get away from God so much as he is running to get out of being a prophet. He is running away from the "presence of the Lord" (1:3, 10). When this phrase is used in reference to prophets in the Old Testament, it has a specific meaning. Prophets are called to "stand before the Lord" (1 Kings 17:1), to enter into the Lord's presence as members of His council. By fleeing, Jonah shows he doesn't want to stand before the Lord as His servant anymore. If being a prophet means helping Assyria, Jonah wants to resign.

But he cannot get away from this either. He doesn't want to be a prophet, but the Lord makes sure that he is. When the storm arises on the sea, all the sailors are "afraid" (1:5) and begin to cry out to their gods. When they learn what Jonah has done, they are "extremely frightened" (1:10). When they throw Jonah into the sea and the seas become calm, they "feared the Lord (Yahweh) greatly" (1:14, 16). By the end of chapter one, they are no longer serving their own gods but Yahweh. Jonah flees from the Lord's presence and resigns his post as a prophet because he doesn't want to run the risk of converting the Assyrians. And the first thing he does is convert a boatload of pagan sailors.

The conversion of the sailors is important in a number of ways. It points ahead to the conversion of the city of Nineveh. Like the sailors, the Assyrians repent and seek the Lord's face. As Jonah's preaching preserves the ship and its crew, so he will preserve the ship of the Assyrian state. The reaction of the sailors also contrasts with that of Jonah. Jonah says he "fears" the Lord of heaven (1:9). Really? The sailors see that Jonah has not only sinned but acted stupidly. He claims to serve the Lord of heaven and of the sea, and yet Jonah is trying to run from Him by getting into a boat. The sailors are also very careful about shedding Jonah's blood (1:14), knowing that they will be punished if they shed innocent blood. Jonah isn't nearly as concerned about shedding blood. Unlike the sailors, he has no compassion on the people of Nineveh or their animals (4:11).

The sailors also contrast with Israel. According to 2 Kings 17, the Lord sends prophet after prophet to Israel, shows them every kindness, and warns them time and again. But they won't listen and make the Lord jealous by worshiping what is not God. The sailors convert when they hear a few words from a single prophet. Israel is more hard-hearted than these pagans.

In spite of his sin, the Lord is kind to Jonah. He prepares a fish for him, delivers him from death in the waters, and raises him up to dry land. The fish saves Jonah rather than destroying him. His sin took him down, down, down, but the Lord brought him up again. Like the sailors, Jonah promises to sacrifice to the Lord and pay his vows.

Jonah's rescue by the fish is a picture of the Lord's promise to Israel. Jonah has fled from his calling and has come near to death, close to the gates of Sheol. Yet the Lord pursues him and saves him and sends him back to preach to the Ninevites. This is exactly what has happened and will happen to Israel. Israel too has turned from the Lord, rejected His call, and refused to be a witness among the Gentiles. Rather, Israel had been imitating the Gentiles, restoring Canaanite worship in the Northern Kingdom. The conversion of the sailors shows what the Lord can and will do through Israel if Israel will but repent. If a reluctant, fleeing prophet can convert a boatload of pagans and the city of Nineveh, what could Israel do if she would give herself wholly to her Lord?

But this is not what is happening to Israel. Instead, because of Israel's idolatry, the Lord is stirring up a great storm at sea. As we saw in chapter one, the sea is frequently a picture of the Gentile nations in Scripture. Psalm 65:7–8 praises the Lord who is able to "still the roaring of the seas, the roaring of their waves, the tumult of the peoples." Isaiah prophesies of Assyria as a nation that will growl against Israel "in that day like the roaring of the sea" (Isaiah 5:30), and in another passage, he prophesies concerning the nations:

> the uproar of many peoples who roar like the roaring of the seas, and the rumbling of nations who rush on like the rumbling of many waters! The nations rumble on like the

> rumbling of many waters, but He will rebuke them and they will flee far away, and be chased like chaff in the mountains before the wind, or like whirling dust before a gale. (Isaiah 17:12–13)

Just as Jonah is thrown into the heart of the sea, so Israel will be flooded by the Gentile nations. Jonah being thrown into the sea is a picture of exile.

Yet, even though He will fling His people into the sea, the Lord is not done with Israel. In the story of Jonah, the Lord delivers the prophet from the sea and the storm by appointing a great fish. Sea monsters in the Bible are sometimes pictures of Gentile rulers. Describing the Exodus from Egypt, Psalm 74:12–17 says, "Thou didst divide the sea by Thy strength; Thou didst break the heads of the sea monsters in the waters. Thou didst crush the heads of Leviathan, thou didst give him as food for the creatures of the wilderness." Jeremiah describes Nebuchadnezzar and Babylon as a sea monster who swallows up Israel (Jeremiah 51:34), but he also promises that the Lord will punish Bel, god of Babylon, and make him vomit what he has swallowed.

Similarly, the book of Jonah tells us that the Gentile powers are "appointed" by the Lord. If the nations swallow up God's prophet and God's people, it is to save them from drowning in the sea. The Lord's rescue of Jonah is a promise of protection during the "three days and three nights" of Israel's exile. Once she comes to her senses, returns to the Lord, sacrifices in thanksgiving, and pays her vows, Israel will be vomited back into the land. And not only that, but the Gentiles will see what the Lord has done for His people, and, like the sailors, will turn to the Lord with exceedingly great fear. When Jonah was thrown into the sea, the sailors turned to sacrifice and give thanks, and in the same way, when Israel is scattered among the heathen, many will come to know the Lord. Converts in Nineveh will be like the fish, rescuing Israel from drowning in the Assyrian sea.

In the long run, the outcome of exile will be life for the world. The world will know that Yahweh is king. But in the meantime, Israel faces stern punishment at the hand of God. To the South, Judah watches fearfully as the Assyrians capture Samaria and take their brothers off into exile. And they ask, "Are we next?"

Review Questions.

1. What nation is the great power during the final days of the Northern Kingdom?
2. When did Jonah live?
3. What was the condition of Israel during Jonah's life? How does this help us understand Jonah's flight?
4. What does the Lord threaten to do in Deuteronomy 32? How does this help us understand Jonah?
5. What is Jonah fleeing from? How does the Lord turn this around?
6. How does Jonah's life picture the threat of exile?
7. How does Jonah's life picture the promise of return from exile?

Thought Questions.

1. Why does Shalmanezer of Assyria take Hoshea away to prison (2 Kings 17:1–3)? What message should this send to the Southern Kingdom?
2. Who is brought into the Northern Kingdom after Israel has been removed (2 Kings 17:24)? What effect does this have on the spiritual climate in the North (2 Kings 17:34–41)?
3. Amos the prophet is prophesying in the days of Jeroboam, the son of Joash, king of Israel (Amos 1:1). According to Amos, what sins characterize the Northern Kingdom (see 4:1–4)?
4. Jonah is ordered as a "two-panel" story. Chapter three begins again where chapter one began. This suggests that there is a connection between the great fish of chapters one and two and the gourd in chapter four. What does the gourd represent?

5. Whom does Nahum prophesy against (1:1)? Why? What has happened between the time of Jonah and the time of Nahum?

[1] Framed by the building of the temple and its destruction, the story of 1–2 Kings can be outlined as follows:

A. Solomon's reign; temple built, 1 Kings 1:1–11:43
B. Northern kingdom, 12:1–16:34
C. Elijah and Ahab, 17:1–2 Kings 1:18
D. Elisha's miracles, 2 Kings 2:1–8:6
C′. Elisha's dealings with Omride dynasty, 8:7–13:25
B′. Last kings of Northern kingdom, 14:1–17:41
A′. End of Southern Kingdom; fall of Jerusalem and temple, 18:1–25:30

[2] This is adapted from David A. Dorsey, *The Literary Structure of the Old Testament: A Commentary on Genesis–Malachi* (Grand Rapids: Baker, 1999), pp. 138, 141.

[3] Structurally, the stories of Elijah and Elisha are at the center of the books of kings and occupy an enormous portion of the text, 1 Kings 17-2 Kings 13. Eighteen chapters out of forty-seven in Kings are dealing with this period, and this covers mainly the reign of Ahab and the aftermath in both the North and the South.

[4] It is worth noting the adoption theme in the story of Elijah's succession. Elisha's request for a "double portion" of Elijah's spirit was a request for the inheritance of a firstborn (2 Kings 2:9; see Deuteronomy 21:15–17). As Elijah was carried away in the whirlwind, Elisha fittingly cried out to his departing "father" (2 Kings 2:12). This passage has evident typological connotations: Those who witnessed the ascension of Jesus received the inheritance of the Spirit, were clothed in the mantle of Christ's authority, and continued His ministry as His sons, co-heirs, and successors. Calvin said that the ascension of Christ and the pouring out of the Spirit were "antithetical," two sides of one event; likewise, Elijah's ascension was Elisha's Pentecost.

[5] The fact that the ravens fed the Lord's prophet "morning and evening" may be a reference to the daily sacrifices of the tabernacle and temple, which included meat and bread that were sacrificed morning and evening (Numbers 28:1–8). As the Lord's representative, Elijah received the tribute of the Gentiles. Similarly, the widow's bread was sacrificial in two senses: first because she fed the Lord's prophet, and second because she gave in spite of her great poverty. Even in exile, the Lord's prophet received honor.

[6] Matthew Henry treats it as a moral lesson like something from Aesop's Fables: "God must be glorified as a righteous God that hates sin and

will reckon for it, even in little children. Let the hideous shrieks and groans of this wicked wretched brood make our flesh tremble for fear of God. Let little children be afraid of speaking wicked words, for God notices what they say." Not a bad moral lesson, but it's not the point of this story.

[7]This interpretation was suggested by taped lectures by James B. Jordan.

[8]The same can be said for the other term used to the describe the forty-two, *yeled*. This word normally means young people or young animals (even fetuses, Exodus 21:22), but it is also used for older persons. Rehoboam consults with the *yeladim* "who grew up with him and stood before him" (1 Kings 12:8). Verse eight shows that they are about the same age as Rehoboam, and 1 Kings 14:21 tells us that Rehoboam is forty-one when he begins to reign. Thus, the "young men" are about forty when they give their foolish counsel. They are called *yeladim* both because they are younger than the elders whose counsel Rehoboam rejects and because they are Rehoboam's subordinates; that they "stood before" Rehoboam suggests that they were his personal servants and confidants, holding the office of "prince's friend." In any case, this passage shows that the usage of *yeled* is not restricted to young children and teenagers.

[9]Structurally, the reign of Joash is included in the section of Kings dealing with Elijah and Elisha. Elijah's ministry begins in 1 Kings 17:1, and Elisha's death is recorded in 2 Kings 13:14–21. These provide the "bookends" around this portion of the book. And Joash's reign, recorded in 2 Kings 11–12, is included within the bookends.

[10]Notice, by contrast, Elisha's willingness to help Naaman, also an enemy of Israel (2 Kings 5).

6
The Last Days of Judah

When Samaria, the capital of the Northern Kingdom, falls to the Assyrians in 722 B.C., it is a warning to the Southern Kingdom. The people of the Northern Kingdom worship idols and won't listen to the prophets. So the Lord removes them, and only Judah is left (2 Kings 17:18). The fall of Samaria is not the first sign that the Lord is angry with the Northern Kingdom. David subdues many of the nations around Israel, including the Moabites, Syrians, Ammonites, and Edomites (2 Samuel 8:12). But during the time of the divided kingdom, Israel loses more and more of this land. 2 Kings begins with the revolt of the Moabites. Jehoram of Israel wins a partial victory (2 Kings 3:21–27), but the Moabites continue their rebellion. Edom and Libnah also revolt against Israel (2 Kings 8:20–22), and the Syrians or Arameans invade Israel and force her to pay tribute (2 Kings 12:17–18). Yahweh is chipping away the Northern Kingdom, bit by bit.

The Lord is warning Israel and Judah not only through the prophets, but through the events of the time. And the message is clear: If you turn from the Lord, the Lord will remove you; instead of subduing your enemies, your enemies will subdue you; instead of receiving tribute, you will be forced to give tribute. 2 Kings 17 sounds like the story of the conquest from the book of Joshua. This time, though, it is not Israel that takes the land, but Assyria. What is described as a new conquest amounts to a reversal of the conquest.

Judah has good reason to take these warnings seriously, since Judah is no better than Israel. According to 2 Kings 17:19, "Judah did not keep the commandments of the Lord their God, but walked in the customs which Israel had introduced." Judah has come under the influence of the worst of the Northern kings. Ahab is the most evil king of the North, but his daughter, Athaliah, marries the king of Judah (2 Kings 8:18). Later, Ahaz of Judah also "walks in the ways of the kings of Israel"; he even copies an altar from Syria and puts it in the temple in place of the altar of the Lord (2 Kings 16:10–16). If the Northern Kingdom has been taken into exile, will the Southern kingdom be far behind?

A New David, 2 Kings 18–20; Isaiah 36–39

Some kings of Judah do take the warnings seriously, and during the century after the fall of Samaria, Judah has some of its best kings. The first of these is Hezekiah. He becomes king six years before the fall of Samaria. He sees what is happening and listens to the prophets Isaiah and Micah. Hezekiah is the best king of Judah since David (2 Kings 18:1–3). Like David, he fights against the Philistines, who have barely been mentioned since the time of David. Under Hezekiah's rule, Judah expands its land, in contrast to the Northern Kingdom, which has been getting smaller and smaller. Hezekiah restores true worship to the Southern Kingdom. Hezekiah is the first king to get rid of the places of worship on the "high places." Worshiping at high places is against the commandment of Deuteronomy 12:10–14, where the Lord commands Israel to worship at only the one sanctuary. He breaks down sacred Asherah pillars throughout the land and crushes the bronze serpent of Moses, to which Judah has been burning incense (18:4). Like David, Hezekiah crushes the serpent.

Because of his faithfulness, the Lord blesses and protects Hezekiah from the Assyrians (2 Kings 18–19; Isaiah 36–37). Like Hoshea, the last king of Israel, Hezekiah revolts against the Assyrians, and the Assyrians invade and lay siege to

Jerusalem. Judah faces the same end as the Northern Kingdom. The Assyrians taunt the men of Jerusalem, saying that they should not expect Hezekiah or Yahweh to save them, since no gods have been able to stand against Assyria. But Hezekiah's response is far different than that of the Northern kings. He takes the letter of Sennacherib into the temple, lays it before the Lord, and calls upon Him to hear the blasphemies of the Assyrians and defend Himself.

This event occurs at the very center of Isaiah's prophecy and deserves a close look.[1] The threat from the Assyrians takes place in the "fourteenth year" of King Hezekiah (36:1), and Hezekiah's sickness takes place soon after: "in those days" (38:1). The whole series of events, then, is included under the heading of the "fourteenth year." This is a clue that shows us that the events of Isaiah 36–39 are like Passover, which takes place on the fourteenth day of the first month (Leviticus 23:5).

Judah's deliverance from Assyria is like Passover in several ways. First, there is a threat to the people of Israel. At the time of the original Passover, Pharaoh attacks and enslaves the seed. Moses comes with the Lord's demand that Pharaoh let Israel, the Lord's firstborn, go. In Isaiah, the threat is Sennacherib's siege of the city of Jerusalem. The conflict between Assyria and Israel is a contest between the gods of Assyria and Yahweh, God of Israel. Rabshakeh, a servant of Sennacherib, warns the people of Jerusalem that they should not trust their gods to deliver them since the gods of other nations have not stopped the Assyrians. Hezekiah recognizes these words as blasphemy and calls on the Lord to defend His name (36:18–20; 37:1–7). In the end, the Lord humbles the gods of Assyria as He humbled the gods of Egypt (36:21–29; see Exodus 12:12). This theme of humiliation of the gods of the nations continues into Isaiah's exodus prophecies, which follow in chapters 40–55. Isaiah's attacks on the idols of the nations are part of the exodus story that Isaiah describes in these chapters (cf. 40:18–20; 41:6–7; 44:12–20; 45:1–7; 46:6–7). As at Passover, the "angel of death" goes through the Assyrian camp by night and slaughters 185,000 (37:36; Exodus 12:29–36). Sennacherib himself survives but returns home only to be assassinated. The sword of the Lord reaches even into "Pharaoh's" house.

The destruction of Sennacherib's army fulfills the prophecy of Isaiah 9:1–5. The "gloom" cast over the land of Zebulun and Naphtali is the Assyrian devastation of the Northern Kingdom (see Isaiah 8:1–7). The Lord promises, however, to lighten the gloom and break the yoke of Assyria (9:4) with a victory similar to the victory of Gideon over the Midianites (9:5; 10:24–26), a victory that also reflects the Passover theme of a night deliverance (Judges 7:19–25). In Isaiah 9 and again in chapter thirty-seven, Isaiah uses the phrase, "the zeal of the Lord of hosts will perform this (9:7; 37:32). Isaiah's prediction that the war materials will be burned (9:5) fits well with the Lord's unassisted victory over Assyria. Isaiah implies in 9:5 that the Lord will be the Victor by saying that the spoils will be consecrated to Him by fire (37:26; see Joshua 6:24).[2]

Isaiah 38 tells the story of Hezekiah's sickness and recovery, a story that also makes sense as a Passover story. Sickness and recovery is a kind of death and resurrection, as Hezekiah's psalm of thanksgiving makes clear (38:10–11). Isaiah 38 thus displays the positive side of Passover: The angel of death slaughters the Assyrians but passes over Hezekiah, the representative of the nation of Israel. Judah has experienced a new Passover with the angel of death delivering her from another "Egypt."

Yet Hezekiah's reign does not end well. After being delivered from the Assyrians and from sickness, Hezekiah receives a group of visitors from Babylon and shows them the treasures of the temple. Isaiah tells Hezekiah that this is a mistake and that someday the Babylonians will come back to take the treasures that Hezekiah has shown them. But Isaiah says that this will not happen in Hezekiah's lifetime. In 2 Kings 20, Hezekiah's sickness and the visit of the Babylonians are right next to each other, and both follow the same pattern: There is an incident (sickness/visitors), a word from the prophet, and a delay of judgment. The two stories belong together. Sick kings often picture a "sickness" of sin within the kingdom, and Hezekiah's "death and resurrection" is a sign that Judah too will recover from her illness. Hezekiah gets well, but he has only fifteen more years of life. Judah has been delivered from Assyria, but Judah's recovery is not permanent. Someday the Babylonians will come back.

Hezekiah's sins are nothing compared to the sins of his son Manasseh. Everything that Hezekiah does is undone by Manasseh. Manasseh's name means "Forgetful," and during his reign, Judah is forgetful of God's law and covenant and of Hezekiah's faithfulness. Manasseh is the Ahab of the Southern Kingdom. He is the only Davidic king who is compared to Ahab, and his resemblance to Ahab comes out in many ways. Like Ahab, he erects images of Baal and Asherah (1 Kings 16:32–33; 2 Kings 21:3). In fact, Manasseh's idolatry is even more openly sinful. Ahab erects Baal and Asherah in Samaria, but Manasseh sets up altars for Baal in the Lord's house (21:4) and carves images of Asherah right before the face of God. Idols in the land are terrible, but idols in the place where God set His name are abominations, like the sins of Hophni and Phinehas. Idolatry never stays within the temple but always has an effect on the way people live. One of Ahab's great sins is taking Naboth's vineyard and shedding innocent blood. Manasseh too fills Jerusalem with innocent blood, from one end to another (21:16). He especially attacks the prophets of the Lord.

Manasseh is also compared to the Amorites whom Joshua drove from the land (21:9, 11). Again, Manasseh's sins are worse than those of the Canaanites. As Israel does under Ahab, the Southern Kingdom is becoming a Canaanite nation, and again the Lord plans to wipe out the Canaanites. Because Judah has followed the ways of Israel, they will be judged like Israel. As the prophets say, Jerusalem will be measured with the line of Samaria. The Lord will give His inheritance over to the plunderers to plunder it (21:10–15).

The Book of the Law, 2 Kings 22–23

After the brief reign of Manasseh's son Amon, Josiah comes to the throne at the age of eight, and there is another great change in Judah. Josiah, like Hezekiah, is compared to David (2 Kings 22:2). Like Hezekiah, Josiah purges the land of idols, removes the high places, and thus starts to turn Judah back to the Lord. He also reunites Israel and Judah, so that, like David and Solomon, he rules over a single kingdom (2 Chronicles 35:16–19). During his reign, the Book of the Law is found in the temple, perhaps left there during the half-century reign of the "Forgetter," Manasseh. When the law is read, Josiah and all Judah repent and renew the covenant with the Lord. Yahweh promises to wait before bringing the final judgment against Jerusalem and Judah (2 Kings 22:14–20). Despite Josiah, though, the Lord is still angry over the sins of Manasseh (2 Kings 23:26–27; 24:4). Though Judah has turned to the Lord, He does not turn from His anger. During the reign of Manasseh, Judah passed the point of no return. Judah will suffer the fate of her sister Israel. As with Pharaoh in Egypt, the Lord is determined to judge Judah. They must not hope for that Judah to continue. She will die, and there is no hope but resurrection.

In Kings and Chronicles, Josiah is a faithful and diligent king. But the prophet Zephaniah gives a different picture of the reign of Josiah (Zephaniah 1:1).[3] This prophet, a descendant of King Hezekiah, warns Judah of a coming "day of the Lord" that will be

> A day of wrath . . .
> A day of trouble and distress,
> A day of destruction and desolation,
> A day of darkness and gloom,
> A day of clouds and thick darkness,
> A day of trumpet and battle cry,
> Against the fortified cities
> And the high corner towers. (Zephaniah 1:15–16)

The Lord will punish everything in Judah: Men and beasts on

the earth, the birds of the sky, and the fish of the sea (1:2–3), because the people "bow down on the housetops to the host of heaven" and "swear by Milcom" and "turn back from following the Lord" (1:4–6). Josiah is a great king, but in spite of his best efforts, Judah continues to follow the ways of the nations.

By this time, Babylon has replaced Assyria as the dominant power of the Ancient Near East. Babylon and Egypt are fighting about who will control Judah. The closing days of the Southern Kingdom are like the end of the Northern Kingdom: One king follows another in quick succession, and most are forced to pay tribute to Egypt or Babylon. When Pharaoh Neco comes from Egypt, Josiah foolishly attacks him and is killed at the battle of Megiddo (2 Kings 23:28–30). Neco puts Jehoiakim, one of Josiah's sons, on the throne of Judah, but soon Nebuchadnezzar of Babylon comes into Judah and forces Jehoiakim to become his servant. After serving Babylon for three years, Jehoiakim rebels. Nebuchadnezzar comes back to Judah, but before he can conquer Jerusalem, Jehoiakim dies and is replaced by his son, Jehoiachin. Nebuchadnezzar attacks the city, captures Jehoiachin, and takes him back to Babylon along with eight thousand soldiers, craftsmen, and artisans. Nebuchadnezzar puts Zedekiah, another son of Josiah, on the throne, but after nine years of serving Babylon, he too rebels. Nebuchadnezzar decides to teach Judah a lesson, so he returns, captures the city, breaks down its walls, and destroys Solomon's temple. And so Judah goes the way of Israel into exile.

Review Questions.

1. What was Judah supposed to learn from the fall of Israel?
2. What does Hezekiah do during his reign?
3. How is Judah's deliverance from Assyria like the Passover?
4. How does Hezekiah's reign end?

5. What does Manasseh's name mean? What does this show about his reign?

6. What does Josiah do during his reign?

7. After Josiah's reign, why is the Lord still angry with Judah?

8. List the kings in the last days of Judah.

Thought Questions.

1. What does the Rabshakeh offer Israel (2 Kings 18:31–32)? Explain his offer in the light of God's promises to Israel. How does this add to the blasphemy of the Rabshakeh?

2. Discuss the similarities and differences between Josiah and Joash.

3. Remember that the temple is a picture of Israel. With this in mind, why is there so much emphasis on the temple vessels that Nebuchadnezzar removed from Jerusalem (2 Kings 25:13–17; see Daniel 1:1–2)?

4. What is the political situation in Isaiah 7–8? Who is threatening Judah? Why?

5. Isaiah 12:2 quotes from Exodus 15:2. In the context, explain why Isaiah would quote from this song.

***Another Shiloh,* Jeremiah**

Jeremiah is living in Jerusalem during these final days of Judah. Things are changing very quickly, and the threat from Babylon is growing stronger all the time. One of Jeremiah's first visions pictures this (1:13–16). Jeremiah sees a pot "boiling" with its mouth away from the north. The pot falls on its side and is beginning to be burned in the fire.[4] The word used here for "boil" is not the usual word; this word usually means "blow." The picture is of a smoking pot with the wind blowing a cloud of smoke toward the South.[5] The Lord gives the meaning of the vision in 1:14–16. The vision shows that the Lord is bringing evil from the north to punish the evil of Jerusalem. Yahweh punishes evil with evil, eye for eye. Judah is being punished for worshiping false gods, and the people from the North (Babylon) will come and set up thrones in Jerusalem, taking over the city. This happens later on. When the wall of Jerusalem is broken down, the officials of Babylon sit in the middle gate and pass judgments (Jeremiah 39:3).

Jeremiah is a priest from Anathoth, a Levitical city in the tribal land of Benjamin (Joshua 21:18; 1 Chronicles 6:60). This is the city to which Solomon exiles Abiathar and his family (1 Kings 2:26–27). Solomon removes Abiathar from the priesthood because he joins a plot to put Adonijah on the throne. But 1 Kings 2:27 says that Abiathar, a descendant of Eli, goes to Anathoth to fulfill the word of the Lord concerning Eli and Shiloh (see 1 Samuel 2; 3:11–14). Anathoth is the place where the descendants of Eli are exiled. Mention of Anathoth brings back memories of the destruction of the shrine at Shiloh and the ruin of the high priestly house of Eli. Jeremiah lives among these priests.

This is not the only reference to Shiloh in Jeremiah. All through the book, there are reminders of the ruin of the Mosaic tabernacle by the Philistines. When Jeremiah preaches at the temple, he says:

> Go now to My place which was in Shiloh, where I made My name dwell at the first, and see what I did to it because of the wickedness of My people Israel. And now, because you have done these things, declares the Lord, and I spoke to you, rising up early and speaking, but you did not hear, and I called you but you did not answer, therefore I will do to the house that is called by My name, in which you trust, and to the place which I gave you and your fathers, as I did to Shiloh. (Jeremiah 7:13–14; see 26:6–9)

In Jeremiah 12:7, the Lord says "I have forsaken My house," as He forsakes His house at Shiloh. Jeremiah accuses the false priests and prophets of adultery. They are like Hophni and Phinehas, the sons of Eli (23:14–15). When Jeremiah talks about the calamity coming on Jerusalem, he says it will make the people's ears tingle, and Samuel uses the same words about the destruction of Shiloh (1 Samuel 3:11;

Jeremiah 19:3). At the end of Jeremiah, Zedekiah the king loses his sons and his eyes are poked out, just as blind Eli lost both sons on the same day. The message is clear: Shiloh is happening all over again.

The Lord is forsaking His house because Judah has forsaken Him. Judah has become a faithless bride, a prostitute. She has forsaken her Husband and gone after other gods, so the Lord is going to forsake her. She has refused to listen to the Word of the Lord through the prophets, so the Lord will cease to listen to her (2:1–8; 2:20–24; 3:1–25; 4:23–31). Judah has become a whorish Jezebel (4:30).

In this desperate situation, Jeremiah is called to be a prophet, and the story of his call tells us a lot about Jeremiah and his work.[6] Jeremiah 1:4–8 records a conversation between God and Jeremiah, and there are many reminders of Moses. Like Moses, Jeremiah is reluctant to accept the call, saying he cannot speak well. As with Moses, the Lord places His words in the prophet's mouth (see Exodus 4:11–16; Deuteronomy 18:18). Moses is mediator of the covenant at Sinai, and Jeremiah announces a New Covenant that will not fail like the Old Covenant (Jeremiah 31:27–34). Jeremiah is a "prophet like Moses." Of course, the ultimate "prophet like Moses" is Jesus, but Jesus was mistaken during his life for another Jeremiah (Matthew 16:14).

In some ways, Jeremiah is not like Moses. Moses is hardly a "youth" when he is called at the burning bush (see Jeremiah 1:6). That takes place near the end of his sojourn in Midian, and he was eighty when he went to Pharaoh (Exodus 7:7). If we remember that Jeremiah comes from Anathoth, we can see that Jeremiah is being compared to the youthful prophet who spoke of the ruin of Shiloh: Samuel. Jeremiah is a new Samuel, who is, in turn, a new Moses. Like Samuel, Jeremiah is consecrated to the Lord from the womb (Jeremiah 1:5; see 1 Samuel 1). Like Samuel, Jeremiah talks about the ruin of the sanctuary (1 Samuel 3:1–18). Samuel not only prophesies of judgment on Eli and Shiloh but also advises and announces judgment on Saul (1 Samuel 13; 15).

Similarly, Jeremiah serves as an advisor to Zedekiah, the last king of Judah, who, like Israel's first king, is slow to listen to the prophet's words. Like Saul, he seeks a word from the prophet but disobeys when things get tough.

This comparison with Samuel has an interesting twist. Remember that Samuel tells Saul of two sins: when Saul sacrifices without waiting for Samuel and when Saul doesn't carry out the ban against the Amalekites (1 Samuel 13:13–14; 15:17–23). Yet, Samuel confronts Saul one other time. When Saul goes to the witch at Endor to learn about his future, Samuel comes back from the dead to tell him he and his sons will die in the coming battle with the Philistines (1 Samuel 28). Something very similar happens between Jeremiah and Zedekiah. Zedekiah speaks with Jeremiah three times. He sends a delegation to Jeremiah to ask for prayer (Jeremiah 37:3), and later Zedekiah secretly talks with Jeremiah, asking for a word from the Lord (37:17). Their last conversation takes place after Jeremiah has been thrown into a pit and pulled out again (38:1–28). After the prophet's "death" in the pit, he "rises up" to speak to the king one last time. After the "resurrected" prophet confronts this new Saul, the king fades from the scene and the next chapter records Zedekiah's death.

Against this background, Jeremiah 15:1 takes on a deeper significance. The Lord says that even if Moses and Samuel intercede before Him, He will not turn from His wrath. Why are these two men singled out? It is not simply because they are great intercessors and prophets, but also because Jeremiah is like them and is in a similar situation. Jeremiah, like Moses and Samuel before him, is a prophet during a time when one order of things is ending and another is beginning. Jeremiah is set "over the nations" in order to "pluck up, break down, destroy, and overthrow, and also to plant and build" (1:5, 10). "Pluck up" and "plant" are words from gardening. Israel is pictured as a garden or a vineyard that the Lord has planted in the land (cf. Psalm 80; Isaiah 5), hoping she will produce fruit for His delight. Judah has no fruit, so the Lord is threatening to uproot her (2:21; cf. Ezekiel 19:12). Later in Jeremiah's prophecy, the Lord promises to replant a remnant of the people in the land. Looked at one way, Judah's history is about land. Judah is planted, plucked up, and planted again. The words "tear down" and "built" are associated with building. Here, Judah is being pictured as God's house or God's city. The Lord built her up, but He is now coming to tear her down. Later, the Lord says, He will rebuild her. Looked at this way, Israel's history is a story of the building of God's house. The word spoken by the prophet plucks up and tears down, plants and builds. The prophetic word of God clears out the rubbish and makes a new world. Like the Word of the Lord in Genesis 1, this word has power, turning what is formless and void into a splendid new creation.

The first vision that Jeremiah sees confirms his call and encourages him to be a faithful prophet. He sees a rod from an almond tree, and to understand the vision of the almond rod, we need to see that there is a play on words. The Hebrew word for almond is *shaqed*, and the word for "watching" is *shoqed*. The "watching" rod shows that God is "watching" over His Word to make sure that His Word is done. The word that the Lord watches is the word that He puts into Jeremiah's mouth (1:9). The Lord is telling Jeremiah that He will make sure that this word will come to pass.

But verse eleven is odd. "Rod" is a good translation but not what we would expect. We would expect a stick from an almond tree to be called a "branch." The word "rod" is only once used for a "branch" (Genesis 30:37), but normally it is used for a walking stick or shepherd's staff (Genesis 32:10; 1 Samuel 17:40). Why does the Lord show the prophet a "rod" made from an almond tree? In a sense, this makes the connection of Jeremiah and Moses stronger. Both Moses and Jeremiah are shown "rods" to confirm the Lord's call (Exodus 4:17). There is also a reminder of the rod of Aaron, which blossomed with almonds as a sign that Aaron was the chosen priest (Numbers 17). In Numbers 17, too, there is a play on the word for "almond." Aaron's "almond" rod shows that Aaron is qualified to "watch" God's house. So here, Jeremiah is a watchman who announces the coming of the judgment. He is qualified to stand in the council of the Lord and hear his Word.

In Jeremiah's time, it is as if the story of Judah is going in reverse (see 4:23). As the kingdom falls apart, many things happen that remind us of the beginning of the kingdom era. Solomon's temple has become like Shiloh, and Judah's king is another Saul. But the reversal is even bigger than that. Jeremiah, a new Moses, is warning about a reversal of the Exodus and conquest. After the Exodus, Israel is planted in the land and built there, but now Israel is being uprooted and torn down. The Lord breaks the yoke of Egypt (2:21; see Leviticus 16:13), but Jeremiah tells the people to take on the yoke of Babylon. In the end, Jeremiah gives the people hope, but the hope is for a rebirth after a long period of exile and "death."

The Suffering Prophet

Jeremiah is not a bystander watching the death of Judah without feeling. His prophecy contains a number of prayers that show how deeply he feels the pain of Judah's fall. Jeremiah, the "weeping prophet," suffers along with Jerusalem and Judah, and in this way, he is like Jesus, who also weeps over the coming destruction of Jerusalem. We'll look at one of Jeremiah's prayers here. In Jeremiah 11:18–12:4, the prophet is supposed to go to the cities of Judah reminding the people about the Sinai covenant. He tells the people that if they listen to the voice of the Lord, the Lord will be a God to them (vv. 1–8). Yet there is a conspiracy against the Word of God (vv. 9ff), so the Lord is bringing the curses of the covenant upon the people. The people refuse to listen, so the Lord refuses to listen to their prayers. And Jeremiah may not even pray for them; they are too far gone to be helped by a prophet's prayers (vv. 14–16). The Lord has planted and built Israel (notice the key words from chapter one), but now He's kindling a fire to burn her down (vv. 16–17).

When Jeremiah delivers these words to the men of Anathoth, they plot against him to kill him. As a later "Jeremiah" found, a prophet is not welcome in his home town. In two prayers, Jeremiah cries out to the Lord for help.[7] When he prays, Jeremiah is acting like a lawyer. He appeals to the God who judges righteously (11:20) and brings his "case" to the Lord (11:20). In 12:1, he again appeals to the Lord as a just judge, pleading his case, and two verses later, he requests that God act in vengeance to bring justice (12:3). As a prophet, Jeremiah may stand in God's council and bring complaints before the Judge. But Jeremiah is not really complaining about the men who plot against him. He is complaining against the Lord, who seems to sit and do nothing while the wicked prosper and plan to slaughter the Lord's own prophet. In the Psalms, there are many similar complaints. Normally, at the end of such pleas, the Lord gives some assurance that He will take care of things. Jeremiah does not get any reassurance. The Lord's answer is not, "I'll take care of it," but "It's going to get a whole lot worse" (vv. 5–6). God doesn't defend His actions, and He doesn't answer Jeremiah's questions about justice. He just tells Jeremiah to get ready for worse persecutions and calls him to trust his Master.

Jeremiah and the Kings of Judah

Remembering that Jeremiah is living through Israel's history in reverse helps us understand what he says about the kings of Judah in Jeremiah 21:1–23:8. He speaks against the kings after a visit from a group of Zedekiah's aids (21:1–2). Nebuchadnezzar is beginning to lay siege to the city, and the king of Judah wants a word from the Lord. Zedekiah is a weak man who cannot stand up against the Jews who want to fight it out with Babylon. In the end, he rebels because he's afraid of what the Jews will do to him if he surrenders to the Babylonians, as Jeremiah tells him to do (38:17–23). He's controlled by the Jewish leaders and lacks the faith to trust the Lord. But notice how Zedekiah refers to the Exodus in verse two. Zedekiah hopes that the Lord will perform another act like the Exodus. Jeremiah agrees that there will be an exodus, but it won't be the kind of exodus that Zedekiah expects. Instead of fighting Babylon, the Lord is going to turn His weapons against Judah (vv. 3–7). As in the Exodus, Yahweh is going to act with an outstretched hand, but His hand will be stretched out against Jerusalem, not for her. Jerusalem will be struck with "plagues," as Egypt was. The people of the city will die by a great "pestilence." The word for "pestilence" is *deber*, which sounds like the Hebrew word for "word." The pestilence fulfills Jeremiah's word of judgment against Judah.

In 21:9–10, Jeremiah continues talking about the exodus. Jeremiah, like Moses, gives Judah a choice between the way of life and the way of death. Following the way of life means obeying and trusting God. If Judah does this, they will prosper, and the Lord will fulfill His promises to Abraham: "You may live and multiply, and the Lord your God may bless you in the land where you are entering to possess it." Turning to other gods is the first step along the way of death: "You shall surely perish, and you shall not prolong your days in the land" (Deuteronomy 30:16, 18). These are the words of Moses, but Jeremiah turns things around. He tells the Jews that they should "go out" (v. 9), and the word here is used throughout the Old Testament to refer to the Exodus. Jeremiah is a new Moses urging the people to follow him in a new Exodus. But now Jerusalem is Egypt, Judah's king is Pharaoh, and the Lord's hand is stretched out against His daughter. Jeremiah's exodus is not an exodus *into* Jerusalem but an exodus out of Jerusalem, into the waiting arms of Nebuchadnezzar. For Moses, life comes by fighting against the Canaanites. For Jeremiah, life will not come by conquest but by surrender.

Zedekiah is looking for the wrong kind of exodus. But this is normal for Zedekiah. After telling Zedekiah's officials that they should surrender to Babylon, Jeremiah speaks about the sins of the kings of Judah. Jeremiah begins by showing what kind of king Judah is supposed to have (21:11–22:9).[8] Kings in Judah should do justice, defend the helpless from the wicked, and especially help strangers, orphans, and widows. (Notice how often Jeremiah uses the word "justice" here. It's leading up to something.) If the kings don't act justly, the Lord will do justice Himself. The fire of His wrath will flare out against the house of the kings (21:12–14). The "forest" in verse fourteen is the palace of the kings of Judah, which was built by Solomon from the cedars of Lebanon. To say that the Lord's anger will burn the forest is to say that He will burn the house of the kings.

Jeremiah then tells of the sins of all the kings of Judah during his lifetime. What he says about Jehoiakim and Jehoiachin is especially important. Jeremiah says that Jehoiakim has built his house on injustice (22:13–23). He has done a lot of expensive building projects, but he does not pay the workers, since he is greedy for dishonest gain. He will die the death of a donkey, with no burial or mourning. His lovers, the nations on whom he relies for help, will be taken away, and no one will be left to protect him. In 22:24–30, Jeremiah turns to Jehoiachin, who is called "Coniah" here. The Lord is ready to throw Coniah away, even if he is a precious ring. He will be taken to Babylon with his mother and will die there. Worse, he will be left childless. 1 Chronicles 3 tells us, in fact, that Jehoiachin has children. Jeremiah is focusing on the kingship, and the last part of verse thirty is the important part of his prophecy: None of Jehoiachin's descendants will sit on the earthly throne of David. His line is cut off, like Saul's. But this dead royal house will one day be raised, when Jesus takes the throne of David at the right hand of the Father (see Matthew 1:11–12).

After the mentioning of Josiah, Jehoahaz, Jehoiakim, and Jehoiachin, we expect a word to the last of the kings of

Jeremiah's era, but there is a surprise in chapter twenty-three. First, there is a prophecy against all the "shepherds," or kings. Because the kings have not "attended" to the flock, the Lord is going to "attend" to the kings (v. 2). But verses 3–8 give unexpected hope. The last three kings of Judah are unjust kings and are going to die or end up in exile. But the Lord promises to gather the people again and give them shepherds who will protect and feed them, who will defend the lame and seek out the lost. The promise is that a new Solomon will rule Judah, a "sprout" from David. His name will be the "Lord our righteousness," which is, in Hebrew, "Yahweh-Zedeknu." We expect an attack on Zedekiah, whose name means the "the Lord is righteous." Instead, we find a promise that someday there will be a *true* Zedekiah, a truly just king, a king who will be worthy of the name.

Who Stands in the Lord's Council?

Unjust kings are one reason why Judah is dying, but the prophets have also sinned and led Judah into sin (23:9–40). Jeremiah is almost alone during his lifetime. Though he has supporters, mainly from the house of Shaphan, the vast majority of the people turn a deaf ear to his words. Instead, they listen to false prophets. The false prophets are promising that the Lord will deliver Jerusalem from Nebuchadnezzar. They are saying that there will be peace and that there will be no exile. Jeremiah disagrees with all of this. He says that Nebuchadnezzar will take the city, that there will be no peace, and that the exile will last seventy years. Nobody wants to hear what he has to say, and it's easy to see why. With Babylon beginning a siege against the city, everyone thinks it's time for all the Jews to work together. Jeremiah seems to be dividing the people, and some Jews think that Jeremiah is discouraging the army (Jeremiah 38:4). He is even accused of going over to the Babylonians. But Jeremiah doesn't change his message. He insists that the prophets who attack him are "false" prophets.

Falsehood is something that Jeremiah talks about a lot. The word for "false" (*sheqer*) is used 111 times in the entire Old Testament and thirty-six times in Jeremiah. For Jeremiah, falsehood is the sin from which all other sins arise. Lies are an acid that corrodes Judah and makes it impossible for people to live together in peace. Lies prevail in the land; no one speaks the truth. And because falsehood prevails, trust goes out the window. If you can't trust your neighbor or your business partners, you cannot get along or trade. Jerusalem is dissolving because of the acid of falsehood (9:1–6). Falsehood also destroys worship, and so Jeremiah attacks false gods as much as he attacks the false prophets. These gods are false because they are not real. And they are also false because they mislead the people who worship them. They say they can save, but they cannot (cf. 1:16; 2:11; 2:28 ["let your gods save you"]; 5:7, 19; 11:10–13; 16:11–20; 18:15). Jeremiah talks about the greatness of the Lord and the foolishness of idol worship. Gods who are only wood and gold, the work of craftsmen, will perish before the Lord (10:6–11). When God brings Israel out of Egypt, He humiliates the false gods of Egypt. When God brings His faithful remnant out of Jerusalem, He will humiliate their gods too.

Like other forms of falsehood, false prophets pollute the whole land (23:9–13). Jeremiah accuses the false prophets of adultery and falsehood. This may be actual adultery, but sometimes the prophets use "adultery" to refer to idolatry. Judah commits adultery when she leaves her Husband for other gods. The false prophets are speaking a lie, a vision of their own hearts (23:16), and the heart, Jeremiah knows, is deceitful above all things and desperately wicked (17:9). False prophets have not stood in the Lord's council to hear His words, and yet they go through the land pretending to deliver the word of Yahweh (23:18, 22).

What lies do the false prophets tell? On the one hand, there is the promise of "peace" from Babylon (23:17). They tell the people that Jerusalem will not be destroyed. Even though the people have forsaken the Lord, calamity will not come on them. They try to heal a sick nation with lies (8:11). False prophets say everything is okay. But everything is not okay. Things are falling apart. False prophets think everything is okay because they believe Yahweh will protect His people and His house, no matter what Judah does. When Jeremiah preaches in the temple, he mocks the people who trust in the temple rather than in the Lord who dwells in the temple. They chant "the temple of the Lord, the temple of the Lord, the temple of the Lord" (7:4), as if that will save them. But when they leave the temple, they steal, murder, commit adultery, swear false oaths, and worship idols. In this way, the temple has become a "den of robbers." The temple is like the place where robbers retreat for safety after their crimes. But they are not safe in this den. Just as the Lord left Shiloh and let the Philistines destroy it, so He is ready to abandon Jerusalem and leave it to Nebuchadnezzar.

Against the false prophets and kings of Judah, Jeremiah says that the exile will happen and that it will be long. This is the message of the vision of the figs in Jeremiah 24. This vision comes shortly after Nebuchadnezzar's second invasion, when he captures Jehoiachin and takes him to Babylon along with other Jews (including Daniel). Jeremiah sees two baskets of figs in front of the temple, which are there as offerings to the Lord. In one basket are good figs; in the other are rotten figs that cannot be eaten. Of course, the Lord will delight in the figs in the first basket but reject the figs in the second.

The two baskets of figs represent two different groups within Judah (see Jeremiah 2:20–21). Israel is like a vine or tree that the Lord has planted in the land. She is supposed to produce fruit that the Lord can "eat." The vision shows that since Jehoiachin has been taken into exile, Judah had been divided into two baskets. One basket is in the land under Zedekiah, the other in Babylon under Nebuchadnezzar. The question is, Which is God pleased with? The people who remain in the land believe they are the true Israel. Isn't the land the place of blessing and promise? How can Jews be blessed if they are not in the land? But Jeremiah sees things differently. The ones who submit to Nebuchadnezzar have chosen the way of life. The choice, good figs are those that have "gone out" in an "exodus" out of the land. The ones in Babylon are the ones who have been delivered from "Egypt."

God tells the good figs that He will care for them and deliver them. He is sending them into the land of Chaldeans, He will regard them as good, and He will bring them out, build them up, and plant them. No matter how things look now, the exiles who have been plucked up will be planted. God even promises to give the exiles a new heart to know God. They won't have deceitful ("false") hearts anymore. On the other hand, the figs that remain in the land are bad and cannot be eaten. The Lord takes no pleasure in them, but they will instead become a terror and evil, suffering the threefold judgment of sword, famine, and pestilence, which will destroy them.

The bad figs are going to be destroyed from the land because they shed the blood of the Lord's prophets (Jeremiah 26). When Jeremiah preaches about Shiloh in the temple for the second time, Judah's priests take Jeremiah to the princes of Judah for a trial. They say he is guilty of a capital crime for prophesying against the city of Jerusalem. Some of Jeremiah's friends among the elders speak up on his behalf. These leaders from the time of Josiah remind the rest of the princes about Micah of Moresheth, who prophesies against Jerusalem and Zion during the days of Hezekiah (see Micah 3:12). Hezekiah does not kill Micah but turns to the Lord and repents, and the city is spared.

There is still hope for Jehoiakim too. If Jehoiakim will be like Hezekiah and fear the Word of the Lord and listen to the prophet, Solomon's temple will not become like Shiloh. Yet, though he spares Jeremiah, Jehoiakim is no Hezekiah. Instead of fearing the Word of the Lord brought through the prophet Uriah of Kiriath-jearim, he seeks to kill him. Not satisfied when the prophet flees from the land, Jehoiakim sends men to Egypt to kill him there, as Jezebel sought to kill Elijah. Jerusalem and her king spill the blood of the prophets, and they will be destroyed.

Nebuchadnezzar, a New Adam

According to Jeremiah 25:11–12, Babylon will rule for seventy years.[9] Yahweh is the Lord and possessor of all the earth and everything in it, both man and beasts (27:1–5), and He has given the world into the hands of Nebuchadnezzar (vv. 6–7). The king of Babylon is a new Adam, ruling not only the nations, but the beasts of the field. This means that Judah should submit to Babylon's king and not rebel (v. 8). Jeremiah pictures this by wearing a yoke of wood on his shoulders (27:2). The message is that Judah should accept the yoke of Nebuchadnezzar and serve him. Not everyone wants to hear this message. A prophet called "Hananiah, son of Azzur," stands against Jeremiah. Hananiah's name means "the Lord is gracious," and this is a good summary of his message. He believes that the Lord is so gracious that He will never punish Judah. Hananiah says that the exile will last only two years. After that, the vessels of the Lord's house and the king will return. The Lord will break the yoke of Babylon quickly. To make his point, Hananiah takes the yoke off Jeremiah's neck and breaks it, saying that in the same way the Lord will break the yoke of Nebuchadnezzar in two years' time. But the Lord's Word is different. Hananiah has broken a yoke of wood, but in its place, the Lord will give a yoke of iron. Because Hananiah, like all the false prophets, resists the easy yoke, the Lord makes the yoke burdensome.

Jeremiah not only tells the people in Jerusalem to submit to Nebuchadnezzar. He also writes to the "good figs" in Babylon to tell them how they should live during exile (Jeremiah 29). The letter uses the key words "build and plant" (vv. 5, 29). Jeremiah says that they should continue life as usual: They should plant, have children, multiply and not diminish, and seek the welfare of Babylon. They are to settle in and grow the way Israel did in Egypt. The immediate issue is that the exile is going to be a long one, and the exiles are to settle down and live in the land of their exile. They are to work hard so as to prosper and multiply even while in exile. So long as they live peacefully, Babylon will be their protector: Babylon's peace means peace for the exile. Jeremiah says that surrendering to Babylon is like a new exodus. Here, Jeremiah not only promises that the people will be built and planted *after* the exile but says that during the exile they should be building and planting. Babylon will become like the garden-land of Canaan, where the Jews will enjoy the blessings of the land even while outside the land. Babylon will become an Edenic place for the faithful Jews. They are to become Adams and Eves living under the lordship of the great Adamic Emperor, Nebuchadnezzar. Leaders such as Daniel, Mordecai, Esther, and Nehemiah take these instructions to heart, and the Lord keeps His promise.

Days are Coming

During its period of power, Babylon will carry out the Lord's judgments. In Jeremiah 25, the Lord gives the prophet the cup of God's wrath and tells him to make all the nations drink from it. Jeremiah is the cupbearer to *the* King. By prophesying that Babylon will dominate the world, Jeremiah is making the nations drink the wine of the Lord's wrath. According to 51:7, Babylon itself is the cup in the Lord's hand. Babylon makes the nations drunk and mad with wine. Wine is a good thing in the Bible, but too much wine makes you unable to stand up. In this sense, Babylon is the cup of God's wrath. The Lord pours out each nation's portion. They become drunk, vomit, fall, and never rise again. But Babylon won't be the cup of the Lord forever. Jeremiah 25:26 tells us that "the king of Sheshach shall drink after them," and this refers to Babylon. After Babylon makes all the nations of the earth reel in madness and fear, she too will drink the wine of the wrath of God, become drunk, and fall. Elsewhere, Jeremiah predicts that the Lord will give the wine of His wrath to Babylon and cause them to fall asleep. While they are in a drunken stupor, the Lord will lead them off to slaughter (51:39–40). Similarly, Isaiah predicts that Assyria will be punished after the Assyrians have completed the

Lord's work of punishing Samaria (Isaiah 10:12–19; see Jeremiah 50:18, 29).

Nebuchadnezzar is a monster who eats Jerusalem (Jeremiah 51:35). As in Jonah, exile is pictured as Israel being devoured by a great monster. But eating Israel is a dangerous thing. Already in Jeremiah 2:1–3, Jeremiah has talked about Judah as the Lord's firstfruits. Firstfruits are holy food that should not be eaten by anyone but a priest. Judah, too, is holy food, so that anyone who devours her is taking the Lord's food for himself. Nebuchadnezzar has devoured Israel and is going to be held guilty. Babylon, like Babel, will be left a heap of ruins. The Lord's cup of wrath will make the sea monster vomit Judah back to dry land.

Though the people are to settle in Babylon for the long haul, they are not to despair of returning. In 29:12–13, Jeremiah says that the people's heart has been far from the Lord, but the discipline of exile will force them to seek the Lord with all their heart. These instructions not only presume that the exile is an exodus but also that the exile is preparation for a new exodus and a new conquest. Babylon will be a fruitful land for the faithful Jews, as Goshen was for their forefathers. They will multiply, as the Israelites multiplied in Egypt. But eventually they will return, as their fathers did. What has been plucked up will be planted; what has been broken down will be built.

Review Questions.

1. What does the vision of the "blown pot" mean?

2. How is Jeremiah like another Moses? Another Samuel?

3. What event does Jeremiah refer to in his temple sermon in Jeremiah 7? What's the point? Why is it important that Jeremiah delivers this message?

4. How is Zedekiah like Saul?

5. Explain how Jeremiah turns words about the exodus inside out.

6. What do the false prophets teach? Explain the confrontation between Jeremiah and Hananiah.

7. What does the vision of the baskets of figs mean?

8. How does Jeremiah describe Nebuchadnezzar?

9. How are the exiles supposed to live? Why?

10. What does Jeremiah promise will happen after the exile?

Thought Questions.

1. What does the prophet warn Judah about in 3:1–5? What is Yahweh preparing to do?

2. Jesus quotes Jeremiah 7:11 in Matthew 21:13. What is Jesus suggesting by quoting from this passage?

3. Look at Jeremiah 14:19–22. Who does Jeremiah remind you of? How does this fit with larger themes of the book?

4. When is the "New Covenant" in Jeremiah 31:31–34 going to be established? Look at the context.

5. In Jeremiah 38, the prophet is thrown into a pit and then drawn out by Ebed-melech ("servant of the king"), an Ethiopian. This reminds us of Joseph being thrown into the pit and brought out. How are the two incidents similar?

[1] David A. Dorsey offers the following outline of Isaiah:

A. Condemnation of Israel and promises of restoration, 1:1–12:6
  B. Oracles to the nations, 13:1–27:13
    C. Woes: Don't trust in princes, 28:1–35:10
      D. Jerusalem delivered from Assyria, 36:1–39:8
    C´. Yahweh supreme over idols, 40:1–48:22
  B´. Servant messages, 49:1–54:17 (contrast with proud nations)
A´. Condemnation and future restoration, 55:1–66:24

The Literary Structure of the Old Testament: A Commentary on Genesis–Malachi (Grand Rapids: Baker, 1999), p. 234.

[2] One problem for this view is that Isaiah 36–37 describes *Jerusalem's* deliverance from Assyria, while Isaiah 9:1 speaks of a light dawning over portions of the Northern Kingdom. It is very possible, however, that

following Sennacherib's devastating defeat at Jerusalem and his subsequent assassination, Assyria's hold on the North was seriously weakened. During Josiah's reign, moreover, the Northern Kingdom was reuinified with the South, so that both kingdoms came together in a common Passover (2 Chronicles 35:16–19). Further, it is clear that the time horizon of Isaiah 9:1–7 is not confined to Hezekiah's reign but points to the dawning of the true light in Galilee (Matthew 4:15–16).

[3] It is possible, of course, that Zephaniah was prophesying about conditions before the discovery of the law. In 1:4, however, the Lord threatens to "cut off the remnant of Baal from this place," which might imply that Baal has already begun to be cut off by Josiah.

[4] My interpretation of this vision is based on William Holladay's commentary on Jeremiah (*Jeremiah* [2 vols.; Hermeneia; Philadelphia: Fortress, 1986, 1989]) but diverges in some ways. As Holladay points out, Jeremiah's vision is similar to two prophecies in Ezekiel. In Ezekiel 11, the prophet says that the city is a pot, and the people are the flesh that are going to be cooked in the pot. In Ezekiel 24, the pot is again the city, but here the prophet focuses on the rust, which pictures the blood of innocent people killed in the city. God is going to raise the temperature in the city until the rust is burned away.

[5] The only other place where this verb is used with "pot" is Job 41:20, which describes smoke coming from Leviathan's nostrils as from a blown pot.

[6] The call narrative is structured as a chiasm:

A. Call of Jeremiah, 4–10
  B. Confirming vision, 11–12
  B′. Vision of pot, 13–16
A′. Promise to Jeremiah, 17–19

[7] These two prayers are arranged chiastically:

A. Lord showed deeds, 11:18
  B. "Lamb led to slaughter," 11:19a
    C. Conspiracy: destroy tree, 11:19b
      D. Jeremiah presents his "case," 11:20
        E. Persecuted by men of Anathoth, 11:21–23
      D′. Jeremiah presents his case, 12:1
    C′. Wicked are planted and bear fruit, 12:2
  B′. Make them like sheep, 12:3
A′. Land mourns because men do not see their end, 12:4

[8] This section has the following structure:

A. Administer justice, 21:10–11
  B. Lord kindles fire in forest, 21:13–14
A′. Administer justice, 22:1–4
  B′. Lord will kindle fire in house, 22:4–7

[9]This seventy-year period apparently begins with the death of Josiah in 608 B.C. and extends to the fall of Babylon to Cyrus in 539 B.C., a literal seventy -year period. Daniel clearly understood it as a literal period (Daniel 9:1–2). Zechariah 1:12 speaks of another seventy-year period, during which Jerusalem will be trodden under the feet of Gentiles. Zechariah 1 is dated in the second year of Darius, which would be about 520 B.C. This seventy-year period begins with the destruction of Jerusalem in 587, though preparations for the siege of Jerusalem began as early as 589. This is almost exactly a literal seventy-year period. Although both of these seventy-year periods were literal, there is also evidently a symbolic import.

7
Exile and New Exodus

Daniel is brought to Babylon in the first deportation and quickly becomes an important man in Nebuchadnezzar's court. Ezekiel, a priest, comes to Babylon the second time Nebuchadnezzar invades the land. Ezekiel and Daniel are in Babylon at the same time that Jeremiah is preaching in Jerusalem and at the same time that Zedekiah is king in Jerusalem. Both of them trust the Word of the Lord given through Jeremiah and work for the peace of the city. And, as the Lord promises, in Babylon's peace, they find peace.

Ichabod and Return, Ezekiel 8–11, 40–48

The book of Ezekiel begins with a vision of the glory of Yahweh beside the Chebar river in Babylon. Yahweh comes to tell Ezekiel that he is going to be a prophet to the stubborn and rebellious people of God (2:1–7). The cloud that leads Israel out of Egypt and through the wilderness has come back as Israel is being taken into captivity. This is the cloud that had been in the tabernacle and then the temple (Exodus 40:34–38; 1 Kings 8:10–11), the same cloud that hovers over the waters in Genesis 1:2. But the temple is unclean and now the cloud has come to be with the exiles in Babylon. Though they are cut off from the temple, the Jews in Babylon are not cut off from the presence of the Lord. They are the "good figs" of Jeremiah's vision. They are going to be the beginning of a "new creation."

Ezekiel first sees the cloud in Babylon, but his next major vision takes him back to Jerusalem: While he is sitting in his house in Babylon, the "hand of the Lord fell on me," and "the Spirit lifted me up between earth and heaven and brought me in the visions of God to Jerusalem" (8:1, 3). In Jerusalem, he sees "the glory of the God of Israel" again, and it is "like the appearance which I saw on the plain" in Babylon (v. 4). Ezekiel's vision in Jerusalem is going to show him how the cloud leaves the temple and how it gets to Babylon.

Ezekiel's vision of events in Jerusalem takes place in four stages.[1] In the first vision, Ezekiel sees what is happening behind the scenes in the temple. The walls of Solomon's temple are carved with pomegranates and palms. The temple is like the garden of Eden. But now, the walls are covered with carvings of "every form of creeping things and beasts and detestable things, with all the idols of the house of Israel" (8:11), and the seventy elders of Israel are offering incense to the idols (v. 12). At the entrance of the Lord's house, he sees women weeping for Tammuz, a Babylonian god who dies and rises again each year (vv. 14–15). In the inner court are twenty-five men. These are the High Priest and the heads of the twenty-four priestly clans set up by David. They have turned their backs on the temple and are bowing toward the sunrise. They are not facing west—the direction of return to the garden—but east, the direction of exile (vv. 16–18).

All these things are taking place before the face of Yahweh, for His glory is still enthroned above the cherubim of the Most Holy Place. But the Lord only takes these insults for so long, and then He leaves His house. What Ezekiel sees are "abominations that bring desolation," like the abominations of the sons of Eli in 1 Samuel 2. When the Lord leaves His house, nothing and no one can protect it. Over the next several chapters, Ezekiel sees the Lord leaving the temple and the city being destroyed. Yahweh does not leave His house all at once. First, the glory moves from the cherubim to the threshold of the temple (9:3; 10:3–4), then it moves to a place above the living creatures that form the

Lord's chariot (10:18–19). Finally, the cherubim lift their wings with the glory hovering above it and leave the city and the temple to take a stand on the Mount of Olives, east of the city (11:22–24).

While Yahweh's glory is leaving the house, riding on the backs of the cherubim, the Lord is preparing to destroy the city. Instead of guarding the city, the Lord is attacking it. In chapter nine, Ezekiel sees a "man clothed in linen" who is told to mark out all those who "sigh and groan over all the abominations" of Jerusalem (vv. 3–4). Those marked on the forehead will be saved when men with weapons are sent throughout the city to "slay old men, young men, maidens, little children, and women" (v. 6) without pity (v. 5). Long ago, the Lord told Joshua to kill all the Canaanites without pity. This is called "the ban." Now, in another "Passover," Yahweh the Warrior is sending His troops to carry out the ban against Judah, which has become an "Egypt" and a "Canaan." The Lord tells the men with weapons to "defile the temple and fill the [temple] courts with the slain" (v. 7). In the Old Testament, touching a dead body makes you unclean (Numbers 19). Piling up dead bodies in the temple makes it very unclean. Judah has made the temple unclean by worshiping idols there. The Lord judges her by making the temple even more unclean.

Ezekiel's vision of the Lord leaving His house is followed by a series of actions and messages. Each of these ends with the Lord saying that He is doing all this to Judah "that they may know that I am Yahweh." The Lord scatters them to the nations "so they will know that I am Yahweh" (12:15). Cities will be laid waste, and the fruitful land turned to wilderness "so you will know that I am Yahweh" (12:20). The Lord will show that the preaching of false prophets is false so that "you will know that I am Yahweh" (13:23). This repeated phrase comes from the book of Exodus, where Yahweh brings plagues on Pharaoh and Egypt because Pharaoh says he does not know Israel's God: "Who is Yahweh that I would obey His voice to let Israel go? I do not know Yahweh"

(Exodus 5:2). Yahweh answers by saying, "You don't know me? Let me show you who I am. I am the God who turns the Nile to blood, who fills the land with stinking frogs, who blots out the sun, who dries the sea and drowns Pharaoh's armies" (cf. Exodus 6:7; 7:5, 17; 8:10, 22; 9:14, 29; 10:2; 14:4, 18). In Ezekiel, however, *Judah* is saying, "Who is Yahweh? I don't know Yahweh." So the Lord shows who He is by sending the plagues of Egypt to His own people.

There is hope here too. Those marked on the forehead are saved (9:6), and the glory of the Lord is traveling east toward the exiles. Just as in 1 Samuel 4–5, Yahweh joins His sinful people in exile, the Lord shows who He is not only in judgment but in mercy. He will "spare a few of them from the sword, the famine, and the pestilence" so that they may know that He is Yahweh (12:16), and He shows His character by delivering His people from the hand of false prophets (13:23). Here, as at Sinai, Yahweh reveals His glory by showing that He is a "compassionate and gracious God, slow to anger and abounding in lovingkindness and truth" (Exodus 33:18–19).

Ezekiel's vision of the fall of the city and temple are in the middle of his prophecy. In chapter twenty-four, Ezekiel's wife dies, and the Lord says that he has to keep the High Priest's rules for mourning. He is to "make no mourning for the dead" nor go barefoot or cover his mustache (Ezekiel 24:16–18; cf. Leviticus 21:10–12). The death of Ezekiel's wife is symbolic of the fall of the sanctuary. The Lord uses the same words to describe Ezekiel's love for his wife ("the desire of your eyes," 24:16) and his concern for the sanctuary ("the desire of your eyes, the delight of your soul," 24:21). And, just as Ezekiel is told not to mourn for his bride, so he is told to be silent about the coming end of the temple until "that day" when the city and temple finally fall (24:27). Ezekiel is not completely silent. But he is silent toward Judah and the exiles. Meanwhile, he sends messages to seven Gentile nations (chapters 25–32). This is the "sign of Jonah" once again: Yahweh provokes Judah to jealousy by sending His word to the Gentiles. It also shows that the judgment that comes on Jerusalem shakes the whole world, because Jerusalem is at the center of the world.

Once the city falls, Ezekiel opens his mouth again to speak to the people of God (33:21–22). His opening words condemn the "shepherds" or rulers of Judah (chapter 34), but most of the last part of Ezekiel promises salvation and return. In Ezekiel 36, he says that the Lord will clean Israel and take her back to her land:

> I will take you from the nations, gather you from the lands, and bring you to your own land. Then I will sprinkle clean water on you, and you will be clean; I will cleanse you from all your filthiness and from all your idols. Moreover, I will give you a new heart and put a new spirit within you; and I will remove the heart of stone from your flesh and give you a heart of flesh. And I will put my Spirit within you and cause you to walk in My statutes, and you will be careful to observe My ordinances. (36:24–29)

This prophecy comes true when Jesus comes, but Ezekiel's message is first of all a message to Jews in exile. It is a very encouraging message: Empty cities will be full of people, waste places will be rebuilt, wilderness will turn to garden. All the nations will see what has happened to Judah, "and they will say, 'This desolate land has become like the garden of Eden'" (36:35).

Like the prophecy in chapter thirty-six, the vision of bones raised from the dead in the following chapter is first of all about a resurrection from the death of exile. Yahweh explains the vision to Ezekiel by saying, "These bones are the whole house of Israel." The message of the vision is that the Lord will "open your graves and cause you to come out of your graves, My people; and I will bring you into the land of Israel" (37:11–12). The risen people will not be like the people who went into the grave, who for centuries have been divided into two kingdoms. The Lord promises to heal the division between the Northern and Southern Kingdoms. Judah and Ephraim will be like two sticks tied together with "one king" for both of them. They will "no longer be two nations, and they will no longer be divided into two kingdoms" (37:19–22). Raised by the power of the Word of Yahweh, Israel and Judah will be made into "one new man;" the two will become one flesh.

Once risen Israel is planted in the land, Ezekiel's prophecy goes on to say that she will face an attack from the nations, led by someone called "Gog of the land of Magog" (Ezekiel 38:2). It is not easy to tell what events Ezekiel is talking about here. Many Christians believe that Ezekiel is talking about a battle at the end of the world (see Revelation 20:8). But Ezekiel has been talking for several chapters about Israel coming back from Babylon. This battle with the nations must have something to do with that. Some Christians say that this battle is the one found in the book of Esther, or Ezekiel might be talking about the battles that Ezra and Nehemiah have to fight when they return to the land. Whatever Ezekiel is referring to, it is clear that the battle ends with a great victory for Israel. The Lord tells Gog, "You shall fall on the mountains of Israel, you and all your troops, and the peoples who are with you; I shall give you as food to every kind of predatory bird and beast of the field" (Ezekiel 39:4).

Even if we cannot be certain about exactly what Ezekiel means, the story is one we have seen before: Israel comes out of a Gentile land and enters her own land (chapters 36–37); she fights with and defeats the nations (chapters 38–39); then she builds a house and divides the land (chapters 40–48). This is a retelling of the story of exodus and conquest. The return from Babylon is a replay of Israel's earliest history.

In the first Exodus, the goal is to build the Lord's house and worship the Lord in the land. The exodus from Babylon has the same goal. The last nine chapters of Ezekiel are a very complicated description of a new temple. We can't look at all the details, but let's notice a few things. First, Ezekiel 43 ends the story of the travels of Yahweh's glory. A man with a measuring rod is marking off the holy space of the temple. As Ezekiel stands at the gate of the temple facing east, "behold, the glory of the God of Israel was coming from the way of the east." The glory "came into the house" and entered the inner court until "the glory of Yahweh filled the house" (43:1–5). The people who build the second temple never see the glory return to the Lord's house. But Ezekiel has seen the glory come back in a vision. The worshipers at the second temple are to believe that the prophet's vision is true: Yahweh is once again enthroned above the cherubim, making His house holy by His glory.

Second, the Lord's return not only sanctifies the temple, but makes the whole city holy. The temple itself is "like a city" (40:2), and there is also a "holy allotment" surrounding the house.[2] At the center of the holy allotment is a square that is 25,000 cubits on each side (v. 20). Moving from North to South, this portion of land is divided into three sections:

Northernmost:	Levites	25,000 cubits X 10,000 cubits	vv. 12–13
Middle:	Priests	25,000 cubits X 10,000 cubits	vv. 9–11
Southernmost:	City	25,000 cubits X 5,000 cubits	vv. 15–17

This means that the city of Jerusalem as a whole is now holy space (vv. 18, 20). Ezekiel shows this by giving the dimensions of the city. In the Bible, only holy places have exact dimensions. Plus, the city is "in the midst" of the southern portion of the allotment, just as the sanctuary is "in the midst" of the priestly portion (v. 10). The exits of the city are named for the tribes, with three gates on each of the four sides. This reminds us of the wilderness camp in Numbers. Since the camp is a holy place, Ezekiel is telling us that the city, like the camp, is now a holy city. The name of the city tells us it is the city where Yahweh dwells (v. 35), and this means it is a holy city.

The new house of the Lord makes the whole land clean and fruitful. In chapter forty-seven, Ezekiel sees water flowing from the house toward the East. As Ezekiel follows the river, it gets deeper and deeper and restores the land and sea.

Water from the temple turns the land back into Eden: "By the river on its bank, on one side and on the other, will grow all kinds of trees for food. Their leaves will not wither, and their fruit will not fail. They will bear every month because their water flows from the sanctuary, and their fruit will be for food and their leaves for healing" (47:12). As in the story of Joash, restoration flows from the house of God.

Review Questions.

1. Where was Ezekiel when he was prophesying? What was happening in Jerusalem at the same time?
2. What was Ezekiel's first vision?
3. What does Ezekiel see in the temple?
4. What is the Lord planning to do to the people of the city?
5. What is important about the phrase "that they may know that I am the Lord"?
6. After his wife's death, in what way is Ezekiel silent? Why?
7. What is the vision in Ezekiel 37 about?
8. How is the story that Ezekiel tells like the story of the Exodus and conquest?
9. How does Ezekiel show us that the city of Jerusalem is a holy city?
10. How does the temple revive the land?

Thought Questions.

1. Ezekiel sees a man in linen enter the cherubim cloud and get a handful of coals, which he scatters over the city (Ezekiel 10:1–2). Compare to Exodus 9:8–12 and Revelation 8:3–5 and explain the parallels between the passages.
2. Who are the ones who plaster the walls with "whitewash" (Ezekiel 13:8–16)?
3. Explain the allegories in Ezekiel 16 and 23. How is Judah pictured?
4. Look at Ezekiel 33:30–33. How is this passage like Matthew 11:17?

5. What is the purpose of Ezekiel's description of the temple (43:10–12)? Explain how he accomplishes this purpose.

Times of the Gentiles, Daniel

Even more clearly than Ezekiel, Daniel learns the lessons of Jeremiah. Daniel is also taken to Babylon by Nebuchadnezzar, and he is trained for service in the Babylonian government. He becomes a very important ruler in Babylon, and when the Babylonians are taken over by Persia, Daniel remains as a leader. As Jeremiah instructs, Daniel is seeking the peace of the city.

But Daniel does not seek the peace of Babylon by disobeying God and going along with everything the Babylonians tell him to do. When obeying the king of Babylon means disobeying the King of Israel, Daniel disobeys the king of Babylon. Every time he does this, the Lord saves him and blesses him. Then Daniel is given a high position, and even Gentile kings confess that the God of Israel is the true God. This happens over and over again in the early chapters of Daniel. During his training, Daniel and his three friends refuse the king's food. Instead of becoming weak, they are stronger than any of the others (1:14–15), and at the end of their training, they are the best in the class (1:19–20). When Nebuchadnezzar has a dream, only Daniel can interpret it. As a result, he is made "ruler over the whole province of Babylon," and the Babylonian king says that Daniel's God "is a God of gods and a Lord of kings and a revealer of mysteries" (2:47–48).

When Daniel's three friends are told to bow down before the image that Nebuchadnezzar makes, they refuse and are thrown into the fiery furnace. The Lord saves them, and Nebuchadnezzar praises the "God of Shadrach, Meshach and Abednego" and warns that anyone who speaks evil of the God of Israel "shall be torn limb from limb and their houses reduced to a rubbish heap." After this deliverance, Shadrach,

Meshach and Abednego "prosper in the province of Babylon" (3:28–30). Later, Darius the Mede tells everyone to pray only to him, but Daniel continues to pray to the Lord. The Lord delivers him from the lion's den, and again a Gentile king praises the power of the Lord:

> I make a decree that in all the dominion of my kingdom men are to fear and tremble before the God of Daniel; for He is the living God and enduring forever, and His kingdom is one that will not be destroyed, and His dominion will be forever. He delivers and rescues and performs signs and wonders in heaven and on earth, who has also delivered Daniel from the power of the lions. (6:26–27)

This is what Jeremiah wanted all Israel to do: Go peaceably to Babylon, accept the discipline of the Lord, and be a faithful witness before the Gentiles. If the Jews seek the peace and welfare of Babylon, they will be saved from all their enemies, and kings of the earth will marvel at the power of Yahweh.

These stories are not in the Bible just to tell us how great Daniel is. Every one of them is also a promise to Israel. Moses says that at the Exodus God delivers Israel "out of the iron furnace" (Deuteronomy 4:20). In Daniel 3, the three men represent all Israel in the furnace of exile in Babylon. If Israel is as faithful as Shadrach, Meshach, and Abednego, the Lord will make sure that not even a "hair of their head is singed" (3:27). Throwing Daniel into the lion's den is like the sheep of Israel being cast to the ferocious Gentiles. Daniel is like the "son of man" in chapter seven who triumphs over the beasts. Eventually, the Lord will bring Israel out of this furnace as He brought them out of the furnace of Egypt. He will send a shepherd to deliver His flock from the lions. And all the kings of the earth will see the Lord's power and bless His name.

The message pictured in the stories of Daniel and his friends is also the message of Daniel's visions. As in Jeremiah, Daniel's visions show that a new world has come, a world where Israel will not be a separate nation but will be under a world empire.[3] And like Jeremiah, Daniel's visions show that these Gentile nations will someday fall. Then, the Lord will set up His kingdom that will last forever. In Daniel 2, Nebuchadnezzar dreams of a statue made of four different kinds of metals. Daniel sees that the four metals picture four Gentile kingdoms: The gold head is Babylon, the silver chest is Persia, the bronze belly and thighs are Greece, and the legs of iron and feet of clay and iron represent Rome (2:36–45). A small stone cut without hands hits the feet of the statue, and it collapses into powder. The stone then grows into a mountain that fills the whole earth. This growing stone is the kingdom that "the God of heaven will set up," one that, unlike the kingdoms represented in the statue, "will never be destroyed" (v. 44).

Daniel's vision of the four beasts in chapter seven tells the same story. Beasts from the sea are Gentile powers, and these four beasts are the same four powers described in chapter two. But their power will be taken away and given to "one like the Son of Man," the Last Adam, who will master the bestial empires of the old world and receive all their dominion and authority to share it with the "people of the saints of the Most High" (7:13–22, 27). Daniel's visions teach Israel patience during exile. Someday the Lord will bring in His own empire and His king will rule the nations with a rod of iron. For now, Israel is living in the times of the Gentiles, and she should patiently wait for the Lord to come set up His kingdom.

From Zealot to Witness, Esther

Not everyone wants to wait. The false prophets in Jerusalem do not believe that they are living in a "time of the Gentiles." They tell the people that the Lord will save Israel and set up His kingdom *now*. Even some of the people who go into exile have a hard time accepting a "time of the Gentiles." They don't want to submit to Gentile kings or accept the yoke of

Babylon or Persia. Mordecai in the book of Esther starts out this way, and the book of Esther shows what happens to Israelites who won't submit. But the book of Esther also shows that the Lord is merciful toward His people and will deliver them. When they repent, He will triumph over the serpent and exalt His people over their enemies.

When Esther begins, Cyrus has already sent the Jews back to the land to begin rebuilding the house of God. Mordecai himself had returned to the land (Ezra 2:2), but in Esther, he is back in Susa, the capital of the Persian Empire. Unlike Daniel, who rises to a high position in Babylon and Persia while being faithful, Mordecai has become compromised. His name means "worshiper of Marduk," the chief god of the Babylonians. After Vashti's fall, he instructs Esther not to tell anyone she is a Jew, whereas Daniel always tells Gentile kings that the God of Israel is the true God. Unlike Daniel, Esther accepts food from the king's table (2:9–10). Mordecai wants Esther to become queen, but he does not want her to help the Jews; he won't let her tell anyone she is a Jew. He wants Esther to become queen because it will make him powerful. Daniel does not seek power; he wants to be faithful to the Lord, and the Lord gives him power. Mordecai seeks power, but in trying to exalt himself, he nearly loses everything.

In order to bring Mordecai to repentance, the Lord raises up an adversary, Haman the Agagite. Agag was the king of the Amalekites who had fought with Saul. Originally, the Amalekites appear in Exodus 17:8–16 when they attack Israel while she is leaving Egypt, attacking the weakest Israelites who marched in the back (Deuteronomy 25:17–19). From that time, the Lord vows to wipe the name of Amalek from the earth. Israel is to carry out the ban against the Amalekites. Like the Canaanites, they are supposed to be completely destroyed. Saul fights against the Amalekites, but he spares the best animals, along with Agag (1 Samuel 15). Haman is one of the descendants of this Amalekite king, while Mordecai is from the tribe of Benjamin, like Saul. The fight between Haman and Mordecai is the final battle in Yahweh's war against the Amalekites.

Israel has not carried out the ban against the Amalekites, and now Haman plots to carry out the ban against Israel. He wants to utterly destroy them. Haman becomes angry at Mordecai because Mordecai foolishly refuses to bow to him. Instead of being faithful like Daniel, Mordecai makes a big show to make it appear that he is faithful. But Mordecai's rebellion against Haman is rebellion against the king, since the king has commanded everyone to bow to Haman (3:1–2). He should have known better: When Vashti refuses to obey the king's command, she is removed from her position. Mordecai's disobedience may have the same result. Because of Mordecai's folly, Haman seeks to destroy the entire nation of Israel. Haman tells the king that the whole empire is in danger so long as the Jews remain (3:8), and he makes plans to hang Mordecai on a gallows. Though Haman is wicked and a hater of God's people, we must not forget that it is Mordecai's foolish zeal that threatens Israel. Mordecai, fortunately, sees the error of his ways and repents in sackcloth and ashes (4:1–3). He tells Esther that she now has to reveal that she is a Jew. He realizes now that the only safe thing to do is to confess the Lord. Esther, after hesitating, finally agrees. She puts herself in the Lord's hands: "If I perish, I perish" (4:16).

At this point, another character takes the main role in the drama, a character that remains unnamed throughout the book of Esther: God. Having brought His unfaithful people to the brink of disaster, having driven them to repentance, having forced them to confess Him or die, He begins to bless and deliver them. In fact, He has been working all along in the shadows. Haman casts lots to determine the best time to attack the Jews, and the lot falls on a date nearly a year in the future. As the Proverb says, the lot is cast into the lap, but its every decision is from the Lord (Proverbs 16:33). When Haman's lot is delayed, it means that the Lord is delaying the destruction of Israel to give them time to repent. When

Esther approaches the king, he raises the scepter and permits her to enter his inner court (5:1–4). As Proverbs says, the heart of the king is in the hand of the Lord, He turns it like a watercourse wherever He will (21:1).

God's hand in saving Israel is clearest on the night before Haman plans to execute Mordecai on his gallows (6:1–14). King Ahasuerus cannot sleep, so he asks for the chronicles of his reign to be read. The chronicle tells how Mordecai foils a plot against the king, and Ahasuerus wants to honor Mordecai. Just at that moment, Haman "happens" to enter the court in order to get permission to hang Mordecai. Before he can tell the king why he's there, the king asks him what to do to the man the king wishes to honor. Haman, thinking the king is talking about him, tells the king to dress that man in the king's robe and lead him through the streets on the back of a horse the king had ridden on. Haman is thoroughly humiliated when he finds out that the king wants to honor Mordecai, his archenemy. Mordecai tries to exalt himself and is abased. Now, having abased himself, he is exalted, while Haman is shamed. In the middle of the night, the Lord turns everything upside down. It is another "Passover."

Esther arranges for two banquets where she reveals her identity to the king and accuses Haman of attacking the Jews. Haman is hung on the very gallows set up for Mordecai, as the Lord causes the wicked to fall into their own trap. Esther wins the favor of the king, and he gives the Jews permission to defend themselves against those who attack them. The day of destruction for the Jews becomes a day of deliverance and a great victory: "On the day when the enemies of the Jews hoped to gain mastery over them, it was turned to the contrary so that the Jews gained the mastery over those who hated them" (9:1). Not only are many Jews not destroyed, but the Lord's hand is so obviously with the Jews that many Gentiles throughout the Persian empire turned to the Lord (8:17). Like the stories in the book of Daniel, Esther is a picture of the Lord's deliverance of His people from exile: If His people repent and confess Him among the Gentiles, He will exalt them and give them victory. And the Gentiles will turn to the Lord in fear.

Review Questions.

1. Give some examples of how Daniel stays faithful to the Lord while in exile.
2. What happens when Daniel and his friends obey God?
3. How do the stories of Daniel picture God's promises to the exiles in Babylon?
4. What are Daniel's visions about the "times of the Gentiles"? What message does this send to the exiles?
5. At the beginning of Esther, is Mordecai a faithful man? Why or why not?
6. Is Mordecai right when he refuses to bow before Haman?
7. Who is Haman? Why is this significant?
8. Give some examples of the Lord acting to save his people in the book of Esther.
9. What is the message of Esther to the exiles?

Thought Questions.

1. What is Belshazzar doing on the night that Babylon is taken by the Persians (Daniel 5:1–9)? Why?
2. Daniel 9:24–27 contains the famous "seventy-weeks" prophecy. When does the period of "seventy weeks" begin? When does it end?
3. Look at the uses of the phrase "latter days" in Daniel 2:28 and 10:14. When do the "latter days" begin?
4. Compare Esther 5:11 with 1:4. What does this suggest about Haman's view of his own prestige?
5. Explain how the feasts provide a structure for the story in Esther.

Second Exodus, Ezra and Nehemiah

We think of the Exodus as the founding event of Israel's history. This is quite proper, since the Exodus is what made

Israel Israel. But Isaiah says that Israel's return from Babylon is going to be an even more important event in Israel's history. In Isaiah 11:15–16, the Lord promises to gather Israel from the nations where they have been scattered, strike the sea of Egypt, and make His people cross on dry land. After this new crossing of the sea, the Lord will make a highway appear in the desert for Israel's return, as there was a highway in the first Exodus, complete with fast food and rest areas along the way.

Again in 43:14–21, Yahweh identifies himself as the Lord of the Exodus:

> Thus says Yahweh,
> Who makes a path through the sea
> And a path through the mighty waters . . .
> Do not call to mind the former things,
> Or ponder things of the past.
> Behold, I will do something new. (vv. 16, 18–19)

The second exodus will be so great that it will make Israel forget about her deliverance from Egypt. And in 44:24–28, the Lord says Israel can be sure that the Lord will raise them from the death of exile, since He is the Lord who creates the world by His Word and who dries up the depths of the sea and makes rivers dry. Now, by the same Word, the Lord promises to bring Israel back, to make creation new once again. Here Isaiah predicts that Cyrus will be a shepherd to Israel. Cyrus will repeat the Word of Yahweh that Jerusalem and the temple will be rebuilt (see Ezra 1:1–4).

The exile and restoration follow another story from earlier in the Bible. Jeremiah says that Jerusalem has become Egypt, and the true Israel has to escape before "Egypt" is destroyed. Leaving Jerusalem is another exodus. This means that the exile in Babylon is like Israel's wandering in the wilderness. During that time, Israel is purified; an old generation dies and is replaced by a new generation. And this new generation enters the land to conquer it. So, the restoration is not only a new exodus but a new conquest of the land. The story even continues to the rebuilding of the temple with Zerubbabel playing the role of a "new Solomon."

It isn't only Isaiah who sees the similarities between the Exodus and the return from Babylon. Ezra and Nehemiah see things the same way. Their books describe the return from Babylon following the story of the exodus and the conquest. As Israel leaves, they are encouraged by "those around them" or "their neighbors," Gentiles who give them silver, gold, cattle, and other valuables (Ezra 1:6). This is just what happens when Israel leaves Egypt. There they plunder the Egyptians (Exodus 11:2–3; 12:35–36), and here Israel again "plunders" the Persians.[4] In addition to the silver and gold from the Persians, Cyrus returns the gold and silver things from Solomon's temple. The riches of Persia and Babylon are going to be used to build the house of God, just as the plunder of Egypt was used to construct the tabernacle. Ezra 2 lists the clans or families who return and the numbers from each. This is like a miniature book of Numbers. But there is an important difference. Israel leaves Egypt with over 600,000 men of fighting age, but Ezra 2:64 says that only 42,360 return from Babylon. Some Jews remain behind in Babylon, and some have never left the land.

If leaving Babylon is a new "exodus," entering the land is a new "conquest." The goal of this new "conquest," like the first, is to set up the Lord's house in the land and to establish true worship. They will bring the land to rest and build the place where the Lord's name will dwell. As in the first entry into the land, Israel meets opposition. They have to contend with the "people of the land," whom they must overcome. Even some names are similar; Joshua leads Israel during the conquest, and the High Priest who leads the people after the return from Babylon is also named Joshua.

These similarities also bring out important differences between the two situations. Pharaoh lets Israel go free only after being beaten by plagues for the better part of a year. Cyrus lets the people go as soon as he takes over Babylon, encourages them with gifts, and gives them permission to build the Lord's house. The Egyptians give silver and gold to Israel because the fear of God has fallen on them and they want Israel to get out of town as quickly as possible. The Persians give their silver and gold as a freewill offering (Ezra 1:6). Because the Jews have repented of their hostility to the Gentile empire, there are good relations between Israel and the Gentiles. As Hiram of Tyre did in the reign of Solomon, Gentiles are helping to build the Lord's house.

Another difference is that there are almost no miracles or signs in this "second exodus." Isaiah prophesies that the sea will be divided, but we see nothing of this in Ezra or Nehemiah. There's no pillar of cloud and fire to lead the people through the wilderness. In Ezra 6:16–18, Israel finishes building the second temple. By contrast with Exodus 40 and 1 Kings 8, the glory of the Lord does not appear in the Most Holy Place. This is not because Yahweh is absent from the temple or because He does not accompany his people back to the land. Instead, God begins to guide His people in a different way. He guides Israel less by visions, miracles, and spectacular signs, and more by the written word and through the teachers of Israel. This is the beginning of the "New Covenant" that Jeremiah promises.

Cyrus gives Israel permission to build the Lord's house, and this rebuilding takes place in several stages. We can get a handle on how this happens by looking at the outline of Ezra-Nehemiah, which is a single book:[5]

- A. Zerubabbel's return and list of returnees, Ezra 1–2
  - B. Building of temple; opposition, Ezra 3–6
    - C. Ezra's return, Ezra 7–9
      - D. Purification of people, Ezra 9–10
    - C´. Nehemiah's return, Nehemiah 1–2
  - B´. Building of walls; opposition, Nehemiah 3–7:3
- A´. Zerubbabel's return and list of returnees; final reforms, Nehemiah 7:4–13:31

Before the Jews build the temple, they first build an altar in order to begin offering sacrifices and celebrating feasts of

Israel (3:1–5). This effort is led by Joshua and Zerubbabel (a descendant of David). Once the altar is in place, the people celebrate the Feast of Booths. The second task is to rebuild the temple itself. Joshua and Zerubbabel lead this phase also, but rebuilding the temple proves more difficult than building an altar. Opponents of the Jews send letters to the king of Persia, warning him about Jewish plans. Jerusalem, they claim, has been a rebellious city, and if it is rebuilt, it will rebel again. The emperor searches his records and finds that Jerusalem has, in fact, been a rebellious city. So he stops the work on the temple, and it is left until the second year of Darius (Ezra 4:1–24).

What sparks the people to return to work on the temple are the prophecies of Haggai and Zechariah (Ezra 5:1–2). Haggai 1:1–11 gives the gist of his prophecy. The Jews are not prospering, he says, because they have stopped working on the Lord's house. The people dwell in paneled houses, but the house of the Lord is in ruins. This shows that they think more of their own homes and comforts than the temple. The temple is in ruins (v. 4), so God will bring "drought." In Hebrew, the word for "drought" uses the same consonants as the word for ruin. In response to the ruin of His house, the Lord brings ruin on Israel. Zerubbabel listens to the prophet and leads the people to return to work on the temple.

Zechariah's prophecy is harder to summarize, but it is dealing with the same set of problems. Zechariah 1:1–6 tells us the prophet's setting and main purpose. The first verses of the book are delivered in the eighth month of the second year of Darius. At 1:7, a second prophecy begins, consisting of a series of night visions that Zechariah receives in the eleventh month of the same year. Chapters 7–8 are delivered in the fourth year of Darius (7:1). The last six chapters of Zechariah's prophecy have no dates. Haggai 1:1–15 contains Haggai's sermon to the people in the sixth month of the second year of Darius, and this is the time when the people return to work on the temple. Zechariah's first prophecy, then, is given a little more than a month after the work on the temple has begun again.

Zechariah 1:1 tells us something about the prophet himself. Here he is called the son of Berechiah, the son of Iddo (see Ezra 5:1). His connection with Iddo is important. In a list of the priests and Levites who return from exile with Zerubbabel (Nehemiah 12:4), Iddo is mentioned. Zechariah is named as the head of Iddo's house (Nehemiah 12:6). Zechariah the prophet is also Zechariah the priest. The names in verse one are also significant: Zechariah's name means "Yahweh remembers," and Berechiah means "Yahweh blesses." Zechariah will tell the people that Yahweh has remembered them in their affliction and is going to keep His covenant to bless them.

Zechariah's first brief sermon highlights the word "turn" or "return," a single Hebrew word translated in several different ways (cf. 1:3, 4, 6). Zechariah's sermon is a call to the people to repent and return to the Lord of hosts. Zechariah begins with a brief history lesson. He reminds them of what happened to their "fathers" (vv. 4–6). Verse six says that the curses of the covenant "overtook" the fathers, and this means especially the curse of exile. Zechariah is telling the Jews that they should not forget their history but should learn from the experience of their fathers. The curses overtook the fathers because they did not "turn" when the prophets warned them. Now, the people are in danger of falling into the same sins as their fathers. If they don't turn, they too will be overtaken by curses.

What is it that Zechariah wants the people to repent of? After all, they are already at work building the second temple. Zechariah is saying that even though they have started building God's house again, something is not right. They have not, with their whole heart and soul, returned to the Lord Himself. Building the temple by itself doesn't guarantee that the Lord will favor them. Their fathers believed that the temple of the Lord would protect them, no matter how they lived. Jeremiah says that the false prophets trust in "the temple of the Lord, the temple of the Lord, the temple of the Lord." Zechariah wants the people to avoid falling into this sin. They need to return to Yahweh and not merely to His house. Only this kind of turning will bring the Israelites the blessing promised in verse three. The only thing that will bring the Lord back among them is a change of heart. But the example of the fathers is not only a warning but a promise of salvation. Even though the fathers refused to listen to the word, and even though their sins brought curses on Israel, the Lord has not left Israel. He invites this new generation to turn to Him. And if they do, He will turn His face toward them.

The first six chapters of Zechariah's prophecy are a series of visions that are very complicated and difficult to interpret, but we will look at one of them. Near the center is a vision of Joshua the High Priest standing before the Lord, dressed in filthy garments (Zechariah 3). He is being accused by Satan before the Lord. Remember that Zechariah is prophesying when Israel is at work rebuilding the temple. The vision shows that Joshua is a defiled High Priest. Because he is unclean, he may not serve in the Lord's house. Normally, an unclean priest could become clean by offering sacrifice. But to offer the right kind of sacrifice, there has to be a temple. Israel may not build the temple without a clean priest, yet the priest may not be cleaned without a temple. Israel is locked in a box with no way out.

Or, with only one way out—God alone can get Israel out of this dead end. And He does. God tells his angels to put clean clothes on Joshua. This means that he is being restored to his position as High Priest; he may go ahead and dedicate the temple and begin making offerings again. In the morning, when Zechariah declares his visions to the people, he will tell them that he has seen the Lord cleanse Joshua, exchanging his filthy priestly garments for garments of glory and beauty. Like a new Moses ordaining a new Aaron, Zechariah the prophet declares the restoration of Joshua.

Inspired by the preaching of Haggai and Zechariah, the people finish the temple in the sixth year of Darius

(Ezra 6:15). Now, it seems that Cyrus's decree has been fulfilled. The house of God has been rebuilt. But we still have several more chapters of Ezra and the whole book of Nehemiah to go. Cyrus's decree allows Israel not only to rebuild the temple, but also to rebuild the whole "house" of God. Rebuilding the house means working to restore the people of God and the city of Jerusalem.

Ezra's work is to restore the people of God, and this comes at the center of Ezra-Nehemiah. Ezra does not appear in the first six chapters of the book that bears his name, but in chapter seven, after the temple has been completed, he comes from Babylon. He is a priest (7:5) and an expert in the law of Moses (7:6). His mission is to study the law and to teach it to Israel (7:10). What does this have to do with building the house of the Lord? First, the house of Israel *is* the house of God, and, as we saw in chapter two, the temple is a picture of the people gathered around the throne of God. Yahweh dwells in the midst of Israel, not merely in the temple. Ensuring that the people of God make a suitable dwelling place for Him is part of keeping the Lord's house. Second, the temple will be clean only if the people live righteously in the land. Solomon's temple is destroyed by Nebuchadnezzar because it is filled with abominations, and it is filled with abominations because of Israel's sins, both in worship and elsewhere. To protect the new temple from being destroyed in the same way, the Israelites are going to have to learn to obey the law of God.

Nehemiah's work of rebuilding the city is also a part of rebuilding the house of God. We can see this from the early chapters of Ezra. The enemies of Judah attempt to stop Jews from rebuilding the *city* (Ezra 4:12), but when the Jews write to Darius later, they ask him to search for the decree of Cyrus. Darius finds the decree that gives them permission to build the "temple" and "house," and he tells them that they may return to building the city. Both the Jews and Darius agree that Cyrus's decree gives Israel permission to restore the city.

How is rebuilding the city related to rebuilding the house? At the very least it means that rebuilding the walls and protecting the city is a necessary part of maintaining Yahweh's temple. But that can't be the whole of it. After all, Jerusalem had strong walls when Nebuchadnezzar came through the land, and those strong walls didn't protect anybody for long. Building the walls is part of building the house because the holy city is part of Lord's house. As we saw above in our study of Ezekiel, the city has become a "holy city," like the camp in the wilderness. In Nehemiah 12:27, the word used for "dedication" of the walls frequently refers to dedications of altars (Numbers 7:10ff) or temples (Psalm 30:1). The walls are dedicated as "holy." Further, Nehemiah brings in Levites from everywhere to "dedicate" the walls of the city, and the Levites have to be purified to participate (v. 30), again showing that the city as a whole is being sanctified. This makes the best sense of Nehemiah 12:40, which otherwise has a strange twist. The verses just before this describe the procession around the walls, and then in verse forty, the choirs suddenly take their stand "in the house of God." If we think "house of God" refers to the temple, the verse doesn't make much sense. How did they get into the temple all of a sudden? But if the "house of God" means the city, the verse is understandable. The two choirs proceed around the walls, one stopping at the Water gate (v. 37), and the other at the Gate of the Guards (v. 39), and having taken their stand *there*, they are taking their stand in the house of the Lord.

It would be great if Nehemiah ended with the dedication of the "house" of Jerusalem. But it doesn't. And Nehemiah 13 is a downer. After all that Joshua, Zerubbabel, Ezra, and Nehemiah have accomplished, Nehemiah still has to enforce the Sabbath (13:15–22), and he finds that some of the Jews, including priests, are still marrying pagans (13:23–29). Like the sins of the sons of God in Genesis 6, this threatens the survival of the Jews in Jerusalem.

And so we come to the end of the history of Old Testament Israel, and things still don't look the way the prophets said they would look. The house of the Lord has been rebuilt, but the temple mountain hasn't risen to become chief of the mountains. Israel is back in the land, but the land doesn't quite look like the garden of Eden. Yahweh has renewed His covenant with His people, but the law doesn't seem to be written on their hearts. Nations have confessed the God of Israel, but the knowledge of the Lord does not cover the earth as the waters cover the sea.

Surely, something better must be coming.

Review Questions.

1. To what does Isaiah compare the return from Babylon?
2. Explain some of the similarities between the return from Babylon and the Exodus.
3. Explain some of the differences between the first and second exodus.
4. What are the different stages in rebuilding the house of God?
5. What is Haggai's prophecy about?
6. What is Zechariah's prophecy about? What does the vision of Joshua in filthy garments mean?
7. What is Ezra's job? How is this related to rebuilding the Lord's "house"?
8. What is Nehemiah's job? How is this related to rebuilding the Lord's "house"?

Thought Questions.

1. What does Cyrus say about the Lord in his decree (Ezra 1:1–4)? What does this suggest about Cyrus?
2. The story of Ezra's return from Babylon includes details of the treasures that Ezra is bringing (Ezra 7:11–26; 8:24–30). Why?
3. In Ezra 9:1, the princes tell Ezra that the people are marrying Canaanites, Hittites, and so on. Many of these people no longer live in the land. Why do the princes call the people of the land by these names?

4. Nehemiah has to deal with conflicts between Jews (5:1–13). What are they fighting about? What laws are they violating?

5. What proportion of the Jews live in Jerusalem after the exile (Nehemiah 11:1–2)? Why?

[1]This is part of a larger seven-section passage:

Vision 1, 8:1–18
Vision 2, 9:1–11
Vision 3, 10:1–22
Vision 4, 11:1–25
Ezekiel's luggage, 12:1–16
Ezekiel's eating, 12:17–20
Message about false visions and divinations, 12:21–13:23

David A. Dorsey, *The Literary Structure of the Old Testament* (Grand Rapids: Baker, 1999), p. 255.

[2]The dimensions of this allotment are described in detail in 48:8–23. This passage forms the structural center of the division of the land described in chapter forty-eight, which is organized by an ABAB pattern:

A. 7 Northern tribes, vv. 1–8
  B. Holy allotment (including city), vv. 8–23
A´. 5 Southern tribes, vv. 24–29
  B´. Exits of the city, vv. 30–35

[3]Intriguingly, the book of Daniel is written partly in Aramaic, the international language of the day, and partly in Hebrew. Fittingly, the Aramaic portions are concerned mainly with the international setting and are arranged in chiastic order:

Introduction: Daniel in Babylon, chapter 1
  A. Nebuchadnezzar's vision of a statue; four kingdoms, chapter 2
    B. Daniel's friends refuse idolatry, chapter 3
      C. Nebuchadnezzar acknowledges Yahweh, chapter 4
      C´. Belshazzar ignores Yahweh's claims, chapter 5
    B´. Daniel disobeys Darius's order regarding prayer, chapter 6
  A´. Daniel's vision of four beasts, chapter 7

[4]Note especially the use of "vessels" or "articles" in verse six; the same words are used in every Exodus passage that mentions the plundering of Egypt.

[5]Dorsey, *Literary Structures*, p. 161.

8
Israel Dead and Reborn

The Old Testament is about God's actions in the world. It is a story of His great acts in saving Israel from Egypt, planting them in the land, and blessing them there. It is the story of God's discipline of Israel for her sins, of exile in Babylon, and of the great second exodus. It is a story of God calling Israel to build His house in His land.

Some Christians read the Bible as if this story ends with the book of Malachi. They think that when Matthew starts his gospel, he is telling a very different story. That's not true. The New Testament is not a different book from the Old Testament. The New Testament tells the end of the story that the Old Testament starts. This means that we cannot understand the New Testament unless we know the Old Testament. Reading the gospel of Matthew without knowing the Old Testament is like reading the last chapter in a novel. You just won't get the point. But it also means that we haven't finished the story when we come to the end of the Old Testament. To get the point of the Old Testament, we need to learn the end of the story of Yahweh and Israel in the New Testament.

This book is mainly about the Old Testament part of the story, and we can't cover the whole New Testament too. Instead, this chapter will look at the end of the story as told by the gospel of John. We'll see over and over that John is telling us that the story of Jesus is the last chapter of the story of Israel.

The Greater Jeremiah, The Greater Solomon

When Jesus asks His disciples, "Whom do people say that I am?" one of their answers is "Jeremiah" (Matthew 16:14). This seems strange to us. Jeremiah is a prophet of doom and judgment. He tells Israel that the Lord is sending Nebuchadnezzar to take Israel into exile. He warns that the temple will be destroyed. He says that Shiloh is going to happen all over again. This is not the picture we have of Jesus. We think of Jesus as a shepherd, as a kind-looking man who heals and helps. But the people who think that Jesus is Jeremiah are onto something important. They see that Jesus, like the prophet, is warning Israel about her sins and telling them that the Lord is about to destroy His house. Like John the Baptist, Jesus tells the people that the "kingdom of heaven is at hand" and that "the axe is laid at the foot of the tree" (Luke 3:7–9). God is getting ready to chop down the vine of Israel.

Jesus' clearest teaching about this comes in the sermon He gives on the Mount of Olives during the week before His death. There, he prophesies that a great judgment is coming, and says that the judgment will come upon "this generation" (Matthew 24:34). When Jesus speaks about "this generation," He is talking about the Jews who are living in Judea and Jerusalem during His lifetime. He's saying that before His generation passes away, Jerusalem and its temple are going to be destroyed. Shiloh is going to happen all over again. Jesus is the greater Jeremiah.

Jesus is the last and greatest of the prophets to tell Israel of her coming doom. Once we see that, we can also see that the biggest battles in the New Testament are about how Jesus' gospel relates to Israel. The conflict between the Christian church and the Jewish synagogue is the main conflict in the New Testament. Paul's letters are full of this. In Galatians, he attacks Christians who are continuing to practice Jewish circumcision and rules about food. In Romans, he asks "Who is the true Jew?" (Romans 2) and "Has God rejected Israel?" (Romans 9–11). The book of Hebrews deals with Christians who are being tempted to return to Judaism.

Acts ends on this note, with Paul leaving off his work among the Jews and going to the Gentiles (Acts 28:23–29).

Jesus is not only a new Jeremiah who announces the destruction of Herod's temple. He is also the greater Solomon, David's greater Son. Matthew introduces Jesus as the "son of David" (Matthew 1:1; see Romans 1:4). Even when the New Testament calls Jesus "son of God" (see Matthew 16:16), it is referring to 2 Samuel 7:14, which says that David's son will be called "the son of God."

This means that Jesus, like Solomon before Him, is going to build a new temple. Jesus Himself says this just after Peter calls Him "son of God"—"I also say to you that you are Peter, and upon this rock I will build My church; and the gates of Hades shall not overpower it" (Matthew 16:18). Jesus says here that He will build a "church," but other passages of the New Testament show us that the church is the "temple of God" (1 Corinthians 3:16–17; 2 Corinthians 6:16; Ephesians 2:19–22). The writer to the Hebrews compares Jesus' building of the church to Moses' service at the tabernacle:

> [Jesus] was faithful to Him who appointed Him, as Moses also was in all His house. For He has been counted worthy of more glory than Moses, by just so much as the builder of the house has more honor than the house. . . . Now Moses was faithful in all His house as a servant, for a testimony of those things which were to be spoken later; but Christ was faithful as a Son over His house, whose house we are, if we hold fast our confidence and the boast of our hope until the end . (Hebrews 3:1–6)

As the true king of Israel, Jesus builds a temple that is more glorious than anything Solomon built. He's building us into His house.

Jesus Among the Jews

Many people read the gospel of John in a different way. They don't believe John is as concerned about the Jews and the temple as the other gospel writers are. But John is every bit as interested in what Jesus means for Israel as any other New Testament writer. We miss the point of John's gospel if we don't see this. John's gospel urges Christians to make a firm break from the temple and synagogue and to continue in the new Way of Jesus.

The early chapters of John's gospel, especially chapters 5–10, are full of debates between Jesus and the Jews. Some of these conflicts are like a legal process. People are questioned, witnesses are called, and a judgment is pronounced. Mainly, the Jews are trying to put Jesus on trial. Jesus is on trial throughout the whole gospel, not merely at the end. Israel wants to put Yahweh on trial.

Who are the "Jews" who are fighting with Jesus? Sometimes, John uses this word to refer to all who follow the practices of the Mosaic law. Not all Jews reject Jesus (cf. 12:9–11). Most of the time, though, the word "Jew" refers to the rulers and leaders of Israel who live in Jerusalem and hate Jesus. In chapter nine, for example, Jesus heals a blind man, and both he and his parents are fearful of the "Jews" (v. 22). The blind man is himself a circumcised child of Abraham, yet he is not part of the "Jews." "Jews" sometimes means chief priests and Pharisees (18:3, 12; 8:13, 18ff). Since these leaders represent the nation, the "Jews" as a people reject the Messiah when the leaders do.

The early chapters show not only that the Jews reject Jesus, but also that Jesus is the one who fulfills all the promises God has made to Israel throughout the centuries. Jesus' miracles show this again and again, but every time Jesus does a miracle, the Jews gang up on Him and start arguing with Him. In John 5, Jesus raises up a man who had been lame for thirty–eight years. The story of the miracle is in nine verses, and the rest of chapter five, nearly forty verses, is about the Jews attacking Jesus for healing on the Sabbath. John pays more attention to the argument than he does to the miracle itself. In chapter six, we have the same thing again. Jesus feeds five thousand in Galilee. The story of the miracle takes up fifteen verses, and from verses 22–71, Jesus is debating about what the miracle means. In chapters 7–8, there is no miracle at all. Jesus goes to the Feast of Booths, and, again, there is a controversy about Jesus that ends with Jesus declaring Himself to be "I am," which is another way of saying that He is Yahweh. In chapters 9–10, which again form a single story, Jesus opens the eyes of a man born blind. The miracle is told in seven verses, and from 9:8–10:21 John tells us about the argument that follows. In chapter nine, the Jews put the man born blind on trial, calling his parents and others as witnesses, and chapter ten is a continuation of the debate. The good shepherd sermon discourse in chapter ten is part of Jesus' answer to the Jews. Jesus says that He is the Good Shepherd, but the "Jews" are hirelings and thieves (cf. Ezekiel 34).

Words that have to do with courtrooms and law are used a lot in John's gospel. The word "witness" is used nearly forty times, and it is used only twelve times in the other gospels combined. Words related to the word "judge" (and "judgment") are used over thirty times. Jesus brings judgment in the sense that He divides the Jews who hate Him from other Jews who believe in Him. And He brings judgment also when He overturns the way things are in Israel. The Jewish leaders think they can see, but Jesus shows they are blind. Meanwhile, Jesus takes a blind man and makes him see. In John's gospel, Jesus does not preach that judgment is coming soon. He preaches that judgment is already starting because He is there. The Spirit in John is called the "Paraclete," a word that in Greek usage is primarily a legal term (John 16:7). A paraclete is an advocate, usually for the defense. Far from being a "spiritual gospel," John is more like a lawyer's brief.

This conflict between Jesus and the Jews that is so important in chapters 5–10 is already being talked about in chapter one. John 1:11 openly speaks of the Jews' rejecting Jesus, who is the light: Jesus comes to His own, and they reject Him. But John has already made that point in 1:1–5. He begins the gospel by reminding us of the creation story in Genesis 1: "In the beginning was the Word and the Word was with God and the Word was God." John borrows the phrase "in the beginning" from the first verse of the Bible. He mentions creation through the Word. And he talks about Jesus as the light, reminding us that light is created on the first day of the creation week. John tells us from the first verses of his gospel that Jesus' coming is the beginning of a new creation.

But the Light who created light shines in darkness, and the darkness does not overcome it (1:5). As we read through the gospel, it becomes clear that the darkness that tries to overcome the light is the Jews. The word "overcome" has a double meaning. It can mean either "overcome" or "seize." The Jews who are in darkness seek to "seize" and "overcome" the light but cannot.

But how are the Jews "darkness"? The reminders of creation help us see what John means. Light and darkness are used in John 1 in the same way they are used in Genesis 1. In Genesis 1, darkness is not evil. God separates light and darkness and still says that both are good (Genesis 1:1–5). Darkness is a part of the creation; it is what comes before the dawn. Since darkness comes before light, it is like the Old Testament period. It is good in itself, but the Old Covenant darkness is always intended to be temporary. It is supposed to last only until the light comes, until day begins. The sin of the Jews is not living in darkness. Before the Light comes, that's the only thing they can do. Their sin is to cling to the darkness when the Light has come. The sin is for darkness to seek to overpower the Light instead of giving way to the Light. The sin is to love shadows rather than the reality.

John's gospel shows that Jesus has to fight against the Jews, and it also shows that the Jews hate Jesus' disciples and followers. John shows us early examples of how the Jews will later persecute believers and kick them out of the synagogue. And he shows us that some of Jesus' disciples, fearing the Jews, turn away from Him.

These things become clear in John 9 after Jesus heals the

blind man. Since the man has been blind from birth, his healing is a new birth. For a blind man to receive sight is to be born anew, from above. As in John 1, there are many reminders of creation in this chapter. Jesus is the Light of the world, the one who enables men to see (9:5). To remake the blind man, Jesus spits on the ground to make clay, just as Yahweh breathed on dust to make Adam (9:6). When the man has been born anew, he is put on trial. The Pharisees ask him questions, and the "Jews" speak to his parents. His parents don't want to speak because the Jews have already decided that anyone who confesses Jesus will be put out of the synagogue (v. 22). Then the Jews question the man again and say he is born in sin (v. 34), something Jesus has denied (vv. 2–3). Then, the healed blind man is cast out of the synagogue. Fear about being cast out of the synagogue keeps some of the rulers who believe in Jesus from confessing him (12:42). John condemns this cowardice, saying that they want honor from men rather than honor from God (12:43). More generally, the gospel speaks a number of times about believers' "fear of the Jews" (19:38; 20:19).

John also shows us many believers who stop following Jesus when things get difficult. After the feeding of the five thousand, some of his followers depart (6:66). Many of Jesus' disciples leave when He begins speaking about eating His flesh and drinking His blood. Another group leaves Jesus in 8:31–59. Jesus is speaking to the Jews who have believed in Him (v. 31), but they still want to trust in their blood connection to Abraham. Jesus says He is greater than Abraham, but the Jews answer by saying He's demon-possessed. This is the context of Jesus' most heated attack on "the Jews" (vv. 39–47), in which he calls them children of the devil, liars, and murderers. But Jesus is not attacking the Jewish people in general, or even their leaders. He is attacking Jews who believe in Him but turn aside from following Him. Those who go out from Jesus are not of Jesus. They are of their father, the devil.

The raising of Lazarus is a key turning point in the gospel

of John. Up to this time, the Jews have been plotting to kill Jesus, but after Jesus raises Lazarus, many Jews believe in Him (12:9–11). This makes the leaders even more anxious to get Jesus out of the way, and the chief priests and Pharisees conspire together to put Jesus to death. What they fear is Rome (11:48). If the Jewish leaders don't deal with Jesus and His disciples, they fear the Romans will take away "our place" (the temple) and "our nation" (11:48).

Even though it doesn't appear in his gospel, John knows about Jesus' sermon about the temple. He knows that Jesus has been warning about a coming attack on the temple. This is clearer in the book of Revelation, which John also wrote (Revelation 1:1). John tells us both at the beginning and end of Revelation that the terrible judgments he sees in visions will take place "shortly" (1:3; 3:11; 22:7, 10, 12). This is exactly what Jesus says in Matthew 24: A great judgment is going to come within "this generation."

In Revelation, John predicts that a great city will be destroyed. Revelation 11:8 names this city as "Sodom and Egypt," and Revelation 17:5 calls this city, which is pictured as a prostitute, "Babylon the Great, the Mother of harlots and of the abominations of the earth." But Sodom was destroyed long before John's day, and Babylon is not much of a problem in the New Testament. John is not talking about these actual cities. John says that the names "Sodom and Egypt" are "mystical" names (11:8), and the name "Babylon" is also "a mystery" (17:5). All of these passages are talking about the same city, but these are not the real names of the city. They are pictures that tell us what kind of city it is. Which city is John talking about? John tells us clearly in Revelation 11:8: The city called "Sodom and Egypt" is the city "where also their Lord was crucified." John is describing Jerusalem, but Jerusalem has gone so far from the Lord that it is more like Sodom, Egypt, and Babylon than the city of God.

Jerusalem becomes a Sodom, Egypt, and Babylon because the Jews attack and kill Jesus, and more importantly, because Jerusalem is "drunk with the blood of the saints, and with the blood of the witnesses of Jesus" (17:6). This is why the angels rejoice when Jerusalem falls: "Fallen, fallen is Babylon the great! And she has become a dwelling place of demons and a prison of every unclean spirit, and a prison of every unclean and hateful bird," an angel cries (Revelation 18:2). And again, "Hallelujah! . . . for He has judged the great harlot who was corrupting the earth with her immorality, and he has avenged the blood of his bond-servants upon her" (19:2).

Heaven rejoices because God's enemies have been destroyed, but there is another reason for celebrating. With the prostitute Babylon out of the way, it's time for a new, true bride to appear: "Let us rejoice and be glad and give glory to Him, for the marriage of the Lamb has come and His bride has made herself ready" (Revelation 19:7). When the bride comes down the aisle, John describes her as "the holy city, new Jerusalem" who is also "made ready as a bride adorned for her husband" (21:2). There is no temple in this city because "the Lord God, the Almighty, and the Lamb are its temple" and because the whole city has become a temple—measured with a golden measuring rod, adorned with precious stones like the High Priest's breastplate, built on the foundation of the apostles. John, like the other New Testament writers, knows that Jesus is the greater Jeremiah, who is preaching against the corruptions of His Father's house. And John knows that Jesus is also the greater Solomon, who will build a new house.

John's visions in Revelation, then, build on Jesus' prophecies about the destruction of the temple and city of Jerusalem, and they show that Jesus is going to build a new city and marry a new Bride. John's gospel shows us that the Jews know Jesus is a threat. But they don't do the one thing that will protect them from the Romans: Turn to Jesus. And because they don't, their worst fears will come to pass.

Review Questions.

1. In what ways is Jesus like Jeremiah?
2. What does Jesus mean when he warns about judgment against "this generation"?
3. Who are the "Jews" in John's gospel? How does John emphasize Jesus' conflict with them?
4. What does John teach us by reminding us of creation in chapter one of his gospel?
5. How does John foreshadow the conflicts between Jesus and the Jews in chapter one of John? How are the Jews "darkness"?
6. What happens to the blind man that Jesus heals? How is this a preview of what happens later in the New Testament?
7. Why are some of the Jews afraid to confess Jesus openly?
8. Why do some of Jesus' disciples leave Him? What does Jesus think of this?
9. What are the Jews afraid of after the raising of Lazarus?
10. What city is destroyed in Revelation?

Thought Questions.

1. How does the miracle of healing in 4:46–54 fit with the conflict between Jesus and the Jews?
2. Whom does Jesus call as His "witnesses" in 5:19–47?
3. What do the Jews plot to do after Jesus raises Lazarus (11:54–57)? How does this fit with the theme introduced in 1:5?
4. Why do the people think that Jesus is a "prophet" when He feeds the five thousand (6:14)? See 2 Kings 4:42–44.

Grace and Truth Through Jesus

John wants people who read his gospel to choose, and he tries to convince them that they should choose Jesus. John does this by showing that Jesus is greater than Moses, Jacob, Abraham, and the entire Old Testament system. The first sign that Jesus does, changing water to wine, shows that He is greater than the Old Covenant (2:1–11). This miracle takes place on the "third day," but it is not clear what it is the third day from. The answer is that the first chapters of John's gospel outline a week. The first four days are noted: 1:19 (day 1); 1:29 (day 2); 1:35 (day 3); 1:43 (day 4). The "third day" is the "third day" after the last mentioned day, and this makes it the same as the seventh day of the week that John is recording. The miracle of Cana takes place on the "Sabbath" of this "creation week." This third day also points ahead to the other third day at the gospel's end, for the last and climactic sign of Jesus is the resurrection.

On this "Sabbath," there is a wedding with Jesus in attendance. Jesus has been identified throughout the first chapter as the Lamb of God, and this is a wedding with the Lamb of God as one of the guests. The wedding feast at Cana points to the marriage supper of the Lamb. In keeping with the marital imagery, in 3:29, John identifies Jesus as the bridegroom who brings joy. Bridegrooms are supposed to give wine to their guests (2:9–10), and at this wedding, the true Bridegroom does exactly that. This is a sign of the coming of a new world that will fulfill and replace the old. The Bridegroom has come, and the wedding feast of the new creation begins.

Water has already been mentioned several times in the first chapter of the gospel (1:26,31, 33). Water is linked to John, the one who baptizes in water to prepare the way for the Man who will baptize with the Spirit. But Jesus transforms the water into wine. Based on John's contrast between baptism with water and baptism with the Spirit, the wine is linked with the Spirit: Jesus does not offer water to His guests but offers Spirit(s). Jesus does not merely change water to wine. He changes the "water of purification of the custom of the Jews" into wine (v. 6). Jesus' miracle teaches that He is greater than the "custom of the Jews." Even the number of jars is significant, especially when we remember that this takes place on the "Sabbath." The Jewish water does not bring rest; it did not bring in the wedding feast of the Lamb. Jesus takes the six waterpots of Jewish purification and transforms the water into the wine of celebration on the seventh day.[1]

The stone waterpots also remind us of Moses. In Exodus 7:19, Moses changes the water of Egypt into blood, including the water in the wood and stone waterpots. For Moses, this is the first sign against Pharaoh and Egypt. Jesus, the greater Moses, does not perform a sign of judgment but a sign of blessing, changing water to the blood of grapes. This is one example of how John shows that Jesus is greater than Moses. As John says in the first chapter, the law came through Moses but grace and truth through Jesus Christ (1:17).

The other incident recorded in chapter two shows that Jesus is greater than the temple (2:13–22). Jesus comes to the temple, cleanses it, and takes it over. Again, we see that John's gospel is concerned about the fate of the house of God. In fact, unlike the other gospels, John puts Jesus' cleansing of the temple at the *beginning* of Jesus' ministry rather than at the *end*. Jesus may have cleansed the temple twice, but John tell us about it at the beginning of Jesus' work because he wants us to understand Jesus' whole life in light of this incident. Jesus' whole ministry is an effort to "cleanse" the house of God.

What does Jesus mean by "cleansing" the temple? Some people say that Jesus is upset because the Jews are buying and selling things in the temple. But something else is going on here. By overturning the tables where sacrificial animals are being sold, Jesus stops the temple worship for a time. He even drives the sheep and oxen out of the temple (v. 15). He's not simply trying to clean up the worship of the temple. He's bringing it to a halt.[2] By stopping the temple worship for a few minutes, Jesus is giving a dramatic warning of what's coming within "this generation." He's showing the Jews that their temple worship will be stopped forever unless they repent. This is what Jesus means in verse nineteen:

"Destroy this temple, and in three days I will raise it up." Some readers understand this as if Jesus said, "*If* you destroy this temple," but the phrase is actually a command. Jesus is being sarcastic. By worshiping God hypocritically, they are making the temple a "house of merchandise" and "den of brigands" rather than the house of Yahweh. Jesus says, "Go ahead, keep on doing what you're doing. Keep on destroying this temple."[3]

John shows that there is another side to what Jesus says. Jesus is talking not only about the temple in Jerusalem but also about "the temple of His body." Jesus already knows that the darkness is going to try to overcome the light. He knows the Jews will keep on worshiping God hypocritically, and they will also try to destroy the "temple" of His body. Elsewhere in the New Testament, the "body of Christ" describes the church. This is part of what John meant. The Jews will attempt to destroy Jesus' body by putting Jesus on the cross and persecuting His disciples. As Jesus says, in killing the "body" of Jesus, the Jews will seal their own fate. By destroying the temple that is His body, they will be destroying the temple where they worship.

But destruction is not the end of the story. Jesus sarcastically encourages the Jews to keep right on living the way they are living. They will eventually suffer the consequences of destroying the temple of Jesus' body. But Jesus will not be defeated by the Jews or by death. They can do their worst, but in three days, Jesus will rise again. Darkness will not quench the light. When Jesus says this, He's still talking about two things at the same time. He's not only saying that He will be raised up to new life three days after His crucifixion. He's also saying that His resurrection is the first part of building a new temple. Since Jesus is the temple, in a sense the whole temple is "rebuilt" when Jesus rises on the third day. But since Jesus' body also includes His disciples, in another sense the resurrection lays the cornerstone of a temple that Jesus is still building today.

Jesus is better than the house, and He is also greater than

the house-builder, the prophet Moses. As we've seen, the contrast of Moses and Jesus is already there in chapter two, but it becomes even clearer in John 5. There, a man is beside a pool near the "sheep gate," the gate where sheep are brought into the city. Under Nehemiah, this gate is rebuilt by the priests and Levites. The sheep who enter the sheep gate are being brought to the temple for sacrifice. At this gate lay many who were sick and crippled (v. 3). This description reminds us of Leviticus 20–21, which describes blemishes that make animals unsuitable as sacrifices. These sick are outcasts from the flock of Israel. They are brought to the sheep gate but cannot enter the house. They are waiting by a pool, hoping to be healed when the water is stirred by an angel.

By this time in John's gospel, we know that water is a picture of the old order that Jesus comes to fulfill and replace. This water cannot make men acceptable sacrifices. Only the word of Jesus does this. Jesus comes to the broken sheep of Israel to give them abundant life. The Mosaic order of water and purification cannot heal. Jesus can. Jesus heals a man who has been sick for thirty-eight years, the same amount of time that Israel is in the wilderness (Deuteronomy 2:14). The man's problem is that he cannot go through the waters. He is stuck in the wilderness and cannot pass into the land. The Mosaic system cannot take him into the land, just as Moses himself does not enter. To pass through the waters to new life, the man needs a Joshua. And Joshua (Jesus) comes to him. Jesus takes him out of the wilderness, makes him suitable as a sacrifice, and raises him from Old Covenant death to New Covenant life.

What makes the Jews mad is that Jesus does this miracle on the Sabbath. When we see what Jesus has actually done for the man, the anger of the Jews is amazing. Jesus has enabled a man stuck in the wilderness to enter the land. And entering the land *is* entering Sabbath rest (cf. Psalm 95). Jesus brings true Sabbath to the lame man, but the Jews persecute Him for breaking Sabbath. Just as the Mosaic order leaves the man in the wilderness, so also it leaves him cut off from Sabbath festivity and rest. The Jews actually prefer the wilderness of Moses to the Sabbath festivity of Jesus.

In John 6, Jesus brings a new Passover, a new exodus, and better manna. This miracle takes place at the time of Passover, but Jesus does not go up to Jerusalem. Instead, He stays in Galilee and offers a new Passover feast to those who gather around Him. After the Passover feast on the mountain, Jesus crosses the sea during the night and saves His disciples from the storm, which is like a new exodus. In the morning, the crowds gather to Him. Since this comes after the Passover and the Exodus, the gathering of the crowds is a wilderness scene. It makes sense, then, for Jesus to talk about manna in the wilderness and to say that He is the true bread from heaven. Here again, Jesus is presented as a leader and guide superior to Moses. Moses does not give life to the fathers in the wilderness; the manna is given by the Father. Besides, the manna in the wilderness does not give eternal life; the true Bread from heaven does. Moses is the leader of the people who receive the manna, but Jesus *is* manna. Yet, as with Moses, the people grumble against Jesus (vv. 41, 43, 61). Jesus is greater than Moses, but as with Moses, His own do not receive Him.

This comparison with Moses continues in later chapters of John's gospel, particularly in chapters 13–17. These chapters are like Deuteronomy in a number of ways. First, Jesus gives these talks when He is about to return to the Father (13:1). These chapters are Jesus' Farewell sermon, as are Moses' sermons in Deuteronomy. The book of Deuteronomy contains laws and commandments about how Israel is to live when they enter the land of promise, and Jesus emphasizes in his upper room discourses that His disciples must obey His commandments. Specifically, He commands them to love one another as He has loved them. When the greater Moses is gone, they are to follow the instructions He gives them as they enter the land and conquer. Deuteronomy is not only a book of laws but a book of prophecy. Moses speaks a great deal about the future of Israel. Deuteronomy ends with prophecies about each of the tribes of Israel and a song. Jesus likewise talks about the future of His people and ends with a prayer. Deuteronomy comes when there is a change in the leadership of Israel. Moses is about to leave, and Joshua will replace him. So also, Jesus tells His disciples He is going away, and they will have a new leader and guide, the Paraclete, the Holy Spirit. The Holy Spirit is "another" Joshua who leads the disciples in the conquest of the world.

Once we see that John 13–17 is like Deuteronomy, we can see that Jesus is talking to His disciples, the "new Israel," and telling them what they will face in the years after Jesus leaves. In 13:1, John tells us that the hour is come when Jesus will depart from the world. As His hour approaches, He loves "His own" who are in the world. Who are "His own"? According to John 1:11, the Word became flesh in order to come to His own, but His own did not receive Him.

In this verse, "His own" means the Jews. But some do receive the Word (1:12–13), and these become "His own." As Jesus says in the Good Shepherd sermon, those are Jesus' own who hear the Shepherd's voice, who follow Him, who are known by the Shepherd and know Him (10:3–4, 14). Jesus has a more specific group in mind too. The twelve are singled out as those who stand by Him (see chapter 6), remaining with the Bread from heaven after those who seek the bread that perishes have departed. Jesus' Farewell sermon is a sermon first of all to those disciples who have stayed close to Him in spite of the hatred of the Jews. These chapters still speak to us today. But they are first spoken to the twelve, and they are about the future of the twelve.

The prophecies about persecutions and hard times refer to what the twelve will face. Jesus makes it clear that the Jews will be the persecutors of His church. As He goes on, it becomes clear that "world" means the Jews.[4] In 15:18, Jesus says, "If the world hates you, it hated Me before it hated you." Because the disciples are not of the world, just as Jesus is not of the world, the world hates them. This contrast between "of the world" and "not of the world" goes back to chapter eight. There, the ones who hate Jesus are specifically the Jews (7:7). In chapter fifteen, Jesus is telling His disciples that they will be persecuted by the Jews because the Jews are of the world.

Also in 15:20, Jesus says that if "they" persecuted Me, they will persecute you. Who are "they"? In 5:16, we are told that the Jews persecute Jesus because He heals the lame man on the Sabbath. Further, in 15:21, Jesus says that "they" do not know the One who sent Him, and this is said about the Jews earlier in the gospel. In 8:19, Jesus says the Jews do not know Him or His Father and repeats in 8:55 that the Jews have not come to know Him. In 15:22, Jesus says that if He had not spoken to them, they would not have had sin. He has done works among "them" which no one else did (v. 24), and the "them" is clearly the Jews. The Jews are the ones Jesus has spoken to and the ones who have seen His works.

From John 15:18, "they" are "the world," but everything Jesus says about "them" are things that have already been said about the Jews. In 15:25–16:4, it becomes even clearer that Jesus is talking about the Jews. He speaks of "their law" (16:2), warns that "they will make you outcasts from the synagogue," and predicts that "everyone who kills you will think that he is offering service to God." The hour of the persecution of the disciples will be "their hour" (v. 4). The persecutions that Jesus predicts are persecutions at the hands of the Jews. The enemies of the church, Jesus predicted, would be His own enemies. After the hour of Jesus has passed, the hour of the Jews will come. The Jews are "the world" that is hostile to Jesus and His church.

Jesus also predicts that the world will be convicted by the Spirit (16:8–12). And the "world" that the Spirit will convict must be the same "world" spoken of throughout chapters 15–16. "The world" that will persecute the disciples is the same as "they" in the following verses, and this is clearly speaking about Jewish persecutors of the church. Then Jesus begins to talk about the Spirit's effect on the "world" (16:7–11). What Jesus is saying is that the Spirit will work to convict the Jews who have renounced their Lord. Again, it is important to compare these promises with other things said in John's gospel. In 16:9, Jesus says the world will be convicted concerning sin because "they do not believe in Me," and throughout the gospel, the Jews are the ones who do not believe. Though the Jews have largely rejected Jesus, the coming of the Spirit will convict many and turn them back to their Lord. Jesus promises persecutions from the Jews, but He also promises a revival among the Jews.

Review Questions.

1. How does Jesus' miracle at the wedding feast show that He is better than Moses?
2. Why is it important that John tells about Jesus cleansing the temple at the beginning of His gospel?
3. Explain the symbolism of the miracle that healed the man at the pool. How does this show Jesus is greater than Moses?
4. How does John 6 follow the Passover-Exodus story?
5. In what ways is Jesus' sermon in John 13–17 like Deuteronomy?
6. Who is "the world" in John 13–17? How do you know?
7. What does Jesus say "the world" will do?
8. What effect will the Spirit have on "the world"?

Thought Questions.

1. To what is Jesus comparing Himself in 1:51?
2. John calls Jesus' miracles "signs" (see 2:11; 4:48). Explain this term in light of Exodus 7:3.
3. Who dug the well where Jesus stops in Samaria (4:12)? Why is this significant?
4. In light of the meaning of "the world" in John 13–17, what does John 3:16 mean?

5. When does Jesus "come" to His disciples (14:18)? Look closely at the context.

A King In Israel, John 18–19

In John 13–17, Jesus refers to the Jews as "the world." Once we see this, we can better understand what Jesus means when He says about His trial and death: "Now is the judgment of this world, now is the prince of this world cast out" (12:31). In the gospel of John, this is Jesus' description of His hour. Though the crucifixion seems to be a judgment on Jesus, it is in fact the judgment on the Jews.

Jesus' trial before Pilate (18:28–19:16) is about Jesus as king of the Jews. Jesus is called king eleven times in these chapters. But the question is not only whether Jesus is king. The question is about what kind of king He is and about what kind of king Israel wants. Pilate doesn't understand Jesus' kingdom. He is interested in it only because a Jewish king might be a threat to Rome. Pilate, trying to protect his power, wants to make sure that he keeps the Jews in line. For Jesus, kingship means something different. Though Jesus does not have warriors as earthly kings do, He does not deny that He is a king but says, "I am a king, and I have authority greater than the authority of the Roman governor. But that authority is exercised in a way completely different from earthly kings." Being a king for Jesus means witnessing concerning the truth (18:37), which leads to mockery and unjust torture. Kingship is the authority to lay down one's life as well as the authority to take it up again. Jesus' kingdom is out of this world. This is not the way human kings operate.

The trial before Pilate in John's gospel is divided into seven scenes. These scenes are marked by Pilate's movements into and out of the Praetorium. At the center of the passage, the soldiers whip and mock Jesus. What the soldiers do here is not an accident. They are performing mock coronation, pretending to crown Jesus as king of the Jews. Jesus is first crowned, then covered with a purple robe, then brought out to the crowds to be acclaimed as king (19:1–6). The cross is his throne, with a script above his head that says He is king. Of course, the soldiers do not really want to make Jesus king. They are making fun of Him. The crown is not made of gold or silver but from the branches of a thorn bush. Jesus' purple robe is bloody from His wounds. When Jesus is presented to the crowd, instead of crying "Long Live the King," the Jews call out "Crucify Him, Crucify Him." They do not want this Man as their king.

But the truth is that God is not mocked, and God turns the scorn of the scoffer against himself. What the soldiers mean as mockery tells the truth. Jesus is the King, and one day, Jesus says, the Gentiles will bow before King Jesus without mockery (18:36–37). Pilate himself declares that Jesus is king when he insists on putting a titulus on the cross proclaiming that Jesus is king of the Jews. Despite the Jews' efforts to change the statement, the truth about Jesus is proclaimed not only in Hebrew but in the major languages of the Gentiles.

Jesus is not only the king but also the judge. This point is made by a subtle detail that John records. As John 19:13 is normally translated, it seems obvious that Pilate brings Jesus out, and then Pilate sits in the judgment seat. But the Greek verb can also mean "cause to sit." From the Greek, it's not clear whether Pilate or Jesus sits on the judgment seat. If Pilate puts Jesus in the seat, he surely means it to be in mockery. But the double meaning of the word raises the question, "Who is in charge here? Who is the real judge presiding at this trial?" John's answer, of course, is that Jesus is the presiding judge, not Pilate.

This trial is not only a trial for Pilate; more importantly, it is the trial of the Jews. They are the "world" that is being judged here. Throughout the history of Israel, Israel has been a special nation because Yahweh has been their King. Israel has the temple, the palace of Yahweh, King of heaven, in their midst. This alone makes Israel different from the nations. At this trial, they are being tested about whether they will accept Yahweh as their king. And they condemn themselves by their own confession. The Jews break the covenant by refusing to bow to the Lord of the covenant. Not long after this, Yahweh will take His palace from Israel. But their doom is sealed right here in the trial before Pilate. As in the times of Samuel, the Jews reject the Lord from being king over them. They want to be like the nations and have a king like the nations. They say, "We have no king but Caesar" (19:15). And so they will.

This is shown by the "stone pavement" where the judgment seat is located. In the Old Testament, the Greek word for "stone pavement" is used only a couple of times. Significantly, in 2 Chronicles 7:1–3, after Solomon finishes His temple, the glory of the Lord fills the house. When the Lord takes His throne in the temple, Israel bows down on the "pavement" with her face to the ground and praises her King. But here in Pilate's Praetorium, Jesus is seated as the Word of God incarnate, the Glory of God, the Judge of Israel, before a stone pavement. And the Jews renounce Him. They do not fall on the stone pavement before their king, and so the stone will fall on them and grind them to powder.

Throughout John's gospel, the Jews have tried to put Jesus on trial. And they think they have finally succeeded. They think that this hour is the hour of judgment on Jesus. But John is telling the end of the story about Yahweh and Israel, and the story doesn't end the way the Jews think it will. Instead of putting Jesus on trial, the Jews are on trial, and they are condemned. Israel as the people of Yahweh dies as soon as the leaders say, "We have no king but Caesar." Instead of bowing before the temple of God, the Jews have "destroyed this temple," the temple of Jesus' body. But He will rebuild it in three days.

On the cross, there is a sign that new life will come from the destroyed temple of Jesus' body. When the Roman soldiers find that Jesus is already dead, they do not break His legs. Instead, "one of the soldiers pierced His side with a spear, and immediately there came out blood and water"

(19:34). The other gospels do not include this scene. Instead, they tell us that when Jesus died, the veil of the temple was torn from top to bottom (Matthew 27:51; Mark 15:38; Luke 23:45). The other gospels are telling us that by His death, Jesus has opened the way into the presence of God. But John 19:34 also tells us something about Jesus as the temple of God. Back in John 7:37–39, Jesus promises that those who received the "water" that Jesus offers will have a river of water flowing from them. John tells us that Jesus is talking about the Holy Spirit (v. 39), who will be given to those who believe. The first person we see who flows with "rivers of living water" is Jesus Himself. When Jesus' side is pierced on the cross, water flows from the One who is born of the Spirit (John 1:32–33).

The water from Jesus' side refers back to John 7, but it is also connected to several Old Testament incidents. Jesus is the "rock" that follows Israel through the wilderness (1 Corinthians 10:4), the rock that flows with water for thirsty Israel. Jesus is also the temple from Ezekiel 47. In that vision, Ezekiel sees water flowing from the temple. As it flows, it gets deeper and deeper and eventually transforms the land and the sea. On the cross, Jesus is shown to be that temple. From Him will flow the living water that will turn the wilderness to Eden.

Destroy this temple, Jesus said, and in three days, I will raise it up. Three days later, Jesus is raised. But the water flowing from His side shows that Israel will be raised with Him and built into the new temple of His body. In Pilate's Praetorium, the Jews renounce Jesus, choosing death over life. But the Israel of God is never dead for long. Israel has died before—in the wilderness between Egypt and Canaan, during the time of the judges, during the reign of Ahab, at the Babylonian exile. But when Old Israel dies, Yahweh, the Lord of life, brings a New Israel from the grave. The death and resurrection of Jesus, who is the true Jacob and Israel, who is the temple flowing with living water, is the sign that a New Israel will be born. The Jews have rejected their King and destroyed their temple, but out of their dead bones the Spirit brings forth living stones for a holy house, an army that cannot be numbered.

But that's another story.

Review Questions.

1. How does John describe the "hour" of Jesus?

2. Explain the arrangement of the trial before Pilate. How many scenes are there? How are the scenes marked off from one another?

3. What is at the center of the story? What are the soldiers doing?

4. Explain the double sense of the word that tells us that Pilate "sat down" in the judgment seat.

5. How is the trial of Jesus the trial of the Jews?

6. What is significant about the "stone pavement"?

Thought Questions.

1. What is significant about the Jews' choice of Barabbas (18:38–40)?

2. When Jesus is pierced in the side, blood and water come out (19:34). How is this connected with Jesus' statements in 4:13–14 and 7:37–39?

3. Discuss the scene in John 20:11–18 in light of Genesis 2:18–25.

4. When Peter sees Jesus on the beach after the resurrection, Jesus is at a charcoal fire (21:9). Why? See 18:18.

[1] There are other references to water in the gospel, and in each case, Jesus is seen to offer something better. Instead of baptizing with the water of John, He baptizes with the Spirit. In place of the water of Jacob's well, he offers living water that becomes a well (chapter 4). The lame man in chapter five cannot get to the waters of Bethesda to be healed, but he doesn't need the water since Jesus can heal him with the Word. Water is good, just as darkness is good, but Jesus brings light and wine.

[2] See the discussion of N. T. Wright, *Jesus and the Victory of God*

(Christian Origins and the Question of God, vol. 2; Philadelphia: Fortress, 1996), pp. 413–428.

[3] George R. Beasley-Murray, *John* (Word Biblical Commentary #36; Waco, TX: Word, 1987), pp. 40–41.

[4] This has already been evident earlier in the gospel. In 8:21–30, Jesus tells the Jews that they cannot follow where He is going. He contrasts Himself with the Jews: He is from above, born of the Spirit and born from above, but they are from below, of the earth, earthy. The above/below contrast is parallel to the contrast between being of this world and not being of this world. The Jews are of this world, but Jesus is not. In 8:44, Jesus says that those who have left Him and taken their place with the Jews as persecutors of Jesus (v. 31) are not of Abraham but of the devil. Their father is the devil. For John, origin determines nature: That which is born of flesh is flesh; that which is born of Spirit is Spirit. That which is born from above is not of this world; that which is born from below is of this world. Thus, the Jews are of this world, originating in this world and operating according to the norms of this world and its ruler. The world refers to the Old Covenant system, the Adamic order of things corrupted by sin, and specifically the Adamic order as it has been given specific shape in first century Judaism.

Author Index

Scripture Index

Scripture Index